Riverbank and Seashore
in Nineteenth and
Twentieth Century
British Literature

Also by Gillian Mary Hanson

City and Shore: The Function of Setting in the British Mystery (McFarland, 2004)

Riverbank and Seashore in Nineteenth and Twentieth Century British Literature

GILLIAN MARY HANSON

McFarland & Company, Inc., Publishers
Jefferson, North Carolina, and London

LIBRARY OF CONGRESS CATALOGUING-IN-PUBLICATION DATA

Hanson, Gillian Mary, 1943–
    Riverbank and seashore in nineteenth and twentieth century British literature / Gillian Mary Hanson.
    p.   cm.
    Includes bibliographical references and index.

    ISBN 0-7864-2284-X (softcover : 50# alkaline paper)

    1. English literature—20th century—History and criticism. 2. Rivers in literature. 3. English literature—19th century—History and criticism. 4. Postmodernism (Literature)—Great Britain. 5. Modernism (Literature)—Great Britain. 6. Landscape in literature. 7. Seashore in literature. 8. Setting (Literature) I. Title.
PR478.R58H36   2006
820.9'32146—dc22   2005020848

British Library cataloguing data are available

©2006 Gillian Mary Hanson. All rights reserved

No part of this book may be reproduced or transmitted in any form or by any means, electronic or mechanical, including photocopying or recording, or by any information storage and retrieval system, without permission in writing from the publisher.

Cover photograph ©2005 Photospin

Manufactured in the United States of America

McFarland & Company, Inc., Publishers
   Box 611, Jefferson, North Carolina 28640
   www.mcfarlandpub.com

For my children

Contents

Preface 1
Introduction 3

PART I. RIVERBANK

Chapter One. The Rural River 11

Alfred Tennyson's "The Lady of Shalott," George Eliot's *The Mill on the Floss*, Wilkie Collins' "The Guilty River," H. E. Bates' *The Two Sisters*, Charles Kingsley's *The Water Babies*, Graham Swift's *Waterland*, Kenneth Grahame's *The Wind in the Willows*, and Ted Hughes' *River*

Chapter Two. The Urban River 33

Charles Dickens' *Our Mutual Friend*, Joyce Cary's *The Horse's Mouth*, Penelope Fitzgerald's *Offshore*, Alan Sillitoe's "A Scream of Toys," Patrick McGrath's *Spider*, Iain Sinclair's *Downriver*, and Susan Hill's *The Mist in the Mirror*

Chapter Three. River into Sea 58

PART II. SEASHORE

Chapter Four. The Rural Shore 65

Thomas Hardy's *A Pair of Blue Eyes*, Virginia Woolf's *The Waves* and *To the Lighthouse*, W. B. Yeats' "Fighting the Waves," Mary Lavin's

"The Great Wave," Iris Murdoch's *The Sea, the Sea*, John Fowles' *The French Lieutenant's Woman*, Graham Swift's "Learning to Swim," Susan Hill's *The Woman in Black*, and Jane Gardam's *Crusoe's Daughter*

Chapter Five. The Urban Shore 102
Matthew Arnold's "Dover Beach" and "The Forsaken Merman," Jane Austen's *Persuasion*, Graham Greene's *Brighton Rock*, Patrick Hamilton's *The West Pier*, Samuel Beckett's *Embers*, Alan Bennett's "All Day on the Sands," Alan Sillitoe's "The Road," Edward Bond's *The Sea*, and Susan Hill's *The Albatross*

Evaluation. The Settings of Riverbank and Seashore 130
Appendix A. About the Authors 139
Appendix B. Riverbank and Seashore in Quotation 151
Notes 169
Bibliography 173
Index 179

Preface

Writer Iris Murdoch once said that "starting a novel is like opening a door on a misty landscape; you can still see very little, but you can smell the earth and feel the wind blowing." This is how I felt when I first began the research for *Riverbank and Seashore*, which, although not a work of fiction, does examine some of the great fiction of the nineteenth and twentieth centuries.

The focus is on twentieth century fiction, but we begin with the Victorians because powerful changes were taking place in the social and technological landscapes of nineteenth century England that often became the underlying themes of much of the writing of the time and influenced succeeding writers. These changes included such aspects as the debate between science and faith, the rapid growth of industrialization, the frenzy for social and moral reform, the "woman question," as it was called by Victorians, and the fascination with reading, described by George Eliot: "Even idleness is eager now,—eager for amusement; prone to excursion-trains, art-museums, periodical literature, and exciting novels." But, most importantly for this study, was the idea of individuals searching for identity in a commercial, industrialized society, for as Matthew Arnold wrote in 1853, "the dialogue of the mind with itself has commenced."

The book is divided into two parts—riverbank and seashore. One or both are used as a setting for the works under discussion. The sections are further divided into rural and urban; the riverbank section also includes a third division, "River into Sea," covering the estuary. What I have tried to do is examine these physical settings as they are presented through each author's creative imagination in the development of character and plot. In addition to the primary works, I have drawn on a number of works that address either directly or indirectly the topological aspects of these settings, in order to support some of my own assumptions about the nature of landscape and humans. George Bachelard, some of whose ideas, along with those of H. E. Bates and W. H. Auden, I discuss in Part I (Riverbank), states, "Nature forces us to contemplation.... An endless exchange is produced between the vision and the visible. Everything that makes us look looks." W. H. Auden's discussion of the symbolic aspects of the sea in literature was particularly helpful in developing Part II (Seashore), as were the ideas concerning the carnival and the literary carnivalesque developed by Elias Canetti and Mikhail Bakhtin. Parts of the discussions on Graham Greene's *Brighton Rock* and Patrick Hamilton's *The West Pier* also appear in my book *City and Shore: The Function of the Setting in the British Mystery* (McFarland, 2004).

Writing this book took me on a seductive journey through some rural and urban landscapes of England, one in which I now invite the reader to participate; all he or she needs to pack is a pleasure in reading and an enthusiastic imagination.

Introduction

> "Through literature we can re-discover a sense of the destiny of our lives."
> —Iris Murdoch

The waters of river and sea represent a kind of freedom, the type described by Iris Murdoch as one that enables man "to exist sanely without fear and to perceive what is real."[1] As settings in fiction, riverbank and seashore are rich in potential because they offer a sense of destiny and suggest the possibility for self-truth and self-knowledge. A careful examination of these settings, using a phenomenological approach that focuses on the study of consciousness and the objects of direct experience—one that draws upon new approaches and gives us not only, as Shelley says, "the power to imagine what we know" but also addresses Iris Murdoch's call for "an area of translation, an area in which specialized concept and recommendation can be seen and understood in the light of moral and social ideas which have a certain degree of complexity and yet are not the sole property of technicians"[2]—will lead to a new interpretation of riverbank and seashore as dynamics of exposure.

Through the rural settings of riverbank and seashore, the idea is demonstrated that it is possible, eventually, for one to discover an affirmation of selfhood, as does the Lady in Tennyson's poem "The Lady of Shalott." Constantly straining within its banks, the river represents the self, seeking the freedom necessary for its development. Bachelard talks of water as offering a type of destiny, achievable through the imaginative powers, "an element of materializing imagination."[3] The river pushes the individual towards this liberating sense of destiny with a movement that parallels its own journey to the sea and eventual freedom. There is also something magical about the rural river: "The river held my eyes.... It hypnotized me,"[4] says H. E. Bates in *Down the River* of the River Ouse. In conjunction with its magical aspects, the river has an Ovidian quality that brings with it the possibility for change, for metamorphosis. The Victorian writer Charles Kingsley was aware of this when he wrote *The Water Babies*, which concerns the joyous transformation of the boy, Tom, an unhappy chimney sweep, into a piscine figure through the waters of the River Ouse. Another work that has established certain archetypical aspects of the river and riverbank is *The Wind in the Willows*, a story of riparian life told through the experience of a group of river creatures, most importantly Mole and Rat. Clear influences of these works may be seen in Graham Swift's *Waterland* and Ted Hughes' remarkable collection of poems *River*. In his discussion of the creative aspects of the imagination, Bachelard focuses on the imagination as something that moves writer and reader beyond the phenomenological towards the ontological. This idea is evident in George Eliot's *The Mill on the Floss* and H. E. Bates' *The Two Sisters*, both of which describe the emotional development of two heroines as they move towards self-knowledge through a series of incidents that take place on the rural river. The river is, as W. H. Herendeen describes in "The Rhetoric of Rivers: The River and the Pursuit of Knowledge," "[of] unique symbolic and literal significance which makes it especially suitable for man's self-conscious gropings for knowledge. It is a reminder to look clearly and truthfully at oneself and one's true condition, but it also offers an image of our intellectual and spiritual potential."[5]

Perhaps the most powerful work of fiction that uses the urban river is Charles Dickens' *Our Mutual Friend*, which has influenced many of the later works that focus on the urban Thames, such as two fairly recent novels: Patrick McGrath's *Spider* and Iain Sinclair's *Downriver*, both of which, like Dickens' novel, are set in the shadowy warehouses and murky alleyways than run beside the Thames in London's East End. The urban river may also serve as the unifying image that often functions as a place of revelation and regeneration as it does in such works as Penelope Fitzgerald's *Offshore* and Susan Hill's *The Mist in the Mirror*. The urban river's embankments, bridges, and tunnels often mark specific stages of revelation and movement in the plot as they do in Joyce Cary's *The Horse's Mouth*, Alan Sillitoe's "A Scream of Toys," and Iain Sinclair's *Downriver*, and the canal in Patrick McGrath's *Spider* functions as the channel by which means the protagonist draws his memories into the present in order to confront the past and define his situation. All of these features aid the character on his journey towards the emancipative truth of imaginative freedom. Inevitably, river runs into sea, for, says H. E. Bates, "A river snaking to all points of the compass, has only one destination and one end ... the supreme point of fusion...."[6]

That place where river flows into sea, the estuary, is of topographical and symbolic importance in English literature and is the subject of such nineteenth century poems as Alfred Tennyson's "A River" and Jean Ingelow's "The Four Bridges." British poet laureate Ted Hughes also focuses on the river and estuary in his collection of poems titled *River*. H. E. Bates describes the passage of river into sea in his tribute to the River Ouse, *Down the River*, and Victorian writer Charles Kingsley focuses on the freedom symbolized by the river's confluence with sea in *The Water Babies*. So, too, do contemporary novelists Graham Swift and Iain Sinclair in their novels *Waterland* and *Downriver*.

The rural coastal setting, with its cliffs, tower, and the constant movement of the sea, becomes the site of revelation and generates the energy that brings characters to a new level of self-awareness and an understanding in Thomas Hardy's *A Pair of Blue Eyes*. These aspects are also found in later works, such as Virginia Woolf's *To the Lighthouse* and *The Waves*, W. B. Yeats' "Fighting the Waves," Mary Lavin's "The Great Wave," John Fowles' *The French Lieutenant's Woman*, and Graham Swift's "Learning to Swim." Alfred Tennyson's poem "The Kraken" describes the mysterious forces slumbering beneath the sea, found also in Iris Murdoch's *The Sea, the Sea*, Jane Gardam's *Crusoe's Daughter*, and Susan Hill's *The Woman in Black*. The sea's movement, unlike the river's, is cyclical. As each nascent wave represents the diversity of nothingness and possibility, so the sea represents the eternal flow of life and death, containing all aspects and stages, physical and spiritual, and reflects the mystery and growth of humankind. The river follows a lateral pattern that represents a form of communication between past and present; likewise, the real and the tropistic presence of the sea becomes the catalyst by which means each character is able to establish a connection with the past and embrace the present. The sea's cyclic pattern contains both horizontal and vertical movements to represent these states and to illustrate the dissolution of the self in the universal sea of humanity.

Whereas both the urban and the rural river settings are places of permanence—one lives by the river—the seashore settings, whether urban or rural, are often temporary sites, suggestive of changes both historical and psychological, as we see in Matthew Arnold's poems "Dover Beach" and "The Forsaken Merman." One visits the seaside for a sense of renewal, often promulgated by an event in the form of a carnivalesque reversal. The event occurs in Jane Austen's novel *Persuasion,* as well as in succeeding works such as Graham Greene's *Brighton Rock,* Patrick Hamilton's *The West Pier,* Samuel Beckett's *Embers,* Edward Bond's *The Sea,* Alan Sillitoe's "The Road," Alan Bennett's "All Day on the Sands," and Susan Hill's *The Albatross.* The urban seaside setting often provides the background for murder and deceit, or, conversely, for celebration. As such, it incorporates the all-important carnivalesque which dissolves traditional boundaries and enables a revelation of truth, creating an inversion of norms that allows its participants a brief sense of freedom from restriction imposed by political and social order as well as by life and death. This reversal is imaged by the rhythmic pattern of the waves as they crest, break, and re-form along the shore. In their carnivalesque explorations, those works that involve the urban seashore often contain music and crowds, as well as places of public recognition such as the promenade, pier and station, and a sense of drama and mystery, all of which stand against the background of the sea.

The familiar landscape of both rural and urban riverbank and seashore, as established by earlier works, especially those of the nineteenth century, a time of great social and topographical upheavals, affords the reader a rich variety of metonymic links specific to the modern world and affirms the possibility for a greater understanding of it as these subconscious associations flow into consciousness like the movement of water itself. Writers of fiction, in particular, through their explorations of the potential of riverbank and seashore, and in their use of these settings in specific and symbolic ways to develop such themes endemic to the twentieth century as entrapment, isolation, communication, and contingency, lead the reader to a much-needed understanding of our current times because, as Iris Murdoch explains, "Whereas society in the nineteenth century was either a reassuring place where one lived, or else an exciting, rewarding, interesting place where one struggled, society today tends to appear, by contrast as menacing, puzzling, uncontrollable, or else confining, and boring. And on the other hand, behind and through society we see the whole apocalyptic scene, the traveling rocket, the hydrogen bomb, and all the things which precisely make us want to think in terms of the human condition and the total man."[7] It is a situation which may also apply to the readers of such works. For, in our postmodern world, described by writer Patricia Waugh as a place where "consciousness is adrift, unable to anchor itself to any universal ground of justice, truth or reason on which the ideals of modernity have been founded in the past,"[8] it is necessary to address these concerns. Waugh suggests that what is currently needed in the field of literature is "a renewed criticism ... [one that] will be contextual rather than textual, not primarily concerned with structure or diction or syntax, all of which assumes that the work of art 'really' exists on the page rather than in a reader's passionate apprehension and response."⁹ With these ideas in mind, this study examines the various ways in which twenty-one modern and postmodern writers have managed to make a connection with some of the major intellectual concerns of the twentieth century by using the physical settings of riverbank and seashore and by following the course of river into sea to examine the uses of that "most faithful mirror of voices"¹⁰ to describe and compare each author's unique and appropriate exploration of these settings for his or her works.

Part I
Riverbank

"Under her feet the ground began to slant river-wards, and she felt unable to do anything but follow it, whither it might lead.... The river was near at last."
—H. E. Bates, *The Two Sisters*

CHAPTER ONE

The Rural River

Alfred Tennyson's "The Lady of Shalott," George Eliot's *The Mill on the Floss*, Wilkie Collins' "The Guilty River," H. E. Bates' *The Two Sisters*, Charles Kingsley's *The Water Babies*, Graham Swift's *Waterland*, Kenneth Grahame's *The Wind in the Willows*, and Ted Hughes' *River*

> Clear and cool, clear and cool,
> By laughing shallow, and dreaming pool;
> Cool and clear, cool and clear,
> By shining shingle, and foaming wear;
> Under the crag where the ouzel sings,
> And the ivied wall where the church-bell rings,
> Undefiled, for the undefiled;
> Play by me, bathe in me, mother and child.
> —"River Song," from *The Water Babies*,
> Charles Kingsley

From ancient times to the present day, the river has been used as a symbol for knowledge and history through which we may gain an understanding of our own condition. "Classical and modern writers," says W. H. Herendeen in "The Rhetoric of Rivers: The River and the Pursuit of Knowledge," "responsive to the language of rivers, understood that submerged in it were ideas associated with man's emerging knowledge of the world, his conception of society.... Men such as Camden, Spenser, and Harrison used the rivers to recreate the historical and mythical landscape of Britain in order to comprehend the history and destiny that they personally shared."[1] Representing, as it does, both spiritual and intellectual potential, the river offers a perspective into the soul; likewise, the landscape of the river is, in Jungian terms, the archetypal symbol for a journey and is often used both metaphorically and realistically to instigate and reflect specific stages in the development towards a recognition of self in the lives of certain fictional characters.

The use of the river setting may be understood through two distinct aspects of rural and urban. Of the rural river setting, Bachelard comments: "...the language of the waters is a direct poetic reality; that streams and rivers provide the sound for mute country landscapes."[2] Alfred Tennyson's poem "The Dying Swan" describes this kind of "direct poetic reality" that Bachelard speaks of as it unifies the landscape of the river to "provide the sound of mute country landscapes": "And the wavy well of the soughing reeds,/ And the wave-worn horns of the echoing bank,/ And the silvery marish-flowers that throng/ The desolate creeks and pools among,/ Were flooded over with eddying song." In the function of the rural river setting, streams, especially tributaries, often serve as transitions, both metaphorically and realistically, for each character's journey toward self-knowledge. For Tennyson, this idea of isolation is often suggested by a body of water, either a river or sea, by which the subject of the poem is cut off, in a sense, from reality. This journey might include existential themes such as isolation and the presentation of different modes of time as, for instance, in Alfred Tennyson's poem "The Lady of Shalott," which he based on an early fourteenth century Italian novella, "How the Damsel of Scalot died for the love of Lancelot de Lac." Everything in the poem follows the movement of the river, which, itself, suggests both a historical and a current perspective. When the critic James Donald Welch discusses Tennyson's "predilection for landscape," he talks of the poet's usage of time:

> Two modes of time are central to Tennyson's imagination. In the first, time appears as repetitive or static, without goal or terminus, and is usually associated with isolation ... generally through isolation from mankind at large. The second form is dynamic, purposeful, non-repetitive, and is associated with some kind of contact between the individual and the community.... In the first form of time life is a succession of repetitive actions, frequently accompanied by a sense of decay without the dissolution of death. In the second form of time, death is the terminus and fulfillment of life; and life is usually seen as possessing the natural pattern and rhythm of human existence.[3]

The river also offers creative freedom for the imagination by which means one may achieve his or her artistic fulfillment—but "the material imagination of water," states Gaston Bachelard in *Water and Dreams*, "...is a special type of imagination. Strengthened in this knowledge of depth of a material element, the reader will understand at last that water is also a *type of destiny* that is no longer simply the vain destiny of fleeting images and a never ending dream but an essential destiny that endlessly changes the substance of the being."[4] For the individual, such as the Lady of Shalott, this "destiny of water" becomes a personal destiny, a realization of purpose achieved through a development of true imaginative powers so that, in the Coleridgean sense, it is "organic" and "creative," transcending ordinary fancy, defined by Coleridge as being "mechanic," and "logical."

The Lady of Shalott is confined behind "Four grey walls and four grey towers" where "...the silent isle imbowers" and the river and the stream of life wend past her window as they pass down to Camelot: "By the island in the river/ Flowing down to Camelot." She is an artist figure—a weaver and a singer. Her mirror, much like the river, reflects the world as it passes by. She weaves her "charmed web" by replicating the reflections of the world outside as they appear to her in her mirror. If she joins reality by looking out of the window and seeing it directly, she will die—this is the curse. Her existential choice is one between life and death: Should she remain isolated, her art safe, or should she step into reality? As the poem progresses through a series of colorful images, including various aspects of life—peasants from the fields, an abbot, a pair of newlyweds—the tension mounts. When Lancelot trots by on his horse with the bridle bells ringing, suggesting both a calling and a caution, she cries, "I'm half sick of shadows" and she leaves the tower. The weather changes to signify the move from the subjective to the objective: "In the stormy east-wind straining,/ The pale yellow woods were waning,/ The broad stream in his bank complaining." The fulfillment of the curse comes upon the Lady as she leaves the tower and looks down to Camelot: "And down the river's dim expanse/ Like some bold seer in a trance." The next part of the poem begins her physical engagement with reality, and it takes place on the river after she leaves the tower, unchains the boat that lies on the bank, establishes her identity by writing her name on the prow, and steps in. The tide draws her boat down the river, and she floats down to Camelot, where she dies. Of this poem Tennyson writes: "The new-born love for something, for some one in the wide world from which she has been so long excluded, takes her out of the region of shadows into that of realities."[5]

In another work by Tennyson, "The Miller's Daughter," the woman, Alice, also lives beside a river which, like the Tolliver family's in *The Mill on the Floss*, is the source of her family's livelihood—it turns the mill. She, too, sits and spins by a "mirror where her sight she feeds." She uses her mirror, however, not as the source of her creative output, but to view her own reflection and the life of the river as well as that of her lover, and here the situation is reversed—not she but a man pines for her by the river. The outcome of both poems also varies—the speaker in "The Miller's Daughter" is actually her husband, who reminisces after they have been married for many years.

Other works of the nineteenth century of which, it may be said, established certain antecedents through words and nature in the symbolic use of setting for succeeding writers who have developed similar themes through their characters' specific relationships with the river and riverbank are George Eliot's *The Mill on the Floss* (1880), Charles Kingsley's *The Water Babies* (1863), Wilkie Collins' "The Guilty River" (1886), and Kenneth Grahame's *The Wind in the Willows* (1908) in which, like Bachelard's rural streams and rivers, the river "...seemed a sudden clear call from an articulate voice."[6] Works that seem to envince these aspects include H. E. Bates' *The Two Sisters* (1926), which, like *The Mill on the Floss* and "The Guilty River," describes a bucolic setting and human passions that are paralleled by the river. Ted Hughes' collection of poems *River* (1983) contains powerful metamorphic aspects drawn from the rural river and its setting similar to those that occur in *The Water Babies* and *The Wind in the Willows*. Themes such as the various modes of time and isolation symbolized by the river setting may also be found in Graham Swift's *Waterland* (1983).

In the introduction to *The Mill on the Floss*, Antonia Byatt writes: "It is not, I think, fanciful to suppose that George Eliot, in *The Mill on the Floss* more than any other books, saw herself engaged in an analogous effort to record local particularities of speech, landscape, custom and morality."[7] The River Floss, a fictional river in Norfolk, is the central image that reflects the emotions of the Tulliver family who live by it, as it both divides and unites them. Mr. Tulliver is the miller who resides with his wife and two children, Maggie and Tom, at Dorlcote Mill. So enmeshed is he in continual litigation concerning river rights that he finally brings his family to financial ruin. The river is not only necessary to the well-being of the Tullivers, but also, paradoxically, a source of conflict that tears the family apart; it is through the river that the estrangement of Maggie and Tom takes place, and the river is finally responsible for their tragic death. The river is not only the central image of the story—water is the source that drives the mill and the people who live by it, just as the river drives the narrative—it also marks the three crucial stages in the plot.

The opening scene introduces all of the key elements in the story, and in its description and its presence, the river, which flows through the nearby town of St. Ogg on its way to the sea, foreshadows the major events that take place: "Just by the red-roofed town the tributary Ripple flows with its lively current into the Floss" (9) and unites the themes of passionate love: "I am in love with moistness..." (10) and isolation: "The rush of water and the booming of the mill bring a dreamy deafness which seems to heighten the peacefulness of the scene. They are like a great curtain of sound, shutting one out from the world beyond" (10).

In this opening chapter, the reader is also made aware of the nature of Maggie Tulliver's character as it relates to the river before she appears in the story: "Ah, I thought so—wanderin' up an' down by the water, like a wild thing: she'll tumble in some day" (15), says her mother, who repeats the terrible prophecy as Maggie enters the story: "...where's the use o' my telling you to keep away from the water? ... "You'll tumble in and be drownded some day, an' then you'll be sorry you didn't do as mother told you" (16).

The river makes possible and reflects the pivotal stage in the story and marks the dramatic reversal in Maggie's life: "They glided rapidly along, to Stephen's rowing, helped by the backward flowing tide...." (484). This is the boating scene in which Maggie, now a young woman, spends an innocent night on the river with a young man, Stephen, and loses her reputation and the support of her brother, Tom, who has taken over as head of the family after the death of their father. The change is also suggested by the weather: "...they became aware that the clouds had gathered, and that the slightest perceptible freshening of the breeze was growing and growing till the whole character of the day was altered" (487).

In the final death scene with the angry river ending, when Maggie returns home from St. Oggs, where she has been living, to rescue her brother from the flood, the culmination of catastrophic events in the family's lives and in nature are, again, marked by the tide: "...a new tidal current swept along the line of houses, and drove both the boats out on to the wide water, with a force that carried them far past the meeting current of the river" (537). The river's tide becomes like a human force which she must wrestle, one that parallels her estrangement from her brother: "She must get her boat into the current of the Floss—else she would never be able to pass the Ripple, and approach the house.... For the first time distinct ideas of danger began to press upon her; but there was no choice of courses, no room for hesitation, and she floated into the current ... she was not far off a rushing muddy current that must be the strangely altered Ripple." (539). And, driven by this power, she submits to the river's force—there is no turning back: "She could see now that the bridge was broken down..." (540). When she reaches the mill in this cataclysmic scene, the river becomes a terrifying presence. Tom experiences an epiphany after he jumps into the boat, and the two are reunited by the river: "It was not till Tom had pushed off and they were on the wide water—he face to face with Maggie—that the full meaning of what had happened rushed upon his mind. It came with so overpowering a force—such an entirely new revelation to his spirit, of the depths in life, that had lain beyond his vision which he had fancied so keen and clear, that he was unable to ask a question" (541). Finally, nature and industrialization collide as brother and sister are reclaimed by the river: "Nothing was said; a new danger was being carried towards them by the river. Some wooden machinery had just give way on one of the wharves, and huge fragments were being floated along.... 'Get out of the current!'" (542).

Like the River Floss, the River Roke in Wilkie Collins' novella *The Guilty River* (1886) is a dark and powerful force which permeates the lives of the central characters. The story opens with the return, after several years abroad, of a young man, Gerard Roylake, whose name suggests water, to claim his inheritance upon the death of his father. Part of the large property Roylake has inherited is a mill and its river. Here, most of the action in the story takes place, beginning with Roylake's first visit to the mill where he discovers a childhood friend, Cristel, the miller's daughter, now a beautiful young woman with whom he falls in love. The conflict arises in the story through the figure of another young man, known as the Lodger, himself extraordinarily handsome, who is already renting a room at the mill. He is deaf and has already fallen in love with Cristel. He is given to jealous rages compounded by his inability to hear, and he plots the death of Roylake by trying to poison him. The Lodger has the manuscript of a story, based on an episode in a volume of French trials, in which a young girl is cleverly abducted. He plots to use the plan himself to abduct Cristel, but Cristel's father steals it. All of this action takes place on and beside the gloomy river Roke. The image of the river is established at the beginning of the story; a Poe-like, phantasmagoric atmosphere foreshadows the dark deeds about to unfold: "Broad and muddy, their stealthy currents flowed onward to the sea.... A repellent river in itself, a repellent river in its surroundings, a repellent river even in its name" (249). Roylake reminisces as he begins his account of the affair: "I wonder how my life would have ended, if I had gone the other way?" (249).

Some similarities exist between "The Guilty River" and Charles Dickens' novel *Our Mutual Friend* (1865), set on the Thames and published just twenty-one years earlier. It also has a heroine, Lizzie Hexam, and Lizzie, like Cristel, rows her boat with practical skill and lives with her widowed father, helping him in his trade. Both women are loved by men beyond their own humble social statuses, and both stories are linked to the river.

In each of these works riparian images evoke a sense of unease and foreboding, as in an opening scene of *Our Mutual Friend* when Lizzie Hexam enters the story rowing on the gloomy Thames, similar to the scene in which Roylake first sees the miller's daughter: "I had not advanced far, when the stillness around me was disturbed by an intermittent sound of splashing in the water. Pausing to listen, I heard next the working of oars in their rowlocks. After another interval a boat appeared, turning a projection in the bank, and rowed by a woman pulling steadily against the stream" (250). Cristel, like Lizzie rowing against the tide of the murky nighttime Thames, is also going against the current, signifying the unnatural course of events to follow—deceit, attempted murder, and abduction.

The description of the river intensifies along with the drama in the story: "Our gloomy trees and our repellent river presented an aspect superbly transfigured, under the shadows of the towering clouds, the fantastic wreaths of the mist.... The mist, rolling capriciously over the waters, revealed the grandly deliberate course of the flowing current, while it dimmed the turbid earthy yellow that discoloured and degraded the stream under the full glare of day" (314). None of the three main characters, Roylake, the Lodger, and Cristel, can escape the dark pull of the river. The Lodger watches the river from his room at the mill each night: "I watch the flow of the stream, and it seems to associate itself with the flow of my thought ... dreams come to me. All of them, sir, without exception connect Cristel with the river" (295). And Roylake admits, "I took the familiar road which led me to the gloomy wood and the guilty river. The longing in me to see Cristel again, was more than I could resist" (310). For Cristel, the river also exerts a dark magnetism; the crucial scene when she saves Roylake's life is preceded by a significant action when she threatens to jump from the window into the river: "She crossed the room, and threw open the window which looked out on the river. "'You shan't die alone,' she said." (324). The story concludes by returning to the river and a description much like the beginning of the story. It is signified by a reversal in the boat's direction: "I walked on, by what we called the upper bank of the river.... The night was cloudy and close.... I had just stopped to look at my watch, when I saw something dark floating towards me, urged by the slow current of the river. As it came nearer, I thought I recognized the mill-boat" (339). Now the boat floats along with the current rather than against it, as it did when Cristel rowed it in the opening scene.

Aspects of this work emerge in H. E. Bates' novel *The Two Sisters*, which, like "The Guilty River," is an intensely romantic work involving a local young girl and a strange man who are brought together by a rural river. This novel is set, as is *The Mill on the Floss*, in Norfolk, on the Ouse and its tributary the Leem, which might well be the real names of George Eliot's River Floss and its tributary, the Ripple, and, like *The Mill on the Floss*, Bates' novel also ends with death through the flooding of the river. When it was first published, critic and writer Edward Garnett wrote in the foreword of Bates' novel: "The claim that *The Two Sisters* ... is of a rare poetical order, is attested by the opening scene of Jenny's homeward journey and clenched by the atmospheric truth and the beauty of the angry river ending."[8] The river setting is the Great Ouse, and story begins in a farmhouse set on a small tributary, the Leem, where the central character, Jenny Lee, lives with her sister, Tessie, two brothers, and a tyrannical father. The mother dies when Tessie is very young, and as adolescents both girls try to find relief from their father's despotism—Jenny by withdrawing from reality and Tessie by paying secret visits to the local dance hall. A river man, Michael Winter, who embodies the river itself, comes into their lives. Both girls fall under Winter's hypnotic spell, although it is to Jenny's love that he responds. His death corresponds with Jenny's coming into an awareness of her own self and her relationship with humanity. As Winter drifts on the river in a state of near narcosis, he dreams of Jenny and, for a moment, fights her enchantment before he succumbs. The first acknowledgment of love between Jenny and Winter also takes place on the river after Winter is drawn involuntarily to the river as he tries to marshal his emotions. His actions and feelings are described through riparian images: "Almost without knowing it he steered into the backwater, where the current was scarcely noticeable, and on whose surface floated bright green weeds..." (209–210).

The river is also a place of discovery for Jenny, who goes there for safety after being driven from the house by her father's insane rage and violence which threatens her life. Here, her thoughts of Winter and the river merge. In teaching her to navigate the river—"He taught me to paddle"—Winter teaches Jenny how to navigate her own life, and the river becomes symbolic of human potential, for, as H. E. Bates says of the river in *Down the River*, "...[it] is not merely a volume of water travelling on a set course from one point to another. It has become a living thing, with its own defined and complex character, its own idiosyncrasies and with something very like its own soul."[9] This is true of the Great Ouse, the river that finally claims Winter, who, drawn inescapably to its violent energy, finally drowns in it: "'This flood has kept me.... I have had to be here—watching.... If you could see the river now you would say you had never seen it so full and angry. It is terrible. It will do anything'" (284–285).

As it is for Maggie Tulliver in *The Mill on the Floss*, the river is the central unifying image that guides Jenny Lee through three specific stages on her journey to self-truth, and, as she reaches each of these revealing stages in her life, she is helped through them by her interaction with it. In childhood, the first stage of her journey, the river is Jenny's world: "She was the eldest of a family of four. All her life had been lived within sight of the slow, not always clean, backwater of river threading the valley behind her" (14). She is desperate in her need for understanding and sympathy, and the river offers her a sense of peace. The river marks this early stage in Jenny's development again when she makes her way home from a shopping trip in the local town. Dejected and confused by the recent loss of her mother, she stops inside a church in the local town and is confronted by a priest who exhorts her to pray. Her reaction is to flee to the river for freedom and solace: "'I want to be free!' ... She began to walk rapidly in the direction of the river she could not see but whose distance and position she had become to know after so many hours of sojourn on its banks and on the edge of the valley through which it ran. That river! Tonight!" (30). The silence of the river is truth as it allows Jenny Lee to come to the understanding that she will never see her mother again: "Suddenly, and courageously, she began to approach the water, not by walking, but by means of her hands and knees" (42). The crawling position that Jenny assumes by the edge of the river marks the end of her innocent childhood and is emphasized by the breaking of the beads given to her by her mother: The cord is broken, the beads fall into the river, and she begins the next phase of her life: "She got up slowly, her hands covering her neck, where had come a sensation she could not describe—something cool, different, as if she had taken off all her clothes and had stood with nothing on but the soft evening air touching her limbs. Her whole body had changed! She had changed!" (45). And the nakedness with which she enters her new stage of self-knowledge symbolizes, in Carlylean terms,[10] the shedding of the past.

As Jenny's own "silver chain" of laughter replaces the beads which had kept her tied to her mother, so she herself leaves the dependency of childhood behind, and she does so through the river, the great Ouse, which gives her the strength to enter the second stage. This stage is marked by a specific incident which has about it a nightmarish, almost surrealistic quality. Jenny's younger sister, Tessie, escapes from the house to pay a visit to the local dance hall to which she is drawn almost involuntarily. Anxious for her sister's safety, Jenny accompanies her sister into town. The river leads Jenny toward reality; her apathy becomes confusion as she wanders alone in the dark streets after leaving Tessie at the dance hall: "Under her feet the ground began to slant riverwards, and she felt unable to do anything but follow it, whither it might lead.... The river was near at last" (72). The river in this second stage reflects her emotions; she moves towards it in her confusion and becomes more and more instinctual, smell taking over from sight: "She caught the smell of the river in her nostrils.... She went into the great thickness of the mist and felt rain on her face, the rain smelling exactly as the fog had done, and simultaneously with those first drops of slack rain, she tripped and fell... (75). This fall, during which she briefly loses consciousness, is the dramatic and violent scene that marks the beginning of the second stage in Jenny's journey. Unlike the first, almost idyllic experience by the river which she welcomes with joyful affirmation, this stage is painful, as her injury suggests; it is the pain and confusion that she must pass through in order to become spiritually alive and break free of the numbing withdrawal from life that has been her protection from her father's brutish behavior and has led to her stoicism. The end of the second stage in Jenny's journey towards selfhood also draws on the river and centers on her involvement with Michael Winter. Until she meets Winter, the river has been Jenny's source of solace, as it is for Maggie Tulliver, and a means of escape from her miserable home life. At the end of their meeting, Winter's departure via the river is a foreshadowing of his drowning, and Jenny's "squatting" position on the riverbank as she watches him merge with the reflections on the river's surface marks the beginning of the third stage in her life: "...she squatted on the bank and watched until she could no longer distinguish him from the boughs and the reflections he had disturbed" (225).

The third stage that preludes Jenny's final awakening to self takes place by the river. Anxious because she has not seen Winter for several days because of his work on the flooded Ouse, Jenny goes in search of him, and the expression on her face as she goes into the town to look for him on the wharf reflects the flooded river: "It had the same look of placidity and depth as the vast chain of floods covering the whole floor of the valley on her right hand and which had increased rapidly and alarmingly during the last few days" (275). She looks over the flooded river valley, where the river is the central and vital image that brings her closer to Winter as she reminisces about her romance with him. Jenny now reaches the end of the final stage. Finally able to face her own isolation, she leaves the safety of Winter's house and goes into the wild night to join humanity in the form of the crowds waiting by the river's edge. Here, through the river, which represents life and death, she experiences a kind of death herself: "A great numbness crept over. She could not move. It was as if death were slowly possessing her body" (304–305).

To be alive is to know fear, and Jenny's new awareness of self is heralded by a shriek from the river: "Then came a great cry, weird and piercing, from the darkness over the river, which sent her cold again and paralyzed her hands into a clasp" (306). This fear is the existential dread that necessarily accompanies self-realization, as Kierkegaard explains: "Dread is an alien power which takes hold of the individual, and yet one cannot extricate oneself from it, does not wish to, because one is afraid, but what one fears attracts one."¹¹ It is this dread that announces Jenny's final awakening. Fully alive, she is now ready to move to an integration with humanity: "Unable any longer to remain in her isolated position she approached the cluster of people, touched a man on his elbow and whispered, finding it impossible to raise her voice any higher..." (307). After completing the final stage of her journey, Jenny sleeps and awakens in isolation to a stark new reality in which she must face her own contingency. The end of her journey brings life, but to be alive is to be in torment, and she realizes this as the river gives perspective to her own bleak landscape. Like the fictional river in *The Mill on the Floss*, the River Ouse is the controlling force in this novel; its waters gradually take precedence throughout, culminating in the catastrophic flood at the end, which not only takes the life of Michael Winter but also marks three dramatic and violent stages in Jenny Lee's life, stages that lead her to self-knowledge and a realization of her own potential as an individual human being.

The Victorian poetess Jean Ingelow also uses allegorical imagery to develop the theme of two lovers parted by a river into which the girl is afraid to enter. In her poem "Divided," considered by critics as her best, she uses the river and its tide to symbolize the parting of two lovers. The river is beguine and beautiful in the opening lines: "A flashing edge for the milk-white river,/ The beck, a river—with still sleek tide./ Broad and white, and polished as silver,/ ..." Yet it becomes angry and dangerous towards the end of the poem, much like the rivers in *The Mill on the Floss* and *The Two Sisters*: "But two are walking apart for ever,/ And wave their hands for a mute farewell." Theme and allegorical imagery unify in the closing lines: "The beck grows wider, the hands must sever"/ and later "The beck grows wider and swift and deep:/ Passionate words of one beseeching—/ The loud beck drowns them; we walk, we weep."¹²

In *Poetics of Space*, Bachelard discuss the literary images of space, or "topoanalysis"—what he calls the tophilic—love of place. He suggests that the occurrence of topophilia in a work of art is developed through the memory of a "felicitous space," often experienced in childhood, and explains that this memory is evoked from a setting where the imagination was unfettered by external criteria.¹³ The friendly space is the river and its tributary in Charles Kingsley's *Water Babies*, a Victorian fantasy that concerns the metamorphosis of a little chimney sweep, Tom, when he falls into a stream and is eventually swept into a river.

In the river he turns into an aquatic creature, discovers a new world, and is carried out to the sea.

The first part of the story concerns Tom's escape from his master and contains images of rebirth through nature as he runs miles over the moors and wanders into the stream, where he is thought to have drowned. It is an existential rebirth with attendant aspects of pain, fear, and nausea that are imaged in the riparian landscape he passes through: "Now and then he passed by a deep dark swallow-hole, going down into the earth ... he could hear water falling, trickling, tinkling, many feet below.... Then, when he had found a dark narrow crack, full of green-stalked fern, such as hangs in the basket in the drawing-room, and had crawled down through it, with knees and elbows, as he would down a chimney, there was another grass slope" (30, 36). (This is a passage reminiscent of the scenery of Ware Cliffs that also suggests rebirth in John Fowles' *The French Lieutenant's Woman* when Charles Arrowby stumbles through the undergrowth and emerges into an awakening of his new life with Sarah.) As Tom nears the stream, he experiences the existential nausea that accompanies fear: "He could not get on. The sun was burning, and yet he felt chill all over. He was quite empty, and yet he felt quite sick.... He could hear the stream murmuring only one field beyond it, and yet it seemed to him as if it was a hundred miles off" (37–38). Like the speaker in Ted Hughes' *River* who changes from a man to a fish, here, too, the river offers a sense of mutasis and becomes the medium for metamorphosis, seen through various river creatures which Tom observes and about which the narrator address his audience: "Do not even you know that a green drake, and an alder-fly, and a dragon-fly, live under water till they change their skins, just as Tom changed his? ... And if a water animal can continually change into a land animal, why should not a land animal sometimes change into a water animal?" (54).

Soon, Tom experiences an unrest; existentially, a period of discontent that precedes choice: "He could not tell why; but the more he thought, the more he grew discontented with the narrow little stream in which he lived, and all his companions there; and wanted to get out into the wide wide world, and enjoy all the wonderful sights of which he was sure it was full" (78). And, again, the existential nausea occurs: "And once he set off to go down the stream. But the stream was very low; and when he came to the shallows he could not keep under water, for there was no water left to keep under. So the sun burned his back and made him sick; and he went back again and lay quiet in the pool for a whole week more" (78). With the arrival of a violent storm that signifies change, he is swept into the river: "But toward evening it grew suddenly dark, and Tom looked up and saw a blanket of black clouds lying right across the valley above his head, resting on the crags right and left. He felt not quite frightened, but very still; for everything was still. There was not a whisper of wind, nor a chirp of a bird to be heard; and next a few great drops of rain fell plop into the water, and one hit Tom on the nose, and made him pop his head down quickly enough" (79). The river's tide sweeps him towards his destiny, the sea: "It was the tide, of course: but Tom knew nothing of the tide. He did not care now for the tide being against him. The red buoy was in sight, dancing in the open sea..." (94).

The rural rivers of the Great Ouse and its tributary, the Leem, become the felicitous spaces of childhood memory that Bachelard talks about in Graham Swift's *Waterland*, which is set in the Fens of East Anglia: "The Great Ouse. Ouse. Say it. Ouse. Slowly. How else can you say it? A sound which exudes slowness. A sound which suggests the slow, sluggish, forever oozing thing it is. A sound which invokes quiet flux, minimum tempo; cool, impassive, unmoved motion. A sound which will calm even the hot blood racing in your veins. Ouse, Ouse, Oooooose..." (1). *Waterland* is a first-person narration of the life of Tom Crick, history teacher, now living in London, who grew up with his father and mentally retarded brother, Dick, on the banks of the River Leem. Memory as it is transformed by the secondary imagination to bring about a sense of purpose and destiny is the central theme of the story. The novel begins with Tom's account of the murder of an adolescent boy and childhood friend, Freddie Parr, whose body is found by Tom's father, the lock-keeper, floating by the lock-gates outside the cottage. For Mr. Crick, the river is everything; it is his livelihood and his god. He is the keeper of the lock-gates. When the body of Freddie Parr floats by his lock-gates, his life—his landscape—changes: "...something floated down the Leem, struck the iron-work of the sluice, and, tugged by the eddies, continued to knock and scrape against it till morning" (4). And as Tom watches his father fish the body out of the river and try to bring the boy back to life, he draws a distinction between life and land that is central to the whole story: "And what else was my father doing on that July morning than what his forebearers had been doing for generations: expelling water? But whereas they reclaimed land, my father could not reclaim a life..." (27). From this incident, the novel grows, moving back and forth and transposing past and present as Tom dives constantly into the history of the Fens, searching for answers to his life. The present, for Tom, is London; here, he summons his memories of the past when he is in Greenwich Park, by the River Thames, where the line of 0 longitude that passes through it was once used as a basis for calculated time—Greenwich Mean Time—throughout the world. He tells his story to his students in a kind of experiment, which is really an effort to explore the validity of history as a tool by which the present may be explained. Due to the intensely autobiographical nature of his discourses on his life in the Fens, he is under dismissal by the school authorities. The present is also the failed marriage of Tom and Mary, his Fenland sweetheart, who, unable to conceive children due to an abortion she had as a teenager, goes to a London supermarket where she kidnaps a baby and is incarcerated in a mental institution for doing so. Eventually, Tom is able to modify and live with his memories and discovers a sense of purpose through an imaginative freedom brought about by the memory of the river.

The two rivers, the Great Ouse and the Leem, represent history itself, shaping and governing all its aspects, including sex, love, and suicide. In "Imperial Topographies: The Spaces of History in *Waterland*," the author, Pamela Cooper, explains the importance of the landscape in the story that takes place within it: "In *Waterland* the 'event' which shifts the perceptual paradigm of history is implicitly diffused throughout the text as the mobile geography of the marshes: their circulating liquidity and solidity and the repetitive spectacle they offer of space as empty and full, sterile and fertile."[14] United by the heartbeat of the Fens—the continuous rhythm of the pumps—the story opens with a cosmic integration of landscape and the human psyche which is to remain a predominant theme throughout: "When the traps had been set we lay back on the riverbank. Dick was fourteen and I was ten. The pumps were tump-tumping, as they do, incessantly so that you scarcely noticed them, all over the Fens, and frogs were croaking in the ditches. Up above, the sky swarmed with stars which seemed to multiply as we looked at them" (1). As in *The Water Babies*, it is an existential landscape, defining its own reality from the world around it. "For what is water, children, which seeks to make all things level, which has not taste or colour of its own, but a liquid form of Nothing?" (5). The "nothingness" which has the potential to "become" is represented through water in this rural landscape: "When you work with water, you have to know and respect it. When you labour to subdue it, you have to understand that one day it may rise up and turn all your labours into nothing" (5). But in this nothingness is reality—"reality is that nothing happens" (34)—"Realism; fatalism; phlegm. To live in the Fens is to receive strong doses of reality; the wide empty space of reality. Melancholia and self-murder are not unknown in the Fens. Heavy drinking and madness and sudden acts of violence are not uncommon. How do you surmount reality, children? How do you acquire, in a flat country, the tonic of elevated feelings? ... By telling stories" (15).

The river is also movement; it creates the energy that passes through this flat, monotonous landscape, and, like humanity, it is generative. And, like sexual energy, says Tom, the Fenland water "cannot be subdued but can be pumped into new channels" (76). Tom's brother, Dick Crick, represents this sexual energy—the movement of the river itself. The other characters in *Waterland* are also manifestations of the effects of living in such a landscape. Tom, who eventually marries Mary, moves away from the Fens and their powerful, stultifying forces. Another character, Freddie Parr's father, tries to escape through suicide: "Because he was oppressed by those flat Fenland fields and that wide, exposing Fenland sky. Because he grew tired of looking, every day, unable to move from his post, at featureless river-banks, phlegm-hued river water..." (99). Later, when Tom and Mary have also drifted away from each other, their marriage dissolved and Mary incarcerated in a mental institution, the view of the River Thames from Greenwich Park draws Tom back into the past through a vision of history that reflects the opening scene of the novel in its inclusion of man and landscape: "The river: a steel serpent coiling through clutter—derelict wharves and warehouses, decaying docks..." (112).

The riparian landscape in *Waterland* controls the lives of those who live on it, as it does in *The Mill on the Floss*, "The Guilty River," and *The Two Sisters*, and it finally brings Tom Crick into a painful recognition of the present through images and memories linked specifically to the rural rivers of the Leem and Ouse, for, as Tom says, "Man is one-tenth living tissue ... nine-tenths water." Of the characters that people this landscape, Tom's older retarded brother, Dick, represents the river and the sexuality implied in it as his constant association with the eels implies. He, like Michael Winter, the river man in *The Two Sisters*, and the fisherman persona in Hughes's *River*, is the river itself, and will return, as they do, at the end of the story to the Great Ouse forever because it is the place where he is most at home: "Because scrub and rub though he might, there is still—others can detect it—that residual whiff of the river-bed" (220). His job as a silt dredger on the Great Ouse, always reclaiming that which is threatened to be lost, is Sisyphean. Dick is saving the Fens and in doing so, due to the nature of his work, is saving the present, the here and now. Because of this, Tom sees Dick's job in a heroic light: "And he's the saviour of the world" (307–308).

Dick, like Tom in *The Water Babies*, is a type of mythic character. He is described through fish-like imagery in his contact with the river, which ties in with the whole sexual argument for the landscape as, for instance, on the occasion of the rite of passage Tom experiences by the River Leem at the Hockwell Lode. A game of "tease and dare" takes place between the group of young friends, including Dick. The person who dives from the bridge and swims farthest underwater down the river will be rewarded by a glimpse into the knickers of one of the girls. As they dive, Freddie Parr, who cannot swim, almost drowns and is saved by Dick, only to be murdered by him later on, suggesting the cycle of life and death that the river itself carries on, one that is also the predominant theme in Ted Hughes's *River*. On both these occasions of life and death, it is through the river that Dick acts, affirming Bachelard's statement in *Water and Dreams*: "Thus, water is an invitation to die; it is an invitation to a special death that allows us to return to one of the elementary material refuges."[15] For Tom, the dive into Hockwell Lode is a plunge into a new phase of his life—from childhood to adolescence—and it brings to him a realization about Dick's association with the river as he watches him emerge from the water and likens him to an eel: "the (long, but finless, scaleless) body of my brother..." (165).

Dick's sexual union with the river that unites water and man through the generative powers shared by both is realized by Tom as he watches his brother return to the group: "So that, even now, twisting strands of Dick's congealed seeds are floating down towards the Leem, where they will surely float to the Ouse and thence to the sea" (165). Dick's own rite of passage, which occurs later, also takes place at the river and concerns two meetings between Mary and Dick. At the first meeting of the two young people, Dick is collecting eels from his traps and sees Mary sitting across the river: "The river flows, unblinking, by" (216). So Dick, propelled by his erotic memory, dives and swims to Mary on the far bank. It is a symbolic death, a prelude to his literal death which follows shortly. "To disappear into water" is "to disappear on the distant horizon"[16] says Bachelard in *Water and Dreams*. Dick disappears into water when he takes his life, plunging into the level planes of the River Ouse from his dredger into another world: "A low and liquid world, a scarcely substantial world" (306). But Dick, like history, will always be a part of the present reality as the silt to which he instinctually returns on this final dive, taking on a piscine form of mythic proportions that encompasses man and nature as he plunges into the Great Ouse: "...here indeed was a natural, here indeed was a fish of a man" (309).

Magic is also represented in *Waterland*, described by Pamela Cooper as, "At once a geography and a topography, *Waterland*'s marshes become effectively a phantasmagoria more hallucination than fairy-tale, and here the contradictory physical properties of the Fens acquire other dimensions of significance."[17] There is a sense of metamorphosis in *Waterland* that aligns it with *The Water Babies*; for instance, through Tom's love for Mary, the landscape changes—the rivers and Fens become places of wonderment: "Because, despite everything, despite emptiness, monotony, this Fenland, this palpable earth raised out of the earth by centuries of toil, is a magical, a miraculous land" (101). And when Tom describes his marriage to Mary as "a sort of Fenland" (102), he talks of their past meetings by the river and describes the landscape as one of magical possibilities: "'...do you remember (can you still remember?) how once we lay in the shell of the old windmill by the Hockwell Lode and how the flat, empty Fens all around us became, too, a miraculous land, became an expectant stage on which magical things could happen?'" (101). Also representing the magic of the Fenlands is the old couple Bill and Martha Clay, a primitive pair, as their name suggests, who live in rural isolation beside the river. Martha is a type of local witch, and her husband is the magus of the river: "How, though Bill wasn't the wisest man in the world, he certainly was the most extraordinary. How he ate water-rats; hypnotized animals; how he was over a hundred; how he knew about the singing swans. How, though he left his cottage and lived alone for weeks on end in his tiny marsh-hut, he was still "married" to Martha Clay and they still 'did it' (a remarkable sight it was too) in the open air amongst the reeds" (47). It is to this cottage by the river that Mary and Tom go to seek an abortion. Martha performs what turns out to be a night-long medieval horror amid the gloom and hanging herbs of her cottage. While Martha utters supernatural admonishments, Tom takes the fetus at daybreak and throws it into the river, thus completing the cyclic process on which the story, like Kenneth Grahame's *The Wind in the Willows* and Hughes' *River*, is based.

The rural river enhances the imagination, becoming a site for fantasy or fairy tale because the imagination, as Bachelard states, "...is never wrong, since imagination does not have to confront an image with objective reality."[18] The rural River Thames at Cookham Dene is the setting for Kenneth Grahame's *The Wind in the Willows*, which describes the adventures of Toad, Rat and Mole, a novel which the writer Peter Hunt describes as "...a cultural artifact ... part of its fascination is its many layers and levels..." and calling it "at once a bildungsroman, a thriller, and a farce."[19]

Rat is a water rat, a natural swimmer, and the river is his milieu; he serves as the guide to the river for both the reader and Mole, but the reader is aligned with Mole through Mole's experiences and emergence into a new life on the river as he is introduced to them by Rat. Toad, the third main character in the story, is unaffected by the river. According to Bachelard, "Space that has been seized upon by the imagination cannot remain indifferent space subject to the measures and estimates of the surveyor. It has been lived in, not in its positivity, but with all the partiality of the imagination. Particularly, it nearly always exercises an attraction. For it concentrates being within limits that protect."[20] The river and riverbank are the truly felicitous spaces in the book as opposed to the places where their adventures take place, the Wild Wood and the Wide World. These represent danger for Rat and Mole, but their adventures always return them to the river.

The narrative opens in spring as Mole is introduced to the river by Rat. Mole is suffering from "divine discontent and longing" (1) intensified by the time of the year, and the river offers him renewal and freedom. And, like the river in Ted Hughes' *River*, it is male: "By the side of the river he trotted as one trots when very small, by the side of a man who holds one spellbound by exciting stories; and when tired at last, he sat on the bank, while the river still chattered on to him, a babbling procession of the best stories in the world, sent from the heart of the earth to be told at last to the insatiable sea" (3–4). As with all rural rivers, this one exerts a hypnotic quality over Mole when he first emerges from his dark subterranean home: "All was a-shake and a-shiver—glints and gleams and sparkles, rustle and swirl, chatter and bubble. The Mole was bewitched, entranced, fascinated" (3).

Mole and Rat experience a series of inversions on the river, the first occurring when Rat takes Mole across the river to his new life. The boat strikes the riverbank, and Ratty is inverted with "heels in the air" in the bottom of the boat. This marks the beginning of the journey: "[S]upposing we drop down the river together, and have a long day of it?" suggests Ratty (6). Another inversion is suggested in Rat's summation of the river: "What it hasn't got is not worth having, and what it doesn't know is not worth knowing" (8). And yet another crucial inversion takes place as they return to the other side of the river after picnicking, and Mole's emotions surface in a fit of jealousy over Ratty's rowing prowess: He grabs the oars from Ratty and capsizes the boat: "'Stop it, you silly ass!'" cried the Rat, from the bottom of the boat. 'You can't do it. You'll have us over!'" (15). Mole sinks, and the river covers him, a baptism through which he is freed from his underground dwelling to begin a series of riparian adventures: "Over went the boat, and he found himself struggling in the river" (15). He is pulled to safety by Ratty and concludes his first day thinking of "his new found friend the River" (18).

In Ted Hughes' collection of poems *River*, the rural setting of the river generates a cosmic integration of creature, man, and nature similar to that described in *The Wind in the Willows* and *Waterland*. When *River* was published in 1984, just one year after *Waterland*, J. D. McClatchy wrote in *The New Republic*: "In a way he [Ted Hughes] has always been a restless poet, experimenting now with voices, now with subjects, his head cocked for a new access to imaginative strength, whether ecstatic or elemental. River marks such a change in his career. If it seems a leap forward it has been accomplished by retracing his steps, and so perhaps should be called not a change but a recovery. It is a welcome and an exciting one."[21] In *River*, water is the life-giving theme; it unifies the seventy-seven poems that follow the pattern of the solstitial year, from December to January, beginning with the first poem which describes the vision of the river from an aerial perspective: "The power line, alive in its rough trench,/ Electrifies the anemones" ("Flesh of Light").

The central persona of all the poems is a fisherman who, like Tom in *The Water Babies*, the river man Michael Winter in *The Two Sisters*, and Dick Crick in *Waterland*, becomes one with the ebb and flow of the river's natural cycles as the river gradually leads him to an acknowledgment of his personal participation in the cycle of life and death. With each new poem, nature slowly takes precedence over the individual, and in the last few poems of the book, the river becomes the catalyst for the healing powers of the landscape as it aids and inspires the fisherman persona to focus on the rhythms of nature and frees him from worldly constraints. As does Jenny in *The Two Sisters* when she acknowledges the death of her mother, the fisherman persona moves through stages of ironic detachment to spiritual revelation made possible by his changing relationship with the river. About halfway through his journey, with the forty-second poem, the tone of the fisherman persona changes, and the river brings this about as it traps the fisherman in the river-fetch and forces him to surrender to its voice. It is a situation similar to the second stage of Jenny's journey in *The Two Sisters* when she realizes, through the river's voice, the loss of her mother. From now on, the fisherman persona experiences a different perspective through which he begins a more direct and personal involvement with the river that culminates in the final poem of the book, "Salmon Eggs." In this poem, Heidegger's idea concerning the effect of language upon life as being able to articulate the self in unity with the natural elements, resulting in "world,"[22] is clearly expressed through the imagery and symbolism of the river as it is experienced by the fisherman persona who is now is able to exert a Keatsian effort of negative capability to prepare himself for spiritual renewal similar to Jenny's at the end of *The Two Sisters*, a renewal implicit in the title of this poem.

As they are in *Waterland*, memory and imagination are also the key themes in *River*. Each poem is a lyric to the memory of the river, its currents, its lights and darkness, its life and death, and its inevitable continuity that moves towards a sense of purpose, which is to unite man with the natural rhythms of nature. "The river," says H. E. Bates in *Down the River*, "...is ageless but, at the same time, perpetually young. It travels, but remains. It is a paradox of eternal age and eternal youth, of change and changelessness, of permanence and transience."[23] The river is the revitalizing force of water and light which refreshes and renews through the relived memory of it as the fisherman describes the galvanic arrival of early spring in "Four March Watercolours": "Spring/ Just hesitates. She can't quite/ Say what she feels yet." In "River Barrow," the river combines past, present and future; its community of life unites nature and humanity in a cosmic integration: "...Future, past,/ Reading each other in the water mirror" (37). Reflecting the movement of the river towards the sea, the poems in *River* slowly draw the fisherman towards a revelation of destiny—to be at one with the rhythms of nature. This knowledge of destiny may be understood as what Bachelard calls "valorization": "It is not knowledge of the real which makes us passionately love it. It is rather *feeling* which is the primary and fundamental value. One starts by loving nature without knowing it, by seeing it well, while actualizing in things a love which is grounded elsewhere. Then, one seeks it in detail because one loves it on the whole without knowing why."[24]

The idea is demonstrated through these authors' explorations of rural and urban riverscapes that if a person is to live freely and imaginatively he or she must first arrive at a position of self-truth. In order to recognize this situation, each central character embarks upon on a kind of psychic journey: The Lady of Shalott does this by choosing to leave her tower, Tom and Maggie's journey in *The Mill on the Floss* is brought to fulfillment as the river floods; Roylake, in "The Guilty River," eventually finds peace and happiness after his dark experience on the River Roke brings self-realization. The boy, Tom, in *The Water Babies*, escapes his appalling life as a chimney sweep to find freedom in the river as it sweeps him toward the sea, and in *The Wind in the Willows*, Mole, the archetypal figure for all who are intellectually and spiritually imprisoned, escapes his subterranean dwelling and embarks upon a life of imaginative freedom. In *The Two Sisters*, Jenny Lee's journey toward self-realization is brought about through her experiences with the Great Ouse and its tributary, the Leem, which witness her relationship with the river man, Michael Winter. The journey for Tom Crick in *Waterland* is a historical one as the same rivers lead him into the past so that he may live meaningfully in the present; he relates his past life as it was governed by the rivers Ouse and Leem and in doing so is able to deal with the present. For the fisherman persona in *River*, the river is an archetype for a cyclic journey of renewal and metamorphosis, as man and cormorant merge in a celebration of the redemptive powers of nature. It is a journey through which the fisherman persona is finally able to overcome the stultifying forces of his worldly existence and discover self-truth in a unity with the rhythms of nature as he experiences them through the river and its landscape.

CHAPTER TWO

The Urban River

Charles Dickens' *Our Mutual Friend*, Joyce Cary's *The Horse's Mouth*; Penelope Fitzgerald's *Offshore*; Alan Sillitoe's "A Scream of Toys," Patrick McGrath's *Spider*; Iain Sinclair's *Downriver*, and Susan Hill's *The Mist in the Mirror*

> Dank and foul, dank and foul,
> By the smoky town in its murky cowl;
> Foul and dank, foul and dank,
> By wharf and sewer and slimy bank;
> Darker and darker the farther I go,
> Baser and baser the richer I grow;
> Who dares sport with the sin-defiled?
> Shrink from me, turn from me, mother and child.
> —"River Song," from *The Water Babies*,
>   Charles Kingsley

Unlike the rural river setting where the individual's aggressions may be replaced with the calm certainty of self-truth, the function of urban river setting is quite different in that authors' development of their characters' recognition of imaginative freedom is often brought about through an interaction with urban features pertaining to the river, such as the embankment, the bridge, and the canal, rather than the submergence of the self to the rhythms of nature. These specifically man-made features seem to take on more significance in the urban river setting, becoming symbols that offer insights into the characters' lives and affect their development. During the nineteenth century, embankments such as the Thames Embankment, like their urban seaside counterparts the fronts or promenades, rapidly became an important feature of urban society, one that authors soon began to utilize in their works. Charles Dickens describes the newly built Victoria Embankment in his *Dictionary of the Thames*:

> Victoria Embankment, London, extends along the left bank from Westminster to Blackfriars, a distance of about a mile and a quarter, and was constructed by Sir Joseph Bazalgette, the engineer to the Metropolitan Board of Works. The whole of the space now occupied by the embankment was covered by water or mud, according to the state of the tide, and few London improvements have been more conductive to health and comfort. The substitution of the beautiful curve of the embankment, majestic in its simplicity, with its massive granite walls, flourishing trees, and trim gardens, is an unspeakable improvement on the squalid foreshore, and tumble-down wharves, and backs of dingy houses which formerly abutted the river.[1]

The River Thames flows through many of the works of Charles Dickens, often as a malignant force and is used as a site for nefarious deeds committed on and around it, but perhaps nowhere as powerfully as in *Our Mutual Friend* (1864–1865), the Dickens' last complete novel, published in serial form and filled with decadence and decay, about which the poet, Algernon Swinburne, said in 1902: "This was the author's last great work: the defects in it are as nearly imperceptible as spots on the sun or shadows on a sunlit sea ... the real protagonist—for the part it plays is rather active than passive—is the river.... Of this book it might more justly be said that the genius of the author ebbs and flows with the disappearance and reappearance of the Thames."[2] Here, where murder, mystery, romance and revelation are all connected to the river, the urban River Thames becomes a menacing harbinger of dark secrets reluctant to surrender its dead, and its poison spreads both literally and metaphorically to all those lives living on and around it. It is indeed a "heart of darkness," a vehicle for attempted murder and murder, the foul deed from which the rest of the story develops.

The novel opens on a gruesome scene, ghostly and macabre, as Lizzie Hexam and her father, river man Gaffer Hexam, troll the nighttime Thames for drowning victims in the hopes that they may find valuables on them before turning the corpses over to the police and possibly receiving a reward. Gaffer Hexam and Lizzie are inextricably linked to the river—he through his appalling work and she by emotions she is unable to relinquish. Gaffer says, "I don't suppose anything about it, ... I ain't one of the supposing sort. If you'd got your living to haul out of the river every day of your life, you mightn't be much given to supposing. Am I to show you the way?" (23). Lizzie admits to the river's hold on her: "And as the great black river with its dreary shores was soon lost to her view in the gloom, so, she stood on the river's brink unable to see into the vast blank misery of a life suspected, and fallen away from good and bad, but knowing that it lay there dim before her, stretching away to the great ocean, Death" (70–71). She later tells her brother, Charley: "I am not here selfishly, Charley. To please myself, I could not be too far from that river.... I can't get away from it.... It's no purpose of mine that I live by it still" (128).

The setting and motives described in the opening chapter establish the mood and the main themes for the rest of the story, which concerns the appearance of John Harmon, recently returned from abroad via the river to claim his late father's fortune. His father, a junk dealer trading in the detritus of human lives, has made a condition in his will that his son must marry Bella Wilfer before receiving his inheritance. John Harmon rebels and stages his own death, and the body found by Gaffer Hexam in the Thames is assumed to be that of John Harmon, who has taken on a disguise and a pseudonym. The fortune reverts to the foreman of the junkyard, Nicodemus Boffin. He and his wife bring Bella Wilfer to live with them to assuage Bella's disappointment at losing the hand of a wealthy man. The avaricious Bella is determined to marry a rich man, yet she eventually falls in love with John Rokesmith, who is actually John Harmon, masquerading as a poor assistant to Nicodemus Boffin. The two story lines—the growing romance between John Rokesmith and Bella Wilfer and the changes in the moral development of Bella and of Nicodemus Boffin, whose inheritance moves him from compassion to greed, and its parallel story—that of murder, attempted murder, and other sordid events—are linked by the river, along with the enormous piles of garbage overshadowing its shores—the source of the Harmon fortune: "The wheels rolled on, and rolled down by the Monument, and by the Tower, and by the Docks; down by Ratcliffe, and by Rotherhithe; down by where accumulated scum of humanity seemed to be washed from higher grounds, like so much moral sewage, and to be pausing until its own weight forced it over the bank and sunk it in the river ... the wheels rolled on until they stopped at a dark corner, river-washed and otherwise not washed at all..." (20–21). The river's tide is the negative energy that pushes the story forward and drags it back, as it follows the two story lines of romance and murder: "Thus, like the tides on which it had been borne to the knowledge of men, the Harmon Murder—as it came to be popularly called—went up and down, and ebbed and flowed ... until at last, after a long interval of slack water, it got out to sea and drifted away" (31).

Invincible and unstoppable, the tide regulates the lives of all who live near the river: "The tide, which had turned an hour before, was running down, and his eyes watched every little swirl and eddy in its broad sweep, as the boat made slight head-way against it, or drove stern foremost before it, accordingly as he directed his daughter by a movement of his head. She watched his face as earnestly as he watched the river. But, in the intensity of her look there was a touch of dread or horror" (1). Tidal time is, in fact, the real time in the book: " ...by the run of the tide, it must be one. Tide's running up. Father at Chiswick, wouldn't think of coming down till after the turn, and that's at half after four" (71). And when the two men lie in wait for the return of Gaffer Hexam, "The wind carried away the striking of the great multitude of city church clocks.... Without that aid they would have known how the night wore, by the falling of the tide, recorded in the appearance of an ever-widening black wet strip of shore, and the emergence of the paved causeway from the river, foot by foot" (167). The tide also reflects Harmon's involvement in the story of murder: "Perhaps I might recall, if it were any good to try, the way by which I went to it alone from the river.... The room overlooked the river, or a dock, or a creek, and the tide was out.... I drew back the curtain (a dark brown curtain), and, looking out, knew by the kind of reflection below, of the few neighbouring lights, that they were reflected in the tidal mud" (368–369).

In later works, the description of the urban river setting often inclines towards the symbolic use of the embankment. Through its vista of river and river life the river's embankment becomes a place of entertainment and, conversely, solitude—a place to socialize as well as a place to meditate—and suggests a sense of reversal through which truths might emerge, along with the promise of spectacle attended by the all-important crowd, taking on the carnivalesque properties of street and marketplace. For instance, the embankment and the River Thames are the central tropes for the imagination and its necessary freedom in Joyce Cary's novel *The Horse's Mouth* (1944). Penelope Fitzgerald also sets her novel *Offshore* (1979) in the same area, thirty-five years later. In Alan Sillitoe's short story that takes place in wartime Nottingham, "A Scream of Toys" (1981), the River Trent that runs through Nottingham is the unifying image that functions as a place of regeneration, and both embankment and bridge mark specific stages of revelation and movement in the plot. Also set in London, Patrick McGrath's powerful novel *Spider* (1990) uses river and canal as the central tropes for the channel by which the protagonist draws his memories into the present in order to confront the past and define his situation. In Iain Sinclair's *Downriver* (1991), London's East End and the River Thames echo the same sense of desolation and attendant grotesqueries as that described in *Our Mutual Friend* and *Spider*. Embankment and bridge in Susan Hill's *The Mist in the Mirror* (1992) suggest stages in the narrator's journey, throughout which the River Thames is the dominant image that unites the events in the story.

In Oscar Wilde's poem "Impression du Matin" (1881), recalling Claude Monet's painting *Impression—Sunrise*, the opening lines establish the image of the Thames—which (like Cary's *The Horse's Mouth*) focuses on color: "The Thames nocturne of blue and gold / Changed to harmony of grey." In *The Horse's Mouth*, the river offers creative freedom for the imagination by which means the central character, Gulley Jimson, may achieve his artistic fulfillment, which takes place on Greenbank Hard, beside the River Thames in the East End of London, the setting for *Our Mutual Friend*. Here, sixty-nine-year-old Gulley Jimson, considered to be one of Cary's most successful creations, struggles to paint the visions which come to him as he shuffles, cold and hungry but never dispirited, alongside the river. The novel opens with Jimson walking beside the Thames, where he has just returned to his run-down boathouse studio after being released from prison: "I could see my studio from where I stood, an old boathouse down by the water wall." Near to starvation, ragged, and in ill health, Jimson is oblivious to the necessities of day-to-day living and is kept alive by the desire to articulate his artistic vision. In order to do this, he finds ways, usually devious, to get the materials he needs to paint his visions into pictures. He embarks upon a series of escapades with local cronies—Sarah (Sal), his past lover now grown old and shapeless but still desirable; Nosey, the young and ardent champion of Jimson whom Jimson tries to dissuade from becoming an artist; Mr. Plant, a grassroots philosopher, and Hickson, the art collector, a past patron to whom Jimson often makes nuisance calls. Through these escapades, the novel becomes the story of the imagination set free, and Jimson represents this, demonstrating Cary's belief that each person exists in a condition of absolute freedom and the most valuable human attribute is the creative imagination: "The same creative imagination which is necessary to every human being to decide the simplest problem of conduct, to answer such questions as, 'What exactly in this situation is important for me, and what is not?' 'What will be the effect of my doing so-and-so?' also perpetually invents new arts, new political ideas, new religions, new machines, new fashions, new swindles."[3] It is through the perspective offered by the river that Jimson experiences the imaginative freedom necessary in transforming empirical reality into his own personal artistic visionary expression. The first instance of this change takes place in the opening scene as Jimson, the alchemist, changes the sordid reality of the River Thames into a vision of beauty and energy:

> I was walking by the Thames. Half-past morning on an autumn Sun like a mist. Like an orange in a fried fish shop. All bright below. Low tide, dusty water and a crooked bar of straw, chicken boxes, dirt and oil from mud to mud. Like a viper swimming in skim milk. The old serpent, symbol of nature and love.... Such as Thames mud turned into a bank of nine carat gold rough from the fire. The sun had cracked into flames at the top; the mist was getting thin in places, you could see crooked lines of gray, like old cracks under spring ice. Tide on the turn. Snake broken up. Emeralds and sapphires. Water like varnish with bits of gold leaf floating thick and heavy. Gold is the metal of the intellect [1–2].

Jimson also goes to the river whenever circumstances threaten his imaginative freedom, such as the time when a group of preachers who have gathered at Mr. Plant's house reject Jimson's painting on the grounds that it is does not represent art in any traditional form: "I should have liked to take myself in both hands and pull myself apart" (44). In this agonizing scene, Jimson feels a unity with the river, in its "wrinkled skin" which he compares to his own emotional state "ruffling under my grief." As his sense of self returns, so the images of the river become firmer, relating to love, and energy is finally restored in the closing violent image: "It made me want to sing and hit the lampposts" (45).

The river offers Jimson another form of escape when the threat of incarceration is imminent. This occurs when he is being chased by the police after making one of his nuisance calls to Hickson, and the earlier image of horses with "silk-like muscles" changes to one of "rheumatic old willows" as Jimson feels the threat of his own mortality. The flight from the police intensifies and Jimson, along with three friends, goes down to the actual reaches of the river. Here, with thoughts of his own possible imprisonment, he briefly feels the need to capture the river by painting it, but it is a temptation he resists because to paint the river would imply a kind of stasis for both it and what it represents in terms of the imagination. Thus he leaves it free, "its surface dissolved away into blue-glass sky." This image of infinite nothingness reverses; as Jimson is reminded of his recent stay in prison, so the river reflects his feelings in its movement and texture: "Overhead the sky was as black as Prussian blue.... And the river crawling along, the color of pig iron, like a steam of lava just going solid" (63).

Vision comes to Jimson again through the river when his boathouse is taken over by the indomitable Mrs. Coker. Because he owes her daughter money, Mrs. Coker confiscates the painting he has been working on. In a violent scene when he tries to get it back and is struck by her, he goes to the river and turns his anguish at losing his work into imaginative joy: "You couldn't see for the sparks" (124). Later in the novel, when Jimson's painting is destroyed, and the young boy, Nosey, to whom Jimson is an unwilling mentor, commiserates with him as they walk beside the river, Jimson's understanding and acceptance of this loss comes to him through the fluid, freeing images he sees in the river and in the rain, and he is, once again, enthused with a new vision: "We had come to the end of Greenbank. And it was raining scullery taps. Out of a sky like a battle. Great jagged lumps and balloons of water, with oyster domes and a green splash. We stood among fountains, under waterfalls" (179).

The end of the story and final vision, one that reflects the opening scene, takes place as Jimson walks besides the Thames after starting his last picture—a mural which he is painting on the inside of a disused chapel in Horsemonger's Yard just off the river. The name of the yard indicates that even though Jimson will not finish this painting because the chapel is to be demolished, he has arrived at the truth, straight from the "horse's mouth," and the truth which he has arrived at through his interactions with the river lies in the freedom of the imagination, not in his paintings. As he leaves the chapel, first carefully, and symbolically, shutting inside his artisan's tools—"I closed the window from the outside"—he goes to the river. Here, he becomes part of his own vision, including himself in a cosmic integration of heaven and earth: "An evening by Randipole Billy. Green lily sky, orange flames over the West. Long flat clouds like copper angels with brass hair orange. Old man lying along the water with a green beard, one arm under head, face twisted up—vision of Thames among the pot-houses" (252-253). The urban setting of the River Thames becomes the catalyst for Jimson's creative imagination. and its embankment and walkways the sites where he experiences the realization of imaginative freedom.

The River Thames also represents freedom in Penelope Fitzgerald's *Offshore*, the story of a group of barge dwellers, and that which draws them to live on the river is what makes them unique: "The barge dwellers, creatures neither of firm land nor water, would have liked to have been more respectable than they were.... But a certain failure, distressing to themselves, to be like other people, caused them to sink back, with so much else that drifted or was washed up, into the mud moorings of the great tideway.... Biologically they could be said, as most tideline creatures, to be 'successful.' They were not easily dislodged" (10). It is the tide, the rise and fall of the river waters which announce themselves through the creaks and groans of the barge's swelling timbers, that unites the lives of these people and governs their riparian existence. Living at the water's edge, their barges caught between land and water, the Reach dwellers, each intensely aware of the other's personal sorrows and aspirations, form a separate world of their own. The leader of this group is Richard, a successful businessman on shore, but on the river, a man with a failing marriage anxious to give his wife anything except the one thing she is dying for—to live on land. He struggles to free himself from the pull of the river but is unable to do so: "And if the river spoke to his dreaming, rather than to his daytime self, he supposed he had no business to attend to it" (11). Nenna, another member of the group, is the mother of two precocious little girls, Martha and Tilda. She, like Richard, has marital problems because of her insistence in clinging to her life on the river. Yet even for her husband, Edward, who refuses to live with her and their children on the barge, the river offers relief during a brief sojourn when he visits her; "[it] flowed like the current, with it separate eddies, of the strong river beneath them" (39). But Edward refuses to stay, so Neena struggles along in happy poverty and the company of her children and her friends, the other bargees. One of these, Maurice, a male prostitute and receiver of stolen goods, is her closest confidant whose life is also deeply affected by the river: "If the tide was low the two of them watched the gleams on the foreshore, at half tide they heard the water chuckling, waiting to lift the boats, at flood tide they saw the river as a powerful god, bearded with the white foam of detergents, calling home the twenty-seven lost rivers of London, sighing as the night declined" (45). Their perceptions of the river and how they each choose to let it influence them is an indication of each character's life. The members of the group suffer, in one way or another, a sort of pain, a sense of sadness of something missed through their isolation from the rest of humanity, from which, through their emotional interactions with the river, they either gain strength or to which they succumb. The identities of the characters are reflected in the way each particular barge is maintained, and the bargees refer to each other, not by their own names, but by the names of their barges. Maurice renamed his barge, *Maurice*, after himself. Willis' barge, *Dreadnought*, that he lives on amid amicable clutter, is like old Willis himself, suffering an irreparable leak, which threatens to sink it with every high tide. Nenna's barge, *Grace*, resembles her own life, full of small leaks which she tries to mend to keep her world afloat for herself and her daughters. Richard's barge, *Lord Jim*, is large and immaculate, as are his dealings with the other bargees. It is on his barge that the monthly community meetings are held: "All the meetings of the boat-owners, by a movement as natural as the tides themselves, took place on Richard's converted Ton mine sweeper" (10).

As it functions in *The Horse's Mouth* and "A Scream of Toys," the river in *Offshore* is the touchstone—it marks the growth of each character in his or her association with it. When, for instance, Nina goes on land to visit her husband, the experience marks an important stage towards a revelation of self-truth for her. Lost in the dark streets after being rejected by Edward, she searches for a way back to the river: "Once she had got to the river she would be on her way home" (96). As she wanders through the night, she loses one of her shoes, throwing it at a man who accosts her, and so she moves barefooted through the sleet and rain. Her foot bleeds, and this is the wound, like that she suffers before entering on the new phase of her life away from the river, living with her sister in Halifax. Her old life of insecurity and confusion she leaves behind, thanks to the self-knowledge she has gained while living on the river, and she is ready to move on. To emphasize this change, she loses her old identity, marked by the contents of her purse, and all it represents while wandering in the city: "almost the whole sum of her identity" (129). She is finally rescued from her confusion by a taxidriver, a modern-day Virgil who offers to take her back to the river shore. She is now ready to move on and is helped in this endeavor by Richard who is waiting for her return. He attends to the wound on her foot before taking her in his dinghy to float with the tide down the river. Recognition and change are symbolized in the "darkness lifting" and the wind rising as they set off at high tide, and Richard, who tells Neena that his wife has finally left him to live on land, surrenders his compulsion for order and organization and admits to giving way to chance.

Significant incidents in the lives of these river people take place at high tide when their barges are freed from the mud banks of the reach and are fully afloat. It is a time of detachment and danger for them, often signaled by a ship's hooter, as is the meeting that takes place at the opening of the story: "The silence was eased by a long wail from a ship's hooter down stream. It was a signal peculiar to the Thames river— I am about to get underway. The tide was making, although the boats still rested in the mud" (11). As the meeting opens, danger arises concerning the subject under discussion of Maurice's friend, a deliverer of stolen goods and a child molester, and the tide lifts the barge: "For the next six hours—or a little less, because at Battersea the flood lasts five and a half hours, and the ebb six and a half—they would be living not on land but on water" (12–13). It is also at high tide that Willis finally loses his old barge to the river and is faced with spending the rest of his life on land—a certain death for him: "The main leak had given way at last.... It was like one of those terrible sights of the racecourse or the battlefield where wallowing living beings persevere dumbly in their duty although mutilated beyond repair" (78). A violent blow from part of his dislodged bunk floating in the darkness of the flooded cabin marks the beginning of a new phase in Willis' life, and he comes above to his waiting friends a changed person: "The door opened, and Willis stood there, like a drowned man risen from the dead, his spectacles gone, water streaming from him, and instantly making a pool at his feet" (79). Willis, a marine painter, also has magical powers. Having grown old on its waters, he is the shaman of the river and from childhood has known its tides and its treasures: "The six-year-old boy knew every current and eddy of the river. Long had he studied the secrets of the Thames. None but he would have noticed the gleam of gold and diamonds" (28). He passes this knowledge on to Nenna's daughter, Tilda, herself at one with the river, who, at six years old, sees the river as her entire existence. Like Michael Winter in *The Two Sisters* and Dick Crick in *Waterland* as well as the cormorant in the *River* poem "A Cormorant" which becomes a fish when it dives into the water, she represents the mutative powers that the river exerts over specific characters who exist solely in the present. Like the tide itself (her name is an anagram for *tidal*) Tilda lives only for the present—her beloved river, which she often views from the *Grace's* wobbly fifteen-foot mast: "Her whole idea of the world's work was derived from what she observed there and had little in common with the circulation of the great city which toiled on only a hundred yards away" (28).

When the other members of the group, including her older sister, Martha, are held in awe by the river as its tides threaten to pull apart their leaking barges, or when its storms and floods promise a watery grave, Tilda is exhilarated by it: "Banished to the cabin, she lay there full of joy, feeling the crazy desire of the old boat to put once again into mid-stream" (28). And when the two set out to explore the river shore for treasure, like Michael Winter and Dick Crick, Tilda takes on a mythic appearance of something more akin to the water than a human being: "Martha surveyed her sister doubtfully. With so much specialized knowledge, which would qualify her for nothing much except a pilot's certificate, with her wellingtons over which the mud of many tides had dried, she had the air of something aquatic, a demon from the depths, perhaps" (63). Using the knowledge of the Thames passed on to her by Willis, Tilda seeks the treasures of the river, and although her sister, Martha, goes on these treasure hunts with her, both sisters are aware that it is Tilda who is closest to the river and its tides and who will be the one to retrieve a treasure of some rare ceramic tiles from its muddy reaches, where "[b]eyond the old Church at Battersea the retreating flood had left exposed wide shelf of mud and gravel," a magical place, the setting of one of Gulley Jimson's visions in *The Horse's Mouth*, where the sisters find their own fabulous creatures when they search for broken tiles in the muddy reaches and Tilda spots one: "The sinuous tail of a dragon, also in gold and jewel colors, wreathed itself like a border round the edge of the other tile (66).

The story closes at high tide on the river, during a violent storm: "On the reach itself, there could be no pretence that this would be an ordinary night.... The Thames barges, built of living wood that gave and sprang back in the face of the wind, were as much at home as anything on the river. To their creaking and grumbling was added a new note, comparable to music. As the tide rose, the wind shredded the clouds above them and pushed a mighty swell across the water, so that they began to roll as they had once rolled at sea" (133–134). Neena takes her children to the safety of the shore, and in doing so, ironically, misses the longed-for appearance of Edward, whom Maurice befriends and tries to guide across his own deck to the *Grace* in the teeth of the storm. The confusion that ensues reflects the confusion in Edward's own life that he has come to the river to resolve as he and Maurice are swept towards the sea.

Another urban river, the Trent in Nottingham, is also the central unifying theme that links past, present, and future while offering a possibility for spiritual revelation in Alan Sillitoe's short story "A Scream of Toys," which describes through images linked to water: clouds, rain, and river, the spiritual and sexual awakening of a young woman. The River Trent represents the boundary that Edie, the central figure, must cross on her journey from childhood to maturity. Set in the city of Nottingham, the story uses embankment and the bridge to symbolize this crucial transition. It is told in two parts that describe childhood and adolescence, linked by the River Trent. The first, brief part of the story focuses on the past, the childhood of Edie, and quickly moves to the present, where Edie is now a young working woman of sixteen. Both parts of the book begin and end with water imagery. The water image that opens the story is a small pool. Like the small child, Edie, and the spring section in *River* where Hughes describes the river in spring as inarticulate, it is filled with nascent possibilities: "Edie looked a long time at blue sky in a pool of water after rain before dipping her finger down for a taste. It got wet. The edge of a cloud was bitter with soil and moldy brick, telling her that the old backyard was in the sky as well. It was everywhere, even when she walked out and on to the street, and to the road at the end of the street, for wherever she was she knew she had to go back to Albion Yard because that was where she lived" (93). The child, Edie, is symbolized as a pool of water, a small reflection of the world come from heaven to eventually unite with river in a cosmic integration of sky, nature and child with universe, rain, and world.

With the river, especially the urban river, bridges take on symbolic significance. The physical link they provide, between neighborhoods and uniting communities and individuals, becomes a link between worlds—stages in the characters' development that must be crossed. For instance, in the opening lines of the second part, we find Edie, now a young woman of sixteen and working in a local factory, standing on the bridge, about to meet an Italian soldier, a prisoner of war, with whom she will eventually experience her first sexual encounter. She wanders alone on the river's embankment, where "[a]ll dressed up and nowhere to go, she stood on Trent Bridge looking into the water.... All water was like oilcloth" (95). Throughout the story the bridge, as it stretches across the boundary of the river, suggests the possibility of escape to a new world, but for Edie, as with nearly all of Sillitoe's characters, the physical escape can only be temporary. Edie's first attempt at crossing the bridge into a new world of sexual initiation is not successful:

> ... they walked along wide Queen's Drive toward Wilford Bridge.... You had to pay a ha'penny if you wanted to cross the Trent there, so they called it Ha'penny Bridge. To her it seemed the only real way to get out of Nottingham, to leave home and vanish forever into a land and life which could never be as bad as the one she felt trapped in since birth. But she had only been taken over to play as a child—or she'd gone across for a walk by herself and come back in half an hour because there didn't seem anywhere to go.... Before reaching the bridge she said: 'Let's turn round.' The thought of water frightened her, and she had no intention of crossing to the other side [104–105].

It is as H. E. Bates explains in *Down the River*: "The river triumphs. And, since it is not only indestructible but a thing of destruction itself, it also terrifies. Then again, since it not only destroys but is a means to the creation of life and beauty, it also soothes and stimulates."[4] The river not only marks the stages in Edie's maturation but also becomes the vehicle through which she is able to articulate her emotions. When her parents, confused and angry over Edie's passage from childhood to womanhood, fall into a violent and desperate argument, Edie likens it to the waters of the river: "She heard them arguing downstairs, though not what was said. Their speech sounded like the flood of a river hitting a bridge before going underneath" (113). Through the concept "being unto death," Heidegger believes that every human being is concerned with finding some way in which he or she can feel the *Dasein*, the sense of *being there*, of having lived meaningfully in the face of death and nothingness and established some meaning in life which death cannot take away.[5] Edie is finally able to achieve this, and her emergence into a new awareness is marked, as it is in the opening, by water; here, it is the baptismal image of the river water lapping at her feet as a victory over death. The end of the story returns to the river in a scene that reflects the one in Hughes' *River* poem "Four March Watercolours," which describes a new awareness along with the promise of a new cycle of life. Attended by the moon and united by the cry of the bird and the final image of the embracing river, Edie comes to this realization as she embraces a new stage in her life:

> Grey water slopped on the concrete steps. There was a noise of children playing from the other side of the river.... The streak of green and blue turned into the last flush of the day. Children stopped playing suddenly. They were alone on the embankment with no one to see them.... They were on the lowest step by the water, which, had it come up another inch, would have flowed over her shoes.... She took two ha'pennies from her pocket. The old woman at the gate wore a thick coat and scarf to keep out the damp. The river pushed itself forcefully along, and the other side seemed far off from where they stood.... A sliver of sharp moon showed as if about to come down and cut the river into ribbons.... At the end of the bridge they walked down the lane, no lights showing from any house.... She heard the grating cry of a crow from the river that looped on three sides of them [117–120].

In this story, the River Trent signifies the border between womanhood and childhood; its embankment and its bridge are public places that represent links between the stages of Edie's transitions in her life towards autonomy.

The Thames Embankment becomes the site for awakening and realization in Patrick McGrath's novel *Spider*, in which memory is linked with the creative imagination of the narrator, Spider, a paranoid schizophrenic. Katherine Dunn writes about *Spider* in her review, "The Child Is Father to the Mad": "The tight, sharp focus of this deceptively slim volume keeps us on track despite the speed of both the past and the present plots. And the sensuous world that Mr. McGrath creates is intense in its beauty as well as its grime, a place where joy waits outside in the rain and there is more murder and mystery than even Spider can admit."[6] The story unwinds from Spider's perspective through which the reader is drawn into a web of recurring images, the threads that weave it together: Light bulbs swing with execution-like crackles from frayed cords; splintered rays of faint sunlight refract on dark pavements and walls; maggots, black and white, crawl slimily; potatoes spurt blood; cold rain drizzles incessantly. Permeating all is the pervading stench of gas, which evokes in Spider an uncontrollable fear, and the only constants in this delusional landscape of the paranoid schizophrenic are the canal and the river. Of the type of character he writes about McGrath says: "I'm interested in characters whose negotiations with reality are disturbed, whose points of view are much more restricted and much more distorted and skewed because of the particular forms of denial or emotional bias that they have."[7]

Spider's obsession concerns the death of his beloved mother whom, he is convinced, was murdered by his father when she discovered him in flagrante delicto with a local woman, Hilda, in his small allotment garden overlooking the canal. According to Spider, his mother's head is bashed in with a garden shovel, and he watches as his father buries her body in his potato patch. From this time on, Spider's life spirals down from misery to madness, driven by the memory of his mother's murder and the taunts of his father and Hilda, who takes over his mother's place in the home. Despair, loneliness, pain, and confusion envelop Spider over the following months as he tracks and watches the pair through pub windows, hallways, and shadowy canalside streets where they pursue their drunken lovemaking. Unable to endure any more torment, he ties a string to the gas tap on the kitchen stove, and, by pulling on it from his upstairs bedroom window, gasses Hilda when she returns home intoxicated one evening. For the murder of Hilda, his surrogate mother, he is incarcerated in a mental institution, Ganderhill, and it is only after his release twenty years later that he returns to the same neighborhood and is able to put the past into some kind of gruesome order as he sits on his bench by the canal. The canal and the river are the central tropes for the channel by which means the protagonist-grotesque, Dennis (Spider) Clegg, in a grisly type of Proustian effort, weaves his web of past into present by recording his memories in a journal, charting his life from the dingy attic room of a halfway house for patients discharged from institutions for the criminally insane. Other than Spider, who has enough sense of urgency and survival to hoard his tranquilizers, the other residents of this house of the living dead are heavily medicated and spend their days, zombielike, under the iron rule of their Dickensian landlady, Mrs. Wilkenson. Here, to the bleak and derelict area of London's East End where he grew up, Spider returns as an adult and moves slowly back and forth from attic to canal where, like a character from a Beckett play, he sits bundled in rags and old newspapers on a bench and waits for recollections of the past. Of his novel Patrick McGrath says that R. D. Laing's *The Divided Self* provided the model for schizophrenia that informed it, particularly in rendering the "tremendous fragility" of Spider's sense of self. "Spider constantly uses metaphors of being a light bulb," says McGrath, "being a flickering coil within a very fragile shell. He talks about his fears of being engulfed by life, of being destroyed by the glances of others. He is terribly, terribly delicate. Laing's book talks about this curious, tragic paradox in which the schizophrenic yearns for contact with life and yet is unable to participate and must hide, retreat and encapsulate, encastellate, himself because life, while being that which he desires, is that which threatens him with distinction. 'Dying of thirst in a world of wet'—Laing used that phrase, and I was able to use it in a scene at the end of the book, where Spider is unable to take a drink of beer in the pub because the worm in his lung won't allow him to. Life is there all around him, but he is unable to access it."[8]

As the canal represents a means by which Spider is able to travel back into the past, so the River Thames, to which he slowly gravitates as he encounters his memories, comes to represent for him, as it does for Gulley Jimson in Joyce Cary's *The Horse's Mouth*, a visionary hope that brings with it the recognition of a possible future. And signifying a connection between mind and language, the river becomes the vehicle by which he, like Jimson, is able to articulate his dilemma, and memory is linked with canal as Spider relates his story: "I was that conduit, I was the channel and absorbed the poison" (97). And it is the unchanging reality of the canal that enables him to summon the shifting patterns of the past:

> But at least I'm not far from the canal. I've found a bench by the water, in a secluded spot that I can call my own, and there I like to while away an afternoon with no one disturbing me. From this bench I have a clear view of the gasworks.... This is how it works, you see. I sit on my bench with my back to the wall. The sky is gray and overcast; there is perhaps a spot or two of rain. An air of desolation pervades the scene; no one is about. Directly in front of me, a scrubby strip of weeds and grass. Then the canal, narrow and murky, green slime creeping up the stones [11–12].

Likewise, the onset of the misery and pain that begins with the loss of his mother is also tied to the canal as it represents Spider's own mind. When Spider describes watching Hilda, his father's mistress, and his father making love, the image of his father ejaculating into the canal suggests a cyclic continuum that reflects the memory of his father: "He could see his sperm drifting away through the black water, filmy strings of the stuff, grayish and translucent" (40). The canal, as it runs between the neighborhood of his childhood and the area he now inhabits, also represents a borderline between past and present, one that Spider must eventually cross in order to find his identity: "When I was growing up we lived on Kitchener Street, which is the other side of the canal, east of here.... I haven't yet been back to Kitchener Street; I feel apprehensive about crossing the canal and seeing again those blackened bricks, imbued as they are in my memory with the sounds and smells of the tragedy that occurred there" (16–17). Spider explains his spiritual state in Carlylean images of clothing as he moves through the confusion of the present towards the canal, which is the only place that affords him a sense of reality, of self-definition:

> I am a baggy, threadbare sort of customer, really—my clothes have always seemed to flap around me like a sailcloth, like sheets and shrouds—I catch a glimpse of them sometimes as I hobble through these empty streets, and they always look vacant, untenanted, the way the flannel flaps and hollows about me, as though I were nothing and the clothes were clinging merely to the idea of a man, the man himself being elsewhere, naked. These feelings disappear when I reach my bench, for there I am anchored, I have a wall behind me and water in front of me, and as long as I don't look at the gasworks all is well [20].

As Spider comes to terms with the fear of his memories, especially those of his father and his own guilt, he goes back to the canal after a horrifying incident at the halfway house when he imagines that gas is seeping from his body: "It wasn't until I reached the canal that some semblance of normality returned, and as with trembling fingers I rolled a cigarette, and the minutes slipped by me in that lonely place, so did the events of the night come to seem like a wakening nightmare of some kind; after a while I was able to shrug it off" (30). This smell of gas, is, for Spider, the smell of fear, especially associated with his father; it is central to his Proustian endeavors, and the ever-looming gasworks across from his bench by the canal is the catalyst which generates memories also of childhood nightmares, enabling him to confront the hidden fears of the subconscious—his past dreams: "I was plagued, as a boy, with nightmares; and that night I dreamed about the gasworks canal.... With every cresting wave some new horror was lifted from the depths and exposed to me, and I knew with utter certainty and utter terror that I would be unable to keep my footing on the bank of the canal but would fall in among these bleating horror" (77). The description of the canal of Spider's nightmare is, like his own mind, filled with horrors and trapped in a web of "netting." And, like the canal of reality, this Stygian horror is associated with his father: "Suddenly then the picture of my father in shirtsleeves and a flat cap digging a hole in the middle of his potato patch" (77). The frightful memory of his mother's burial when he witnesses his father digging the grave in the allotment parallels the end of the canal nightmare: "Then I saw that my father was shoulder deep in the hole, damp with sweat despite the chill of the fog. He tossed up the spade, then with some difficulty clambered up after it. The earth crumbled beneath his fingers, and several times he slipped back in.... Worms, faintly visible, gleaming in the moonlight, writhe from the soil in the hole's deep walls" (78).

To disabuse himself of the painful, recently emerged memories of Ganderhill, Spider goes to the river. The scene, which brings together the perspective offered by the river as well as a sense of being for Spider as he carries his umbrella, a symbol of sanity and forethought, brings to mind W. H. Auden's description of a cartoon in which "a little man with an umbrella is engaged in a life-and-death struggle with a large octopus which has emerged from a manhole in the middle of the street: "He is a real individual, yet even with him, the question arises: 'Would he be standing out there in the street by himself if the octopus had not attacked him?' i.e., if he had not been compelled by a fate outside his personal control to become an exceptional individual. There is even a suggestion about his bourgeois umbrella of a magician's wand. Could it be possible that, desiring to become an individual yet unable to do so by himself, he has conjured up a monster from the depths of the sea..."[9] Here, by the river, with his "magician's wand," Spider is able to effect the crucial change, to objectify his life and see himself—his "bony knuckles"—as he does the scenery, where the flight of the gulls across the river becomes an image of the memories of Ganderhill that he relinquishes.

For Spider, as the canal is the means by which he brings to light all his fearful memories, so the River Thames, as it does for Gulley Jimson in *The Horse's Mouth*, offers healing and signifies change through the awakening of the imagination that leads him to a sense of destiny: "The moon was a slender crescent of yellow light, and I imagined that light rippling on the dark swells of the river a mile or so up to the south. I knew I would sleep well tonight, and there would be no more of this business about gas" (45). Spider gravitates more and more towards the river and what it represents through its perspective, and as he does so, he is able to purge himself gradually of his painful memories relived by the canal: "Oh, the river! Great broad swirling stream, of Father Thames in the raw gray day! On the far side, the cranes of Rotherhithe poking at me through the mist like fingers, or insects" (47). When he is finally able to go to the allotment and release the memories that are associated with it, the turning point is marked by a wind of change that comes up from the river as he lays a bunch of flowers on the potato patch: "Overhead thick banks of gray cloud were moving in low from the river, and the wind was refreshing.... After a few moments I felt stronger..." (93). It is this new strength that moves Spider back to the river the next morning to an epiphanic experience: "The next day I went down to the river.... I loved to be alone in that damp gloom with the screaming of the gulls overhead as they wheeled and flapped over the water" (94). River takes the place of canal in Spider's world as present takes over from past, and, through the new perspective afforded him as he sits by the river, Spider's recognition of his own "negotiations with reality" paradoxically suggests a certain saneness. As each of his memories, drawn up through the "canal" of his mind, is presented to the reader, Spider, the alchemist, creates a new reality through exerting his new imaginative powers. For him, it is a kind of catharsis that leads him to self-recognition—a realization of destiny that takes place by the river and a reminder that creative imagination is the most valuable human attribute.

Another work that describes a London setting not likely to be found in the tourist's guidebook, one that reflects and intensifies the environment of Dickens' *Our Mutual Friend* as well as McGrath's *Spider*, is Iain Sinclair's *Downriver*, about which the author explains in his introduction to the American edition: "I wanted to unwind congeries of narrative in the form of a novel ... to travel backwards down a changed and changing river.... What drew me was the Thames, the agitations of light on the oily water, and all those dead voices screaming their auditions.... I wanted to offer my trust to that which was least known: the random convulsions of the river" (xii–xiv). Topographically linked by river, rail, and tunnel but otherwise fragmented like a mesmerizing appliqué with the river as the background against which the stories of these lives are stitched, the book is comprised of twelve chapters—stories, seemingly unconnected except through their proximity to the Thames, part mystery and part a Carson McCullers–like inventory of grotesques who live "downriver." The story is described through the imaginative experience of the narrator as he introduces the reader to an array of characters—derelicts, doctors, drug addicts, perverts, chronic cynics and lost children, all of whom are suffering from some sort of madness, despair, or isolation. As they emerge from the shadows of wharf and warehouse, madhouse and doss-house in the light of the narrator's imaginative vision, the story takes on the eerie darkness of a Fritz Lang movie. Each life, as bizarre as it is heartbreaking, is reflected in archetypal figures from real life and fiction, including Alice from Alice in Wonderland, Jack the Ripper, and Stephen Hawking, in what Michael Moorcock says is a novel that suggests "the angry passion of Blake or Shelley" and "speaks for the alienated, the underdog, the disposed, the eccentric, the bewildered idealist."[10]

The Thames is also both real and archetypal; it is the heart of darkness of Conrad's Congo and the hellish river of Dante's Styx. Canal and river, tunnel and railway line, stations and mental institutions, all become stages in a dark journey that the narrator embarks upon, one that takes him through the mean streets of Stepney and Wapping, down to the estuary and the wasteland of the Essex and Surrey flatlands in what Sinclair calls his "grimoire." It is a kind of grisly Pilgrim's Progress where Dickensian characters suffering every conceivable malaise afforded by the twentieth century emerge from their riparian hellholes. It is Heaven and Hell—partly the glorious London of Gulley Jimson, the artist, and partly the London of the tunnels and gasworks of Spider, the schizophrenic who finds his counterpart herein in the vagrant, Arthur, who holes up in the horrifying Monster Doss House, a home for derelicts where his room, like Spider's "crow's nest," looks to the west, the river and its promise of the sea: "His turret room a literal crow's nest" (133).

In the first chapter, the river becomes the force that turns the city into a place of unbelievable beauty: "He was drowning in physical detail: breathless, aroused.... It was all pouring into him" (51). Like the artist Gulley Jimson in *The Horse's Mouth*, the narrator creates his work by filming a documentary of those who live around the Thames as he travels the sordid environs with his eccentric companions, and brings to his narrative historical references and disturbing predictions as he goes.

The narrator's journey deepens in "Riverside Opportunities," and the Dantesque images intensify as he finds himself under the river in Rotherhithe Tunnel that connects the two banks of east and south London: "It was all to do with Rotherhithe Tunnel ... holding the irreconcilable differences of the two shores in an evil marriage" (53–54). He begins on the Surrey shore: "...diving, after Tower Bridge, into the obscurities of Horselydown, Curlew Street, and Jamaica Road.... I decide to come back across to Shadwell and the homelands by the way of the Rotherhithe Tunnel.... White abattoir walls solicit vivid splashes of blood. You *feel* the brainstem ineluctably dying, reeling, at its margins, dim and flaccid hallucinations" (54). This begins the perilous descent into the story as he advises the reader with a caution that echoes Dante's admonishment above the gates of hell: "If you want to sample the worst that London can offer, follow me down that slow incline" (54). When he emerges, he thinks he has died in the tunnel and now "beached in the suburbs of purgatory ... I willed the skeleton of Tower Bridge to rise from the waters" (56). He finally realizes "I had made the mistake of climbing out of a ventilation shaft on the same side of the river that I had embarked from. In fact, I had never left Rotherhithe. But an involuntary return to the point of departure is, without a doubt, the most disturbing of all journeys" (58). This terrifying image of the circle of hell that holds no promise of cyclic renewal is repeated in the following narration, "Horse Spittle," which introduces the character of Edith Cadiz, another tortured soul. She finds her salvation—"disappearing into the present" (73)—in taking care of lost children in one of what must be the most unforgettable descriptions of a fictional mental intuition in which all of the images of hell are contained in one building:

> The hospital site.... had been designated the dumping ground for all the swamp-field crazies, the ranters, the ultimate referrals. Leave here, and there is only the river.... Looked at from the east end of Victoria Park, or out of a shuddering train, the hospital was minatory and impressive: a castle of doom. The endless circuit of its walls betrayed no secret entrances. Window strips flickered with nervous strip lighting. Grimy muslin strips muted forbidden glimpses of the interior: recycled bandages.... My circuit was complete. I was back where I had started [72–73].

The presence of the river suggests, as it does for Spider, a symbol of hope, of movement: "Edith made her decision. She rescued all the children she found lost within the inferno of the wards..." (74) She finds a room facing the river where "Over the months, Edith coaxed the children towards language. The railway passengers noticed this single window, blazing with light" (75).

Time and the river finally come together at the Old Station Museum, "this unreal terminus" (193) in Greenwich where "they keep artifacts recovered from the river" (193). Here, in a scene that reflects Spider's own liberating experience by the Thames when his realization of spiritual freedom is imaged in the wheeling gulls, "a black gull drifts, a swerving V, hinting that the river is close at hand, accomplice to the whole affair" (195). Past, present, and future finally merge in "The Sexing of Stones," where "The long march to the sea ends at Leysdown.... There is nothing more. Leysdown on Sea is the ancestral dreamsite of a lost tribe: all the aboriginal cockney characteristics, celebrated in fiction and in song, have migrated here.... This is the Last Redoubt, the final stand" (431). The cyclic process suggested in the Danteen images throughout will begin again, and the only consolation offered, here on the estuary, is that the river leads into sea.

The River Thames also becomes the catalyst for the imagination in Susan Hill's *The Mist in the Mirror* through which the narrator experiences confrontations with a ghostly figure. His journey into the past is also signified by the river, as is the narrator's in *Downriver*, and it ends with the same kind of freedom afforded the narrator in Patrick McGrath's *Spider*—a freedom from past, shadows and memories that have occluded the present. The main narrative is set in the early twentieth century, and the story within takes place in the late nineteenth, with all the Victorian props of dense swirling fog, taxi-cab ranks, and dark winding streets. The powerful descriptions of setting and atmosphere are focused around the River Thames, the unifying image that moves through the story and winds its way into the past. The Thames connects all aspects of the plot; in fact, so constant is its image throughout the story that it seems to take on the characteristics of a persona. The story concerns the disturbing memoirs of a Sir James Monmouth, which were given to the nameless narrator and are related by him after Monmouth's death. These memoirs describe the life of Monmouth, orphaned as a boy and brought up by a kindly guardian in British colonial Africa. It goes on to tell of the subject's fascination as a young adult with a traveler named Conrad Vane, a fascination which grows steadily and eventually consumes his life as he follows the same the routes that Vane took earlier. Monmouth spends twenty years trying to discover all there is to know about Vane, and finally ends up in London, still trying to disclose the enigma surrounding Vane's life. Here, in London, at forty years of age, he picks up the search in the vicinity of the River Thames, which marks each significant stage in his journey.

When Monmouth arrives in London, the river is the opening image: "Rain on London's river, and slanting among the wharves and quays" (9). His feeling of strangeness at being in a new and alien land is reflected in the river: "I turned then and gazed back down the long dark ribbon of London's river that led away to the sea, and felt for that moment utterly dejected, and as bleak-spirited and lonely as I had felt in my life" (10). He finds a place to stay by the river, at Cross Keys Inn, and before he enters, a "chill wind" sweeps up the river to suggest the change about to begin while at the same time he sees, fleetingly, for the first time the apparition of a boy, "some twelve or thirteen years old, thin, with a pale face above a dirty collarless shirt" (15) who will appear several times during the story, always near the river.

He explores the area, the twisting alleys and streets of the wharf district that is also the setting for Charles Dickens' *Our Mutual Friend* and Iain Sinclair's *Downriver*, and finally comes to the river where he stands and "for a moment, closed my eyes and breathed in the river smell ... and, mingled with it, the distant smell of the open sea.... A curious sense of belonging here, of having come home, had settled upon me, so that the smell of London's river seemed a welcome, and even an old familiar, one" (22). The smell of the river intensifies his perception "so that I became gradually aware of a hidden life on all sides of me" (22). But returning to the streets he finds: "I was lost. I had wandered and wound my way far from the river, and the Cross Keys Inn, probably by several miles" (23). It is the river, again, that draws him: "The smell of the river, when it came to me at last, and the sight of the dim alley that I knew led up to the street, lightened my heart" (24). Soon after this event he begins to familiarize himself with London through the river: "I gave myself over to it. I walked the length of the Thames" (29). He finds a permanent place to stay, a suite of rooms by the river across from the Thames Embankment at Prickett's Green, next to Chenye Walk, in Chelsea: "...for I had acquired a great affection for London's river, and it would please me to live beside it and become familiar with it in all its phases and aspects" (42). The house at Prickett's Green is described in relation to its proximity to the river: "I found a row of three-storey, stuccoed houses set back behind their own rectangle of garden, with elm trees to either side, overlooking the wide embankment and the River Thames.... Many times I stopped to lean against the embankment wall and look up and down river, enthralled by all I saw upon it.... London, I thought to myself, aware of how deeply I was growing to love it (49). From his rented rooms the river stays with him, and the bridge he sees suggests the next stage of his journey on which he is soon to embark: "Below lay the river, almost completely dark now, but still just flushed over its surface by the last light from the sky ... I saw the bridge, strung out to the opposite bank, across the water" (51). He contemplates the river as it draws him towards this important part of his journey: "I spent many hours during those first days simply watching the river" (53).

The new phase is reflected by a change in the river: "A raw wind blew off the river" as he prepares to visit a house outside of London where he will find new information concerning the traveler, Vane: "To my pleasure, the train ran some way along the Thames" (56). A metaphor of travel, the railway station, situated by the same river, marks his arrival. The bridge in the next stage emphasizes, as it does for Edie in Alan Sillitoe's "A Scream of Toys," that entry into what will turn out to be the deepest part of his journey: "Here, the Thames curved slightly towards me, wide and fast-flowing, and I stood and looked over into the water" (61). He crosses another bridge as the journey becomes more convoluted; the danger he is about to experience in the house where he is staying is suggested by his nearly falling into the river: "We were standing looking at the river towards a graceful wooden bridge that curved across it to the opposite bank.... We walked on, and mounted the bridge. The wooden boards were slippery with frost, so that I almost fell..." (81). Here, he is told that "Conrad Vane was an evil man ... evil and depraved, [a] Jekyll and Hyde" (85, 93). Later in the story, when he eventually finds his ancestral home in a remote location in Yorkshire where his early childhood memories are smothered by a sense of foreboding and evil, memories he is able to finally allay, the river has become purely symbolic: "...the past came flooding towards me like a river, so that I almost drowned in it" (159). Finally, he returns to London and the urban river where his destiny becomes clear to him and he is able to begin his new life aided by the catalytic impulses of the river.

The nineteenth century saw great and rapid changes in the face of urban and agrarian England. No one more powerfully than Charles Dickens incorporated these concerns in his works through the topological and imaginative uses of the urban river. By establishing mythic and archetypal themes into a native setting, he influenced, directly and indirectly, later writers and their characters, such as Cary's Gully Jimson in *The Horse's Mouth*, who describes through the river a journey inward towards creativity and the freedom of the imagination. He comes to recognize through the visions he paints of the river that imaginative freedom, the only true freedom, is internal: "But what you get on this inside, I said to myself, is the works—it's SOMETHING THAT GOES ON GOING ON. Hold on to that, old boy, I said, for it's the fact of life. It's the ginger in the gingerbread. It's the apple in the dumpling. It's the jump in the OLD MOSQUITO. It's the kick in the old horse. It's the creation" (104). For the young girl, Edie, in "A Scream of Toys," the river is the vehicle which will eventually lead her into a recognition of adulthood as she crosses the border, represented by the river, from childhood into womanhood. The power of the river in *Offshore* also draws the characters towards creative freedom and imaginative self-truth and offers the bargees a place to redefine their existence away from the confining shores, with the promise of freedom marked by the tidal swings and movement to the sea. For the mentally disturbed man in *Spider*, the urban waterways of canal and river represent a revitalizing force which gradually propels Spider into the pain of being: "To be awake is to be in torment, and this is the full complete meaning of life" (156). They function as conduits through which come an imaginative realization that he is truly a free and authentic human being. He sits by the Thames and rejoices: "I am the Spider of London, after all! Over the river by Westminster Bridge, the Thames alive with light, sparkling green in the autumn sunshine, and the sight of it did me good" (200). In *Downriver*, the River Thames is a constant reminder of history that flows towards freedom while creating a unity between past and present, as it does for the narrator in *The Mist in the Mirror*. Like history, the river represents change which is often presented as a kind of metamorphosis. Ovidian themes emerge as those characters most closely aligned with the river—Michael Winter, Dick Crick, Hughes' cormorant, a bird that has both a soul of water and a soul of air which, in diving into water becomes a fish, while reemerging again it becomes a bird, and the young girl, Tilda, metamorphose through their relationships with the magical waters of the river. In these works the urban river, with its attendant features of bridges, embankments, and canals, is the dominant motif that represents the archetypal journey on which each of the central characters embark as they move towards an affirmation of selfhood.

Chapter Three

River into Sea

> "The floodgates are open, away to the sea,
> Free and strong, free and strong,
> Cleansing my streams as I hurry along,
> To the golden sands, and the leaping bar,
> And the taintless tide that awaits me afar.
> As I lose myself in the infinite main,
> Like a soul that has sinned and is pardoned again.
> Undefiled, for the undefiled;
> Play by me, bathe in me, mother and child."
> —"River Song," Charles Kingsley

The final confluence of river and sea is a glorious inevitability. Says the speaker in Tennyson's poem, "A River": "Flow down, cold rivulet, to the sea, / The tribute wave deliver: / No more by thee my steps shall be, / For ever and for ever." Jean Ingelow describes her childhood home on the rural estuary in Lincolnshire as a place where "the pools ... welled by the sides of the path, sheltered by green rushes that whispered together as the wind swept through them" as she "gazed towards the sea, for sea and land mingled together in the cool marshes where mist lay thick and nothing was heard but the cry of the skylarks over the estuary."[1] In her poem "The Four Bridges," the merging image of land and sea at the mouth of the estuary is captured: "Watch the green breakers and the wind-tossed foam, / And see the land-fog break, dissolve and clear."

H. E. Bates describes this journey of river to sea:

The sea draws it on and down and finally under, in absolute subjugation, draining the strength of its waters like some too-greedy never satisfied lover. The river is, at last, to be a victim itself of the inexorable magnetism of water. From the source downwards all its turns and prettiness and growth and character have in reality been subservient to this exercise of the sea's magnetism. Its end was resolved before it began ... a river, snaking to all points of the compass, has only one destination and one end.... We stand fascinated by the river's end, foreseen, inevitable as night and day ... we look forward continually to one point: the final moment of subjugation, the end, the supreme point of fusion that is, in a way, a kind of death. We look forward and think forward, in fascination, always to the sea.[2]

The "supreme point of fiction," as Bates calls it, is a kind of death, but also a regeneration, a journey of the self, recognized and renewed, described in Hughes' poem "Flesh of Light": "Spinal cord of the prone adoring land, / Rapt / To the roots of the sea, to the blossoming / Of the sea" (7). In Graham Swift's *Waterland*, Tom and Mary's aborted fetus makes its journey to the sea to join the cyclic process when Toms throws it into the river:

I carried the pail, down to the Ouse. Because Martha said: "You gotta do it, bor. Only you. No one else. In the river, mind. An' when you throws it, don't you look. Nothin' but bad luck if you looks." So I carried the pail across the mist-wrapped, dew soaked meadows. Larks were trilling somewhere above the mist, but I was stumbling through a mist of tears. I climbed the river wall, descended to the water's edge. I turned my head away. But then I looked. I howled. A farewell glance. A red spittle, floating, frothy, slowly sinking. Borne on the slow Ouse currents. Borne downstream" [274].

In fiction, that water passage where river currents and sea tide merge signifies, as its original meaning, "boiling," suggests, a kind of fermentation, and in *The Thames Embankment*, Dale Porter explains the tidal action of the River Thames that foreshadows its merging with the sea:

The weir and locks at Teddington, built four and a half miles below Kingston in 1811, mark the beginning of tidal action. The tide flows about twice daily from the North Sea, carrying a wall of salt water up the river. Incoming tides impede the river's flow.... At ebb tide, the effect is reversed: the river flows faster below Teddington than it does upstream, scouring its channel and the shoreline on the outer edge of each bend. If the tides washed down all the way to the

> North Sea, the river would be cleaned twice daily. But the movement is only incremental, like a ratchet; what goes down river tends to come back up, at least part way. When the tide changes the water comes to a standstill for about an hour.³

This tidal action, which is natural rather than chronological, not only regulates the lives of those who live on and around the river but also becomes a metaphor for freedom and renewal when the river enters the sea, as we have seen in Patrick McGrath's *Spider*, Graham Swift's *Waterland*, and Iain Sinclair's *Downriver*, whose narrator says when he reaches the Thames estuary: "This is not what I expected. This is not the barnstorm finish. I can't come back. I was prepared to confront another self, a fetch. To be carried away, sucked like a prophet into the clouds. It's all too easy. Saltmarshes, tidal flats, water meadows.... A new vocabulary is required.... I begin to let go, to fade from the path; to lose my always fierce sense of individual identity" (434).

The River Thames' powerful tidal sweeps are the controlling theme in *Offshore*, as the regular swing of the river waters affects the lives of the small group of people who live on Battersea Reach, a tidal basin on the River Thames. To face life is to face danger, and at the end of the novel the movement of the *Maurice* toward the Thames estuary where river current and sea tide merge suggests this: "With that last heave, Maurice's anchor had wrenched clear of the mud, and the mooring ropes, unable to take the whole weight of the barge, pulled free and parted from the shore. It was in this way that *Maurice*, with the two of them clinging on for dear life, put out on the tide" (141). The magnetism of the sea is the force in *Spider*, where the halfway house for the criminally insane looks towards the distant promise of the sea: "The house often feels to me like a ship, did I mention this already? It points east, you see, toward the open sea, and here I am on top of the east end of it, like a sailor in a crow's nest, as we slip downstream with our cargo of dead souls!" (14). Spider's final journal entry is a description of death that returns him to the river. It is a vision generated by his newly awakened imagination of a suicide by drowning—his own—which actually becomes a symbol of rebirth in his rejection of the idea of death. It is, for Spider, the affirmation of the spirit now freed from the web of frightful memories that threatened its death:

> I will stand on the top of the slimy steps and watch the moonlight on the river, and I will think of the North Sea. I will think of that

empty sea heaving beneath the moon, as I begin gingerly to descend, and I will picture in my mind's eye the pale light gleaming on its swells, and even as the river churns about these large flat asylum shoes of mine, even as it catches and tugs of the turn-ups of my flapping flannels, even as my leg wrappings turn soggy and my socks get wet—I will think of the silence of the moonlit sea" [218–219].

Since the latter part of the twentieth century, the idea of closure in British literature has gradually become less and less significant; the postmodernist Jacques Derrida states that "closure is not only not desirable, but also not possible," and the postmodernist Brian McHale also talks about a sense of "(non-) ending." With this idea in mind, the river becomes the perfect symbol, for it never ends; rather, it flows into other rivers and eventually into the sea. The narrator in *Downriver* rejoices when he reaches the end of his journey at the Thames estuary: "This is the end of the claims of civilization. The feeble encroachments of humanoid life forms. From this point on, we are free" (434). Just as the river, confined within its straining banks, eventually flows into the freedom of the sea, so each of the characters discussed in these works finally reaches his and her own imaginative freedom through a growing sense of destiny that reflects the movement of the river to the sea.

Part Two
Seashore

"English Literature is a flying fish. It is a sample of the life that goes on day after day beneath the surface; it is a proof that beauty and emotion exist in the salt, inhospitable sea."

—E. M. Forster

Chapter Four

The Rural Shore

Thomas Hardy's A *Pair of Blue Eyes*, Virginia Woolf's *The Waves* and *To the Lighthouse*, W. B. Yeats' "Fighting the Waves," Mary Lavin's "The Great Wave," Iris Murdoch's *The Sea, the Sea*, John Fowles' *The French Lieutenant's Woman*, Graham Swift's "Learning to Swim," Susan Hill's *The Woman in Black*, and Jane Gardam's *Crusoe's Daughter*

"I am being dissolved into a landscape."
—*Crusoe's Daughter*, Jane Gardan

Since Homer wrote *The Odyssey*, writers throughout the history of literature have been fascinated by the seashore and used it as a setting for their works. What is it that makes the seaside setting so ideal? Perhaps it is because it seems to be a place where the individual pushes himself to his physical and psychological limits, a place where the constant and never-ending surge of the tide represents a kind of self-negation, a nothingness constantly renewing itself, a place not only where death produces life but also where feelings of possibility and impending change underlie all else. Throughout history, British writers have used the seaside setting and sea imagery countless times. In Shakespeare's pastoral drama, *The Tempest*, for instance, the struggle between primitive innocence and sophisticated decadence is played out on the shores of an island after the characters representing these forces have been brought together by a violent sea storm. W. H. Auden writes about Shakespeare's use of the coastal setting:

> The handling of the symbols of sea and storm by Shakespeare provides us with a bridge between what, for convenience, one may call the classic attitude and the romantic.... In the earlier plays the stormy sea is more purely negative, a reflection of human conflict or the fatal mischance which provides evil with its opportunity (e.g. *Othello*). In the last plays, *Pericles, The Winter's Tale, The Tempest,* however, not only do the sea and the sea voyage play a much more important role, but also a different one. The sea becomes the place of purgatorial suffering; through separation and apparent loss, the characters disordered by passion are brought to their senses and the world of music and marriage is made possible. There is, however, one extremely important difference in the relation of the actors to the sea from that which our period exhibits, namely, that the putting to sea, the wandering, in never voluntarily entered upon as pleasure. It is a pain which must be accepted as cure, the death that leads to rebirth, in order that the abiding city may be built.[1]

The movement from the classic attitude to the Romantic that Auden describes here is discussed by James Applewhite in *Seas and Inland Journeys* as the theme of psychological death and rebirth in the context of a landscape imagery which has it origins in Romanticism, and, through that "typical tension between conscious structure or figure and wild or unconscious moorland or sea, we are participating in a psychological interpretation that has already been made, in effect, by intellectual and artistic developments in our own century."[2] However, beginning with the Romantics and writers such as Samuel Taylor Coleridge and Mary Wollstonecraft Shelley, this use has gradually become more and more introspective and psychologically representative as well as geographically entertaining, culminating in the writings of the present day. The Kantian view of psychic disintegration as the result of societal malaise described in the works of Coleridge and Mary Shelley has carried through to contemporary literature. Aspects, for instance, of "The Rime of the Ancient Mariner"—its nautical setting and themes of mystery and magic, death and renewal—and of Mary Wollstonecraft Shelley's short story "Transformation," with its elements of evil and magic and change and stasis within the seaside setting, may be seen as occurring most clearly in the novels of Virginia Woolf and Iris Murdoch.

With the Victorians, the emphasis on the physicality of the seaside setting and its corresponding influences on the psychic changes of the individual expanded to include the theme of internal strife brought about by the advent of science and technology. Matthew Arnold uses the sea as a metaphor for a gradually receding faith, which left behind a sense of insecurity and loss. In "Dover Beach," earth and sea withdraw from each other, and the shoreline, that which represents both mutability and stasis, is endangered. In "The Forsaken Merman," mystery and magic, represented by the merman and his children, are lost to the world; faith has now become organized, requiring the cultivation of habit rather than intuition, and the mythical merman witnesses the fracture of his family as, deaf to her cries and those of their children, he watches his wife as she prays in a church on the coast of his watery world. In "The Voyage of the Maeldune," Tennyson uses the seaside setting in a lyric poem which describes, through themes of love and magic, the voyage of a group of sailors as they sail to a series of fabulous islands. A different kind of shore is used in "Break, Break, Break" in which, with tones of irony and anguish, Tennyson mourns the loss of a past that can never return like the sea that seems to mock him as it crashes upon the shoreline with a continuity that he will never be able to experience himself. Other Victorian writers such as William Morris and Charles Kingsley use the seaside setting to express in their poems a disquiet and an incertitude over a rapidly changing society. Gerard Manley Hopkins uses a nautical setting in "The Wreck of the Deutschland" to render an account of a profoundly religious experience, and in "The Sea and the Skylark," he uses the seaside setting to represent God's beauty. Christina Rossetti also uses this kind of setting to express the intensity of her feelings as she speaks of the mystery of the sea in "By the Sea."

Writers of prose in the Victorian era also often used the sea and its coast as their subject matter. In his essay "Effect of Sea after a Prolonged Storm" in *Modern Painters*, Ruskin's long, rolling sentences seem to take on the movement of the sea itself as he discusses Turner's painting "The Slave Ship." And even Darwin's account of his five-year voyage, *Zoology of the Voyage of the Beagle*, must have fired the imaginations of his contemporaries and those of later writers as they came to use the sea setting in their works. But of all the Victorian writers, it is Thomas Hardy who most represents the transition from nineteenth to twentieth century literature in his use of the seaside setting by demonstrating a distinct and consistent use of the local setting, the south coast of England, to represent the psychological transformations experienced by his characters: "Which way did you go? To the sea, I suppose. Everybody goes sea-ward," says Mr. Swancourt in *A Pair of Blue Eyes*.

The rural landscape of sea and cliffs is an important topological and symbolic part of *A Pair of Blue Eyes*, which is set on the northern coast of Cornwall in far southwest England, Hardy's "Wessex." Thomas Hardy writes in the preface to the first edition: "The place is preeminently (for one person at least) the region of dream and mystery. The ghostly birds, the pall-like sea, the frothy wind, the eternal soliloquy of the waters, the bloom of dark purple cast, that seems to exhale from the shoreward precipices, in themselves lend to the scene an atmosphere like the twilight of a night vision."[3] The story of the tragic romance opens on a note of possibility that is reflected in nature with a view of the coast that describes the nascent clouds, much like the innocent young heroine, that drift above the cliffs: "...three or four small clouds, delicate and pale, creeping along under the sky southward to the Channel" (11). *A Pair of Blue Eyes* concerns a young girl, Elfride Swancourt, the girl of the blue eyes, whose father is the vicar of the tiny local parish, and a young architect, Stephen Smith, who has come down from London to restore the tower of Endelstow church. When it is discovered that Stephen Smith is actually the son of two of the local peasants, Elfride's father forbids the relationship, and the two elope. The church tower, which stands on a crucial cliff, takes on particular symbolic aspects, representing at once the paternal and religious authority of Elfride's father, the vicar, as well as civilization amid the fruitful chaos of nature, much like the church tower in Matthew Arnold's "The Forsaken Merman." A strong symbol as the story opens, the tower collapses with the disclosure of a romantic attachment that reveals a key event in Elfride's past that eventually destroys the chance for her future happiness. One of the turning points in the novel occurs when Elfride falls from this tower in an event that signals her imminent fall from grace. Her passage from innocence to knowledge is marked by "bleeding from a severe cut on her wrist" (165), and her realization of mortality foreshadows her own death: "The close proximity of the Shadow of Death had made her sick and pale as a corpse" (163–164).

The coastal setting functions most powerfully in its natural perspective of cliffs combined with the other natural elements throughout that are reflected in the actions of the characters. For instance, when Elfride leads Stephen to the edge of the cliffs, the landscape foreshadows the dangerous outcome of their elopement soon to take place: "She led the way out of the lane and across some fields in the direction of the cliffs. At the boundary of the fields nearest the sea she expressed a wish to dismount. The horse was tied to a post, and they both followed an irregular path, which ultimately terminated upon a flat ledge passing round the face of the huge blue-black rock at a height about midway between the sea and the topmost verge. There, far beneath and below them, lay the everlasting stretch of ocean..." (59). Just before they elope to London, Stephen walks in the lane in front of Elfride's house: "Stephen reached the point of intersection.... Nothing could be heard save the lengthy murmuring-line of the sea upon the adjacent shore" (101). At the last minute, however, Elfride, cannot go through with the marriage, and the two return from London in secret. Stephen goes to work in India in the hopes of making a fortune that will render his position more acceptable to the vicar. During his absence his patron and friend, Henry Knight, an older man, knowledgeable but emotionally naive, becomes Elfride's wooer, and when she saves his life on the cliff, "The Cliff with No Name," the story takes a dramatic turn. Hardy describes "The Cliff with No Name," which functions in the most dramatic and successful part of the story: "One enormous sea-board cliff in particular figures in the narrative; and for some forgotten reason or other this cliff was described in the story as being without a name. Accuracy would require the statement to be that a remarkable cliff which resembles in many points the cliff of the description bears a name that no event has made famous."[4]

Ironically, the love that has been growing between Elfride and Mr. Knight is acknowledged by both when Elfride suggests they walk to "The Cliff with No Name" so she may watch the arrival of Stephen's ship, bringing him home from abroad. Here, the opposing lines of cliff and shore reflect Elfride's emotional conflict: "And it must be remembered that the cliff exhibits an intensifying feature which some of those are without—sheer perpendicularity from the half-tide level.... Thus, far from being salient, its horizontal section is concave. The sea, rolling direct from the shores of North America, has in fact eaten a chasm into the middle of a hill.... I will call the precipice the Cliff without a Name" (209–210). When Mr. Knight slips down the face of the cliff, he comes face-to-face with his own mortality, and, while Elfride runs for help, he is both literally and existentially hanging on for his life. For him, time changes—Knight feels that Elfride has been gone for ten minutes rather than three—and he is forced to face inward and examine his life as he faces a trilobite fossilized in the face of the cliff. Chronological, historical, and geological time come together, bringing emotions to the surface as Elfride and Mr. Knight, fueled by terror, outwardly attest their love for each other. This important event is marked by a reversal in nature: "An entirely new order of things had been observed in this introduction of rain upon the scene. It rained upwards instead of down" (215).

Elfride's former failed elopement, however, was witnessed by a malicious local woman whose son was formerly engaged to Elfride before his death, for which she blames Elfride. She reveals her knowledge to the stern moralist Mr. Knight, who rejects Elfride, wrongly believing that the night she spent in London compromised her reputation. Stephen Smith returns from India, meets up with Mr. Knight, and tells him the real truth behind the innocent night in London. Stephen learns that Elfride is still unmarried. Both travel down to Cornwall and discover in a tragic irony that the train carrying them is also the train carrying Elfride's dead body.

In later fiction that uses the rural coastal setting, such as John Fowles' *The French Lieutenant's Woman* (1970), Susan Hill's *The Woman in Black* (1983), and Jane Gardam's *Crusoe's Daughter* (1985), the characters are also governed by the powerful forces of the setting, which, in turn, is defined through its relationship with the sea. For Virginia Woolf, the sea, with the continuous ebb and flow of the waves, represents life itself. It is, as Susan Gorsky explains in *Virginia Woolf*: "...a reservoir of images referring to birth or death, change or cyclic constancy, the human unconscious, the imagination. In fact, in Woolf's novels it can serve all these functions and more. In the individual wave that breaks just once on the shore, the sea suggests the fragility of human life; but as each wave is part of the whole pattern of the tides, the sea can also stand for the eternal in human life."[5] Woolf's sea represents the eternal flow of life and death, containing all aspects and stages, both physical and spiritual, and reflects the mystery and growth of humanity; it is the medium through which her characters survive to gain insight about life and death, mutability and immutability, the self and the universe. The actual condition of the sea often reflects the psychological states of Woolf's characters, and she uses a cyclic pattern that contains both horizontal and vertical movements to represent these states. As her characters move away from that which represents for them stability and the familiar—in *The Waves* (1927), the six characters move away from the house of their childhood, and in *To the Lighthouse* (1931), the Ramsays sail toward the lighthouse—each develops a sense of retrospect and a perspective that enables him or her to deal with the present Encompassing these linear movements is the continual ebb and flow of the waves. It is a pattern developed in works of succeeding writers, such as W. B. Yeats' "Fighting the Waves" (1934), Stevie Smith's "Beside the Seaside," first published in *Me Again: The Uncollected Writings of Stevie Smith* (1982), Mary Lavin's "The Great Wave" (1961), and Graham Swift's "Learning to Swim" (1986).

Significant features of the seashore setting, especially the rural, are the lighthouse and the Martello tower, described by Shelia Sutcliffe in *Martello Towers*:

> Among the many fortifications built over the centuries for coastal defense, the most historically interesting and architecturally curious are the Martello towers. Solid, low and circular, they were massively built of stone or stuccoed brick with guns mounted on the flat roof. Their purpose was to provide concentrated fire on ships at sea to repel an enemy landing, and they were capable of withstanding a siege of considerable duration. The towers were strategically placed to protect coastal batteries, vital installations and any particularly vulnerable stretch of coast where an invasion might be expected.... The classic period for Martello building was the Napoleonic era and the towers are best known and most frequent on the south coast of England nearest to the Continent of Europe.[6]

Probably one of the best known Martello towers in fiction is the one at Sandycove to the south of Dublin described by James Joyce in *Ulysses* which now functions as the James Joyce Museum. Together these manmade coastal features of Martello tower and lighthouse represent an achievable reality and a sense of permanence amid the flow of life. The lighthouses in Woolf's *To the Lighthouse* and Stevie Smith's "Beside the Seaside" represent a new sense of reality that the characters strive for and do finally attain in their outer, public searches. The counterpart of the lighthouse, the Martello tower, as a war relic, is used in *The Sea, the Sea* and "Beside the Seaside" to represent the inner struggle for self-knowledge.

In Tennyson's poems "The Merman" and "The Mermaid," the sea acts as a vehicle for internalization, imaged by the characters, submarine experiences which suggest a loss of worldly restrictions and an acknowledgment the self. The critic William Cadbury discusses the role of the children in these poems: "[they] confront explicitly the image of the isolated self and move to the celebration of joy and union. Both poems open with a brief stanza that is part invitation, part pure song, emphasizing both the beauty and the loneliness of the magical state of the mer-creatures ... the nighttime life, the life of the complete imaginative self, of irrational fulfillment.... The poems here admit the argument that all men are isolated, but they see that isolation simply as a past of a multiplicity of conditions, a multiplicity, furthermore, which contains not only isolation but happiness and freedom."[7] Images of children at play are reflected in both poems through the descriptions of the sea; in "The Merman" the waves are described as "pale-green seagroves straight and high / Chasing each other merrily," and in "The Mermaid" the mergirl says: We would run to and fro, and hide and seek, / On the broad sea-wolds in the crimson shells, / Whose silvery spikes are nighest the sea."

Virginia Woolf's novel *The Waves* also begins with children who are symbolized by the nascent waves that come to the shore. Of her novel, Woolf stated that what she wanted to do in writing it was to "set my people against time and the sea." That she did, for in this book the references to water—fifty percent of which occur in the monologues—quadruple the references to other images. John Lehmann describes the impact that *The Waves* had on twentieth century fiction, in *Virginia Woolf*: "*The Waves* was indeed, as she had described it at an early age, 'a completely new attempt,' as well as a 'different attempt,' and more ambitious than anything she had set her hand to before. Her aim, one can say, was to give a picture of the whole of life from the earliest dawning of sensation to the end; of its dreams, ambitions, aspirations, achievements and failures, to its final disillusionments, accompanied perhaps by the joyous discovery of wisdom."[8] The story starts out by the sea and takes on the movement of a wave itself as it follows the lives of six characters from childhood to old age. A seventh character, Percival, is never physically present in the story; the memories of him are evoked by the other six. The descriptions of these evocations create a unity between the six and suggest the twentieth century malaise of alienation and fragmentation. Each character becomes a representation of a certain aspect of the sea itself through his or her relationship with it. For Susan, the earth mother, the sea is a natural force; for sexually promiscuous Jinny, the rhythm of the sea is the rhythm of sex. Impressionable Rhoda feels chaos in the sea and a sense of the unpredictable, the unknown. Neville, the homosexual, sees his lovers in the separate waves, and Louis, in his insecurity, senses only danger in the sea—the uncontrollable "stamping beast" that is always lurking there. Bernard, the central figure in the group, speaks for them all in his representation of humanity, for he understands all aspects of the sea, destructive and creative. In this sense, he, like Lily Briscoe in *To the Lighthouse*, unites the characters in the story and in doing so creates a vision of unity between man and the universe. The lives of these characters, as they rise from nubile childhood to energetic maturity and sink into the frailty of old age, depict not only the pattern of a single wave but also patterns of individual waves breaking on time's shores as each life gathers force, crests, and disperses in the "thin line of foam" that Woolf analogizes with both senility and semen to enforce the cyclic pattern of life.

The novel is a series of monologues presented by these six characters at different stages in their lives. Between the monologues appear lyric interludes, prose poems which use the coastal setting to describe a world of nature—sea, sun, birds, plants, and wind—that corresponds to the physical and spiritual growth of the characters. Just as their growth represents also the growth of humanity, so the prose poems represent the passing of time in days and seasons, from sunrise to sunset. Each person is depicted as both an individual wave and as a part of the one universal wave that returns constantly with the tide. Through the interweaving of monologue and prose poem, man and nature, Woolf achieves even more successfully that which she set out to do in *To the Lighthouse*: to unify humanity with the rhythms of the universe through the use of a chronological perspective. Set by the sea, the first passage opens during childhood and is preceded by a corresponding prose poem that reflects these early years with such words as "bar" and "stroke" to describe the as-yet-unformed waves of the dawn, and the "grey cloth" or caul that covers the emerging waves: "The sun had not yet risen. The sea was indistinguishable from the sky" (7). The sea imagery follows through in the opening series of monologues as Louis, in his loneliness, sees "flowers like fish made of light upon the dark green waters" (11). And Bernard, already the spokesman for the group, predicts, "The waves close over us" (16). Rhoda also uses the sea to describe her fears and anticipations as she begins to individualize her situation and gain some sense of perspective: "The waves rise; their crests curl.... Out of me my mind can pour.... Oh, but I sink, I fall! ... Let me pull myself out of these waters..." (16).

In the second prose poem, as the morning comes in and the waves begin to take shape and separate into greens and blues, so in the second monologue the children disperse and go to separate schools as they grow into adolescence: "I begin to feel the wish to be singled out," says Jinny, and, in an acknowledgment of the end of childhood for herself and the rest of the group, she adds, "Now the tide sinks" (46). Also about to confront the world, Louis, too, expresses his uneasiness in terms of the sea and the "chained beast" of dormant sexuality: "...I hear always the sullen thud of the waves; and the chained beast stamps upon the beach. It stamps and stamps" (58). As the three boys step off the train that has carried them to London and away from their childhood by the sea, they step into reality, and Neville speaks for all of youth when he likens the new world he is about to enter to "the surge of the sea," the chaos of which both exhilarates and terrifies: "I feel insignificant, lost, but exalted" (72).

The waves in the third prose poem are full of growing energy as new elements of war and apprehension are introduced. There is also a new kind of unison brought about by group fear—the birds that used to sing their individual songs in the dawn now sing in "chorus shrill and sharp," and an ominous feeling enters the poem as the waves are described through warlike imagery. Extending the build-up of fierce energy, Bernard in the third monologue expresses his new understanding of Neville through sea imagery, and in doing so, declares also a new understanding of humanity: "O friendship, how piercing are your darts—there, there, again there.... Like a long wave, like a roll of heavy waters, he went over me, his devastating presence—dragging me open, laying bare the pebbles on the shore of my soul" (98). And as Bernard awakens to a painful understanding of human relationships, so Louis expresses a painful knowledge of self and the essential isolation of man: "Here is the central rhythm.... Yet I am not included ... I, who would wish to close over me the protective waves of the ordinary..." (94). Jinny, likening her movements to a body of water, finds relief from her emergence into adulthood and society in sexual desire: "I flutter. I ripple. I stream like a plant in the river, flowing this way, flowing that way, but rooted, so that he may come to me..." (103). But Rhoda, antithetically of Jinny's melting sensuousness, feels only insecurity and doubt in the face of her oncoming maturity and likens herself to the foam—the most unformed and vulnerable: "Hide me, I cry, protect me, for I am the youngest, the most naked of you all.... The wave breaks. I am the foam that sweeps and fills the uttermost rims of the rocks with whiteness; I am also a girl, here in this room" (106; 107).

The sea in the fourth prose poem now resembles an army of waves, invincible in its unified strength, each indistinguishable from the other. The sexual energy that is implied in the image of the engine's movements that push it up toward the final crest reflects the force of the emotions and the desire for, paradoxically, both identity and conformity in the young adults: "They drew in and out with the energy, the muscularity of an engine which sweeps its force in and out again" (108). The corresponding set of monologues describes a meeting of the group—themselves, like the waves, gathering forces—for a farewell dinner for Percival, who is going to India. The sexual imagery introduced in the prose poem is extended as the characters examine their feelings about love through imagery of the sea. For Susan, the earth mother aligned to the natural forces, love is a cycle bringing her children who will keep her in touch with life. For Rhoda, love is an unknown fantasy, a blurred white shape on a foreign shore where "Behind it roars the sea. It is beyond our reach" (139). And Louis, braced for the departure of his beloved Percival, sees only chaos in the loss of this friend who unifies the group in their virtual hero-worship of him: "But now the circle breaks. Now the current flows" (142).

Louis' prophecy is fulfilled in the fifth and central prose poem as the energy behind the cresting waves pushes them up and they cascade over the shore. Symbolized by the horses, which have now become "great," the sexual implications in the sea imagery are strongest here, and mark the "cresting" of these characters' lives: "The sun had risen to its full height.... The waves broke and spread their waters swiftly over the shore" (150).

Decline is introduced through the cyclic pattern of the ebb and flow of the sea, and the central meaning of the work becomes apparent as the group now begins to gather a different kind of force—one that will enable each of them to rise and resist the final reality of death while, at the same time, accepting its inevitability. This understanding of death is exemplified in the reaction of each member of the group to Percival's death in India. "My son is born; Percival is dead," says Bernard. Rhoda, as she walks down Oxford Street and enters a music hall, sees all of humanity, now passive and out of touch with the flow of life, in Percival's death, whose finality she is unable to accept. Through sea and coastal imagery she ends her speech with energy and defiance: "...we have been hauled over the shingle down to the sea... Into the wave that dashes upon the shore, into the wave that flings its white foam to the utmost corners of the earth I throw my violets, my offering to Percival" (162–164).

Through each character's reaction to death is implicit his and her views on life as, from now on, the story unfolds into retrospection. And as the intellect in the following monologues takes precedence over the physical, so the waves in the sixth prose poem are on the decline: "The sun no longer stood in the middle of the sky.... The waves massed themselves, curved their backs and crashed" (166). Susan and Jinny depict their acknowledgment of the cusp of middle age in images of shells left upon the shore: "Here, in this room, are the abraded and battered shells cast upon the shore" (175).

The theme of death as part of the natural cycle is developed by the dying of the waves in the seventh prose poem, with shroudlike shadows casting over the new white sand: "The sand was pearl white, smooth and shining" (182). Bernard repeats this pattern of renewal in the seventh monologue as he looks for an answer to the passing of time and the finality of death and finds it in the analogy of a drop of water—falling and refalling but never drying up: "'And time,' said Bernard, 'lets fall its drop. The drop that had formed on the roof of the soul falls.... This drop falling is time tapering to a point.... The drop falls; another stage has been reached. Stage upon stage'" (184, 186). These individual drops of water represent, for Woolf, part of the great wave of humanity which gains its strength in the unification of its parts, as Elias Canetti explains in *Crowds and Power*: "Waves are not the only multiple element in the sea. There are also the individual drops of water. It is true that they only become drops in isolation, when they are separated from each other. Their smallness and singleness then makes them seem powerless; they are almost nothing and arouse a feeling of pity in the spectator.... The pity you feel for them is as though they were human beings, hopelessly separated. They only begin to count again when they can no longer be counted, when they have again become part of the whole."[9] From middle age, Susan looks back at her life and sees it as a series of waves: "The waves of my life tossed, broken, round me who am rooted" (192), and Rhoda sees the passing of a wave as the beginning of a new phase in her life as she admits, on a note of triumph, her acceptance of death.

Towards the end of the eighth monologue, Bernard uses the sea and coastal setting to illustrate the dissolution of the self in the universal sea of humanity: "Rolling me over the waves will shoulder me under.

Everything falls in a tremendous shower, dissolving me" (206). With the eighth prose poem comes darkness and the final decline; only the "livid foam" remains to signify renewal. In conjunction with the decline of the dark waves—the descending darkness of old age—the characters are faced with feelings of isolation and confusion until they are swept up in Bernard's vision which, like Lily Briscoe's in *To the Lighthouse*, enables him to exert a constant affirmation of life in death and admit to the regenerative pattern of life as envisioned through the sea's rhythmic flow. This vision he imparts to the others when they meet as a group for the last time. The energy generated by the characters as they come together carries them through this final affirmation and moves them toward a metaphoric death as Bernard admits: "My little boat bobs unsteadily upon the chopped and tossing waves" (211). The others respond; each speech is a personal objectification of the self through sea imagery. Neville sees himself as "immeasurable"—a net that catches all of time from the old "leviathan" to the new, unformed "white jellies" (214). The joyous acceptance of death that unifies the group is reflected in the unity of land and sea established in the ninth lyric poem: "Now the sun had sunk. Sky and sea were indistinguishable. The waves breaking spread their white fans far out over the shore, sent white shadows into the recesses of sonorous caves and then rolled back sighing over the shingles" (236). In the last soliloquy, Bernard explains his understanding of his place in the cosmos through sea imagery: "Should this be the end of the story? a kind of sigh? a last ripple of the wave? ... But wait—I sat all night waiting—an impulse again runs through us; we rise, we toss back a mane of white spray; we pound on the shore; we are not to be confined" (238, 267). The final joyful consolation in the recognition of the "eternal renewal" of the individual through humanity, like a wave in the ocean, comes to Bernard as he sits alone in a London restaurant and articulates his affirmation of the unity of mankind and the universe. Nature and man are as one as Bernard uses words that repeat the opening lyric poem "There is a sense of the break of day.... The bars deepen themselves between the waves.... Yes, this is the eternal renewal, the incessant rise and fall and fall and rise again" (297).

In *To the Lighthouse*, the setting is a remote island in the Hebrides. It is described by Cam Ramsay, one of the characters, as she views it from the boat towards the end of the story. Through her description of it, she puts her own life into perspective as well: "She had never seen it from out at sea before. It lay like that on the sea, did it, with a dent in the middle and two sharp crags, and the sea swept in there, and spread away for miles and miles on either side of the island" (280). The setting is isolated; its exact whereabouts are unknown, so the story unfolds without the interference of reality. The reader is thus drawn, unaffected by preconception, into the story, at the center of which lies a trip across the sea to the local lighthouse. For all the characters in the story, the sea evokes a sense of nothingness about to become as it enables them to experience a surge of new strength that urges them to move beyond the limits of self. As the sea depicts movement, so the other dominant image in the story, the lighthouse, depicts stability. The story opens with a dispute between Mr. Ramsay and his son, James, over the much awaited trip that Mr. Ramsay never seems quite willing to take. Years later, it is the trip, finally taken, that unites James and his father. During the time before the trip the lighthouse becomes a recurring image that unifies the story in its sense of permanence outside the self and in its immunity to change and movement that juxtaposes the sweep of the waves as they represent the self constantly coming into being.

Before the trip finally takes place, Mrs. Ramsay dies. For her, the reality of life—the sense of continuity—is in her children, James and Cam; they are her lighthouse. The light she sees in James' eyes is the beam from the lighthouse: "something wondering, pale, like the reflection of a light" (94). Mrs. Ramsay delights in the coastal setting, and her character is defined by this. For her, the waves of life are counterbalanced with a reality which, like the lighthouse, is firmly set in the sea, and she understands the necessity for both. The duality of the awesomely destructive and mysteriously generative powers of the sea is felt intuitively by Mrs. Ramsay and reminds her of her own mortality, "like a ghostly roll of drums remorselessly beat the measure of life" (27).

The sea is also always a source of peace, and it offers Mrs. Ramsay a chance for spiritual renewal; it is an endless reservoir of subconscious calm in which she may submerge herself in order to escape, however briefly, from the trials of day-to-day existence without ever completely losing touch with reality: "Losing her personality, one lost the fret, the hurry, the stir" (96). Through her identification with the sea, Mrs. Ramsay is swept out of herself on the ebb tide and returns, replenished like a fresh wave, with the inward flow, "the ecstasy burst in her eyes and waves of pure delight raced over the floor of her mind and she felt, It is enough! It is enough!" (99–100). This sublime state is brought on whenever Mrs. Ramsay recalls a specific memory of the sea that has a special significance for her, and she uses these Wordsworthian "spots of time" to elevate her from the ordinary. Because of this ability, she does not, as do the other characters, feel the need to go to the sea; we never see her walking upon the shore or sailing in the bay. When her daughter invites her to go down to the beach, she declines, but the mere thought of doing so evokes a memory from her girlhood, and she is joyous.

The sea is also used to present an image of peaceful death. When we last see Mrs. Ramsay before she dies, she is standing in the window through which she viewed so much of life and is drawn away from her husband by the almost hypnotic memory of a calm, dark sea: "she remembered how beautiful it often is—the sea at night" (185). Unlike his wife, Mr. Ramsay, the philosopher, is out of sync with the ebb and flow of life as exemplified by the distant, formal relationship he shares with his children. Going to the lighthouse is a painful experience for him, for it means coming to terms with the realities of life, until now viewed only at a distance. It is a situation similar to the one described by W. H. Auden in "The Sea and the Desert": "[In] the putting to sea, the wandering is never voluntarily entered upon as a pleasure. It is a pain which must be accepted as cure, the death that leads to rebirth, in order that the abiding city may be built."[10] Mr. Ramsay is at first loath to embark on this journey across the sea. It is only after the death of Mrs. Ramsay, she who represented the natural forces that balance his pure reason, that he undertakes to do so. This change is foreshadowed at the beginning of the story through both husband and wife's reactions to James' much desired trip to the lighthouse: "'There wasn't the slightest possible chance that they could go to the lighthouse tomorrow,' Mr. Ramsay snapped out irascibly. 'How did he know?' she asked. The wind often changed" (50). Mr. Ramsay is a solitary figure, and his detachment from life is reflected in his relationship with the sea: "the sea is slowly eating away, and there to stand, like a desolate sea-bird, alone.... He stopped dead and stood looking in silence at the sea" (71). And as he is gradually drawn toward the sea, so Mr. Ramsay is drawn toward life itself. This twofold movement begins when he first thinks of his children in a more universal context than he has previously.

The sea also has a life-giving effect upon Lily Briscoe, the artist and guest of the Ramsays, who records her impressions of life through her art. The picture she paints of the coastal scene which includes Mr. Ramsay and his children, who are being rowed across the bay on their visit to the lighthouse, becomes her final vision. It represents a necessary harmony between past and present. While Lily Briscoe is painting, her thoughts turn to the deceased Mrs. Ramsay, and as she works on her painting she begins to unite the past with the present and man with nature. It is at this point in the story that the growing intensity of perspective comes to its height as the voyage out that is being experienced by Mr. Ramsay and his children is juxtaposed by Lily Briscoe's voyage inward. She combines both voyages in her painting to create a fixed tableau that will always remain in the present.

The disappearance of the Ramsays into the coastal setting, symbolic of their spiritual death before coming alive at the lighthouse, is concurrent with Lily Briscoe's unifying introspection of the past as she, the artist who speaks for humanity, sees in the movement of the waves an analogy for life through which death becomes regenerative rather than nihilistic: "...what did it mean to her when a wave broke? ... one had constantly a sense of repetition—of one thing falling where another had fallen, and so setting up an echo which chimed in the air and made it full of vibrations" (294–295). With this objectification, Lily Briscoe adds the last strokes to her canvas. The perspective becomes focused as she achieves her vision, and, with a gesture that unifies the entire story, her painting is complete: "I have had my vision" (310).

Woolf also uses the sea and coastline to develop a unity between specific characters in the story through their shared experiences of the setting. For Lily Briscoe and another guest of the Ramsays, William Banks, the close relationship between the sea and the coast evoke in them feelings of intense sexuality. In the following passage, the phallic image of the "red hot pokers" is completed by the corresponding seminal image of the "fountain of white water": "guarded by red hot pokers ... almost every evening spurted irregularly, so that one had to watch for it and it was a delight when it came, a fountain of white water ... They both felt a common hilarity, excited by the moving waves..." (33–34).

The seaside setting draws Mrs. Ramsay closer to her husband when she likens his strength to a wooden stake, impervious to the buffeting of life's waves, and Lily Briscoe's understanding and awe of the love shared by the Ramsays is likened to a wave which draws up everything in its path and "became curled and whole like a wave which bore one up with it and threw one down with it, there, with a dash on the beach" (73). The sea is also the setting for the final unity between Mr. Ramsay and his children, a setting which becomes a type of universal unity, taking on the motion of a great wave that slowly gathers energy as the wind of change pushes their little boat towards the lighthouse. A perfect revitalizing unity with nature is experienced by the three Ramsays, father and children, as they race upward through the waves toward the lighthouse: "...they were like wild creatures who were perfectly free" (306–307). The wave crests, and the energy peaks. The boat reaches the lighthouse, and Mr. Ramsay steps ashore in new territory. He, like the wave that brought him to the lighthouse, is reformed—reshaped by the flow of the sea: "...he sprang lightly, like a young man, holding his parcel, on to the rock" (308). He brings with him his children and a parcel of provisions for the lighthouse keeper's family—his reformation speaks, as does Lily Briscoe's painting, as a vision for the regenerative powers of humanity whose movement is like that of the waves themselves.

In William Butler Yeats' "Fighting the Waves," Cuchulain, the hero, also struggles with the sea. Cuchulain is a warlike man who has supposedly drowned at sea, and his body, now lying in his wife's house at the edge of the sea, has been taken over by the spirit of Bricriu, the maker of discord. Two women, Emer, Cuchulain's wife, and Eithne Inguba, his mistress, labor over the body, entreating the spirit of Cuchulain to return to it. Finally, Emer is told by Bricriu that if she renounces her love for her husband, Cuchulain will return to his body. At great personal loss she decides to do so. The play opens with a man wearing a mask that resembles the face of Cuchulain. He is fighting the waves, and, says Yeats: "In his frenzy he supposes the waves to be his enemy."[11] He is fighting for his life, and not until he submits to the waves will he be reawakened into a new being. Sea imagery is used also in the opening lyric as the chorus likens a woman to "A strange, unserviceable thing, / A fragile, exquisite, pale shell, / That the vast troubled waters bring / To the loud sands before day has broken" (82). These lyrics open and close the play and function, as do the lyric interludes in Woolf's *The Waves*, by creating a universal, timeless world of cyclic proportions, as A. S. Knowland explains in *W. B. Yeats, Dramatist of Vision*:

> "[P]rologue the first leads us into the world of essences, into the deeps of the mind, and the last epilogue leads us back to the everyday world. The first lyric evokes not only a woman's beauty, its fragility, its exquisite uselessness, and so seems relevant to Eithne Inguba, but loveliness itself; and behind that the energies of the

mind and imagination that create it, energies that are self-generated, in the paradoxical interpretation of quietude and violence, stillness and movement, attraction and repulsion."[12]

The "stormy sea" is seen tossing in the background through the open door as the characters enter the play. As part of his reawakening, Cuchulain loses his identity to the sea and actually becomes part of the sea itself, suggested by his mask, of which Yeats says, "I am deeply grateful for a mask with the silver glitter of a fish, for a dance with an eddy like that of water, for music that suggests, not the vagueness, but the rhythm of the sea."[13] Emer, too, sees Cuchulain as the sea when she says, "[W]e are two women struggling with the sea" (87). Images of fire and water also appear in Emer's speech as she tries to combat the spirit of Bricriu for her husband's body: "The sea is full of enchantment, whatever is on that bed is from the sea, but all enchantments dread the hearth and fire." But it is to no avail; Bricriu advises her that her husband will awaken only if she relinquishes her love for him—the one force that has kept her alive. She chooses to do so, and through this heroic gesture which condemns her to a life of loneliness and pain, she gives her husband life and freedom. Of this type of gesture, Yeats says, "The heroic act, as it descends through tradition, is an act done because a man is himself ... so lonely is that ancient act, so great the patterns of its joy."[14] The sea is also present in the thundering hooves of the sea horses that are ridden by Fand, magical daughter of the sea who draws near to claim Cuchulain for eternity, and we are reminded of the hooves that thundered through the lyric interludes of *The Waves*: "Listen to the horses of the sea trampling! Fand, daughter of Manannan, has come. She is reining in her chariot, that is why the horses trample so. She is come to take Cuchulain from you, to take him away for ever, but I am her enemy, and I can show you how to thwart her" (90). Bricriu goes on to urge Emer to accept his proposal: "[T]hose who love the daughters of the sea do not grow weary, nor do the daughters of the sea release their lovers" (90). With this threat, Emer submits to her heroic act, and Cuchulain awakens in the arms of his mistress and the memory of the coastal setting which she invokes for him: "Cuchulain! Cuchulain! Remember our last meeting. We lay all night among the sand-hills; dawn came; we heard the crying of the birds upon the shore" (92). As Cuchulain comes alive, so Emer comes into spiritual being through her self-denial, and the final lyric echoes her own sadness and that of Fand's as they mourn the loss of Cuchulain's love amid the movements of the dancers.

The central figure, Margaret, in Stevie Smith's story "Beside the Seaside," which is set a few miles from Dungeness on the southeast coast of England, also experiences a spiritual awakening that leads to intellectual freedom through her interaction with the sea and the coast. The opening of the story sets the mood for the ensuing story of spiritual freedom attained by Margaret through exercising her choice as she vacations with her husband, Henry, their two children, and her friend, Helen: "It was a particularly fine day. The calm blue sea at unusually high flood washed the highest ridge of the fine shingle beach. It was a particular moment of high summer" (13). At this point, everything seems very clear, but a little later on, as Margaret steps into the sea and symbolically marks the beginning of her journey inward, this clarity begins to fade. The way Margaret steps into the sea suggests that she is a careful participant, and her tentative understanding of the landscape around her reflects her vague understanding of self: "'I think I shall bathe now,' said Margaret. She stepped into the sea and stood with the sea washing gently round her knees looking out to the horizon of the sea where the heat mists played tricks with the passing ships. The great liner that was passing down channel from Tilbury seemed to be swimming in the high air, because the dark band of mist that hung below her made a false sea border" (16). In *Crowds and Power*, Canetti says, "The sea has not interior frontiers and is not divided into peoples or territories. It has one language, which is the same everywhere. There is thus no single human being who can be, as it were, excluded from it ... it is an image of stilled humanity; all life flows into it and it contains all life."[15] This idea is reflected in the description of horizontal and vertical perspectives as Margaret stands facing her hazy horizon, which, itself, symbolizes her conflict with the natural world that disappears as soon as she submerges herself in the sea and aligns herself with the line of the shore: "Margaret always took a long time to get into the water, when she was at last right in she would begin to swim strongly up and down parallel with the beach in a leisurely way that was full of please" (16).

Margaret is aided on her journey by her friend, Helen, whose impulsiveness, suggested by her rushing "quickly into the water" leads Margaret to a new relationship with her family: "How beautiful the water was, warm and milky; the sun burning through the water struck hot upon their shoulders washed by the sea. Helen turned her back to rise and fall with the swelling sea (there was quite a swell in spite of the calmness)" (16). The effect of the sea upon Helen, who wishes that Harry and the children would join them in the water, is also suggested in her position as she lies half in the sea and half on the shore at Harry's feet, representing a link between the fast-separating worlds of Harry and Margaret: "Helen, who was slopping about in the water again at Henry's feet, her elbows on the shingle ridge to keep her steady and her body afloat in the deep water where the shingle dipped, looked up into Henry's anxious face" (16). Unknown to Margaret's husband, the two women take a trip to Dungeness, and as the end of the journey nears, Martello towers—symbols here, as in Iris Murdoch's *The Sea, the Sea*, of an inner disquiet—appear in the landscape as Margaret struggles to define her existence in relation to the demands of her family. The lighthouse on the peak of Dungeness, to which they are taken by a third woman, Phoebe, a native of the area whose role is much like Evens' in Edward Bond's *The Sea*, symbolizes, as it does for Mr. Ramsay in Virginia Woolf's *To the Lighthouse*, the lengths to which one must sometimes go in order to understand the truth about oneself in relation to humanity and the universe. It is here, as she sits close to the lighthouse, that Margaret begins to feel the pain of her newly awakening inner self, and the paralleled perspectives of natural and spiritual landscapes merge into one: "Where the North Sea met the Atlantic the waves drove up against each other, but in the lee of the land a great calm left the surface smooth to the wind's track" (23). The story reaches a turning point after Henry goes back to town for a while and the two women spend their days on the beach with the children. In preparation for the spiritual change about to take place in Margaret, the women go each night to watch the sea from the hilltops behind the town. Here, Margaret is able to put her emotions in perspective along with the landscape that surrounds her. Through her acknowledgment of self, Margaret achieves a freedom that enables her to face the demands of her family without the conciliatory feelings with which she is usually engulfed: "She ran along the beach picking up some mussels as she ran. The moon was coming up in the twilight sky over to the horizon" (24). Instead, she asserts her freedom by leaving, again without notice, this time to spend the night at Phoebe's house; on the way there, the final image of the sea and coast reflects the unity and freedom that Margaret has won for herself.

The evocation of a particular memory made possible through the imagery of the sea is the key element in Mary Lavin's short story "The Great Wave" (1961), which concerns the visit of a religious dignitary to his boyhood home and the confrontation of a specific memory. Set on the coast of a small island in the Irish Sea, just off the west coast of England, "The Great Wave," like Woolf's *The Waves*, follows the pattern of the wave itself; it is drawn up through memory, peaks, then disperses in the present as Jimeen, the Bishop, is rowed across the sea towards the island where he was born and grew up. Through the coming to terms with this memory, Jimeen is able to come to an understanding of the present. On the trip, the irritability and the reluctance the Bishop shows in coming close to the sea foreshadows the desperate fight for his life that he entered into with these same waves as a boy, and his present actions become the transition into the memories of past conflicts.

As the island bay to which they are heading comes to represent the memory which the Bishop will eventually face, so horizontal and vertical perspectives in the coastal landscape are used to transport the Bishop back to his childhood as the boy Jimeen. The island gains form on the horizon as the memory strengthens: "'How long more till we get there?' he asked, because the island was no longer a vague green mass. Its familiar shapes were coming into focus" (3). Like the pier and the lighthouse, the promontory represents a place between shoreline and sea, a place where the self comes into being as new levels of consciousness are reached. For the Bishop, it also represents a symbol of nature and of a life more powerful to him than his church. As a child, Jimeen is forbidden to go out to sea with the fishing boats; much as he feels the sea's pull, his mother is unwilling to release him from her protection. But at the peak of the herring run, Jimeen is finally allowed to go out to sea with a young visiting seminarian. The sea turns rough and builds up to a menacing, dangerous force as Jimeen faces death, and the incident becomes his rite of passage into manhood, a time when he comes face to face with his own limitations and gains an understanding of his own mortality: "He saw—oh God!—a face, looking out at him, staring out at him through a foot of clear green water.... For a minute the eyes of the dead man stared into his eyes" (18).

Images that signify the birth of a new consciousness come into play as the vast wave approaches the small boat; the hands of Jimeen and the seminarian are torn and bleeding, trapped in nets too loaded with fish to be hauled aboard in the violent sea. The cresting of the wave parallels the movement of Jimeen's revelation which is, itself, counterpoised by his actions: "As Jimeen rose up to his full height to throw the net wide out, there was a sudden terrible sound in the sky over him, and the next minute a bolt of lightening went volleying overhead, and with it, in the same instant it seemed, the sky was knifed from end to end with a lightning flash" (14). The darkness and confusion that descends marks the preliminary to the impending spiritual rebirth: "For they could see nothing. And it was as if they were all alone in the whole world" (15). Through his brush with death, Jimeen comes alive as he awakens the following morning and finds himself washed up with the seminarian on the top of the promontory: "For it was on that promontory—four times the height of the steeple—they had found themselves" (18). The Bishop's memory of his experience is the plot for this story. It is the memory of the great wave that swept him as a boy through death and into being that will remain with the Bishop forever, and it is in his regular visits to the shores of his childhood every four years on his way to baptize young children, that he realizes, as his boat draws nearer to the island, that this is what he comes for—the renewal through which his life takes on the pattern of the waves, constantly coming into being.

In John Fowles' novel *The French Lieutenant's Woman*, the events are also described through symbols and imagery drawn from the sea and the coastal setting where cliffs and seashore represent freedom and hope for the two major characters, Sarah Woodruff and Charles Arrowby. In the center of the novel, John Fowles actually interrupts the narrative to discuss the influence of Thomas Hardy on his work: "I have now come under the shadow, the very relevant shadow, of the great novelist who towers over this part of England of which I write." The major part of the story takes place in the rural area of Ware Cleeves, the rest in the contrasting resort town of Lyme Regis, sites that represent two very different worlds: the world of warmth and passion shared by Charles and Sarah and the coldly regimented world of Victorian morals. Also represented in this landscape are the two worlds of science and nature and the corresponding themes of movement and stasis, hope and despair, and past and present. For Sarah, "Tragedy," the representation is quite conscious; she turns constantly to the sea for solace until, through Charles and the relationship that grows between them in their coastal setting, she is free and moves on. For Charles, the sea works upon him almost like a force that compels him to seek out Sarah through, whom he, too, will eventually experience a freedom in terms of coming into a consciousness of self. And it is the tragedy of Sarah and her life, as she tells it to him, that affords him this opportunity, for as playwright Edward Bond says concerning the importance of tragedy in life in a letter to his director: "We even need a sense of tragedy. No democracy can exist without that. But tragedy as something to use in our lives, that gives us sympathy and understanding of other people. Only a moron wants to grin all the time, and even he weeps with rage in the night. Tragedy in this sense is necessary for moral maturity, it doesn't lead to despair, and it certainly has nothing to do with a catharsis that makes us accept abominations to which there should be political reasons. It leads to knowledge and actions."[16] Bond is talking about exactly what happens to Charles Arrowby. Until Charles meets Sarah and shares her tragedy, accepts her burden, he is a "moron" in the sense that he is as yet unawakened to the pain that gives life meaning, and although he is a Victorian figure held back by the constraints of the period, he is also representative of the twentieth century through his involvement with Sarah; he is change itself. To emphasize this sense of change that permeates the whole story, Fowles brings into it evolutionary aspects, using the coastal setting do so, as A. A. DeVitis and William J. Palmer suggest in "*A Pair of Blue Eyes* Flash at *The French Lieutenant's Woman*": "This confrontation with Sarah does, however, bring upon Charles the realization of his own lack of selfhood; he sees for the first time his own existential impotence. This realization, like Knight's on the cliff, is occasioned in Charles by a fossil."[17] Sarah's strong alliance with the sea as it symbolizes freedom and hope is made clear towards the end of this meeting in the woods when Charles suggests that she leave Lyme Regis. If she leaves the pain of her present situation, she will never be free, but Charles' offer to help her leave is premature at this point. And the reader knows, as does Charles, after this statement, that it is not for the Lieutenant's return that she looks to the sea. With Charles' recognition of this, the mystery around Sarah deepens.

The imagery suggestive of birth continues and is intensified through the coastal landscape as Charles is about to enter a new phase of his life—"Charles began his bending, stopping search" (112)—which reflects the whole evolutionary aspect of the novel. And the scenery that sets the stage for this birth itself symbolizes the "newness" of it through the "lowing of a calf" and the flight of the old life in the birds' flapping wings against the "wash of the tranquil sea"—the amniotic fluid—the waters of life always cleansing and renewing, all of which lead Charles to Sarah as she waits and watches him emerge from the tunnel: "In places the ivy was dense—growing up the cliff face and the branches of the nearest trees indiscriminately, hanging in great ragged curtains over Charles' head. She stood above him, where the tunnel of ivy ended, some forty yards away" (113). And again, after the exchange of the tests at the third meeting, the kneeling pattern is repeated as Sarah delivers her anguished appeal for help just as Charles is about to leave and resume the path without her: "she sank to her knees." By doing so, Sarah saves Charles from turning back to his former self: "The invisible chains dropped, and his conventional side triumphed ... on the point of turning through the ivy with no more word" (117).

When Charles likens Sarah to the mythic Calypso at this meeting, he presents himself, by implication, as Odysseus, the sailor, and reinforces the representation of the sea as freedom. It is towards this sea of freedom that Charles and Sarah instinctively turn as the constraints and pressures placed upon them by the Victorian society in which they live engulf them and threaten their spiritual well-being. If we look at Lévi-Strauss' idea of myth, which he describes in *The Savage Mind*, as being a way of understanding the world in which we live, as a congenital part of the mind rather than as simple narration in that myths "take to pieces and reconstruct sets of events ... and use them as so many indestructible pieces for structural patterns in which they serve alternatively as an end or means,"[18] the secluded setting of the Undercliff and its isolated spots known only to Sarah do suggest a kind of Calypso's cave, for here Charles enters a different world; the dense foliage, the covered paths and natural hideaways resemble a cavelike womb from which Charles emerges a new person. At the end of this revealing and symbolic part of the story, the description of Charles crashing through the wall of ivy on his way downhill uses images that enforce the evolutionary aspects of the novel by associating him with nature rather than society—animal rather than man: "Charles bowed, hesitated, one last poised look, then turned. A few seconds later he was breaking through the further curtain of ivy and stumbling on his way down hill, a good deal more like a startled roebuck than a worldly English gentleman" (119). "Evolution," says Edward Bond, is the record of failure at the same time as it's the record of success.... Evolution proceeds by solving problems. You could almost say that moral evolution proceeds by making mistakes."[19] In this light, we may see Sarah's guilt, from which she frees herself by sharing it with Charles, as another aspect of the evolutionary theme in the novel. This idea is especially significant when we see that the new life Charles has entered upon through his association with Sarah is heralded by feelings of guilt and dislocation: "He felt ashamed as if he had, without warning her, stepped off the Cobb and set sail for China" (120). And soon after, when Charles is back in the town and visiting his confidant, the local doctor, at his house which stands halfway between the worlds of Lyme Regis and the Undercliff, he feels caught between stasis and change—the familiar and the mysterious as they are represented by the ever-changing changeless sea.

Another meeting takes place between Charles and Sarah in the Undercliff, but there is a sense of certainty to this one that emanates from Sarah as she waits, knowing without seeing that Charles is on his way to her. As she waits to give him the tests she has found, butterflies, symbolic in the East for freedom, sail around her and attend Charles on his path toward her, paralleling Charles' earlier reference to China and the author's description of Charles as being "the China-bound victim" (120). A signal from nature marks Charles' entrance into the three stages of recognition, denial, and indifference: "A livid flash of sheet lightning lit the Cobb, the beach, the torpid sea. He turned" (179). After he turns, Charles enters these Carlylean stages and emerges ready to "change his clothes" (189). He goes to the Undercliff for the last time and looks for Sarah, who has been made a complete outcast and is now dependent upon Charles for survival. As he nears the barn wherein she is sleeping, the sea draws closer to signify the imminent freedom that Charles will experience in choosing to help her through his own newfound strengths. From this point, the story unfolds and becomes, for Sarah, a healing process. For Charles, it records a growth into self-knowledge, an awakening into consciousness. One of the important questions raised by the author is that of the state man's spirituality in a fast-moving world where past and present, nature and science, are realigned through evolutionary concepts that concern the very depths of his moral being. In this light, Charles's own revealing words are significant: "In a vivid insight, a flash of black lightning, he saw that all life was parallel: that evolution was not vertical, ascending to perfection, but horizontal. Time was the great fallacy; existence was without history, was always now, was always this being caught in the same fiendish machine" (165). As Charles finally finds freedom through an understanding of self, this image of entrapment is replaced by images of hope and possibility through the symbolism of the sea itself: "He walked towards an imminent, self given death? I think not; for he has at last found an atom of faith in himself, a true uniqueness, on which to build ... upon the unplumb'd, salt, estranging sea" (336).

In Iris Murdoch's novel *The Sea, the Sea*, the empty sea awaits the impressions and changes wrought upon it by her characters in their psychic explorations, which often become journeys toward death, either symbolic or real, and, concurrently, journeys towards self-illumination similar to the one experienced by Margaret in Stevie Smith's "Beside the Seaside." The central character, Charles Arrowby, constantly swims in the sea, and on several occasions faces a sea monster, representative of his own deep fantasies and obsessions, that suggests the sea monster in Tennyson's poem "The Kraken": "Below the thunders of the upper deep; / Far, far beneath in the abysmal sea, / His ancient, dreamless, uninvaded sleep / The Kraken sleepeth." Critic Christopher Ricks explains the symbolic significance of the Kraken:

> The Kraken is quite other than science-fiction or Loch Ness fantasy; its depth of feeling comes from Tennyson's pained fascination with the thought of a life which somehow is not life at all. His poems contemplate such life in drunkenness, and in madness, and in extreme old age, and in stillbirth, and drugged by the lotos, and paralyzed by Art in a world of mirrored shadows like the Lady of Shalott. Indeed the Kraken is like the Lady of Shalott in that he too will awaken only to death. For the Kraken's life till then will be only sleep.[20]

Charles Arrowby's monster, like the Kraken, must eventually die in that it represents his earlier life, one which he has to confront in order to move on. Significantly, the monster is beside him when he almost drowns before finally experiencing a type of thalassic renewal similar to those of the waves themselves in Woolf's *The Waves*. The energy that Charles finds in the sea charges the entire story; it seems to enter his body and mind of its own volition and, because of this, he gives it characteristics of its own, able to do so through his absorbing relationship with it: "Then I had felt no fear. Now I felt fear" (146). And like Woolf's setting in *To the Lighthouse*, Murdoch's remote coastal setting is a place in which she is able to distance her characters from society in order that they gain some perspective in their lives as well as to make their often bizarre experiences more intense through isolation; however, unlike Woolf, Murdoch uses the sea in her novels as much more than a background against which the characters examine their lives in that it actually becomes part of her characters and vice versa; a very real symbiosis takes place, as Zoreth T. Sullivan writes in "Iris Murdoch and the Enchantment of Untruth": "Among the recurring images that control this memoir and serve as external symptoms of internal obsessions, the most striking are those of external and internal enclosures and empty spaces on land and in the sea."[21] History plays an important part in both these authors' works, but, with Murdoch, there is something sinister, not always fully explained, such as the relationship between Charles and Hartley in *The Sea, the Sea*. The reader is left with a sense of mystery bought about, in part, by the characters' understanding of the reality they have created through their retrospection. In Woolf's *The Waves*, the interaction of the characters in the coastal setting is used to bring past into present, and the same is true in *The Sea, the Sea*; however, in her novel, Murdoch also uses aspects of magic realism brought almost to the threshold of actuality.

From an old stone house that sits on the promontory of a rugged, harsh coastline, the story unfolds partially in retrospect and partially in the present as it is presented through diary form by Charles Arrowby. The shape of the house in which Charles carries out some of his hopeless plans stands out dramatically in his description of it: "its awkward tall thin shape appearing against the high horizon of the sea" (100). The story opens in springtime and closes in the early autumn, taking on an overall cyclic form, within which perspectives described in horizontal and vertical lines drawn from the sea and coast are used to indicate the opposing moods and conflicts that develop within Charles as he records his experiences in his diary. For instance, as the story opens, sea and coast are contrasted in the description of the sweep of the horizon and the piles of rocks on the shoreline. The diametrical placement of the horizontal and vertical planes within Charles' perspective of literal and spiritual landscapes gradually comes together with a sense of harmony, but this is not achieved without painful discord. The Martello tower, as a relic from the war, functions as a place where Charles is able to put into perspective the war within. It is set a short way from the house on a dangerous part of the rocky coast where Charles must use a rope as a handrail to drag himself up to it from the sea. After several failed attempts on different occasions, when Charles finally manages to climb out of the sea and reach his tower unaided by this metaphorical umbilical cord, he is healed. The process begins early in the story: "I was sorry to observe, visiting the tower steps this morning, that my curtain 'rope' had also somehow come undone and vanished. I swam nevertheless. I think that my muscles are stronger and I am becoming more skillful at climbing out. I always manage to scrape or cut myself however" (67). When Charles is about to dive into the sea from the top of the cliff, his leap into the horizontal takes on significant meaning so that, finally, as Charles' coastal retreat comes to an end, there is a unity in the landscape of the sea and shore that is described by him as he brings to the "empty sea" his own feelings of peace that encompass all humanity while he watches the seals that sport beneath him like the water snakes of the ancient mariner: "And as I watched their play I could not doubt that they were beneficent beings come to visit me and bless me" (476).

The story of Charles' awakening centers upon the entrapment, by Charles, of the unwitting Hartley, his first love, whom he finds living with her husband on the outskirts of the local village. In his failed attempt at kidnapping her, and in his final acceptance of the fact that Hartley probably never did love him, Charles comes to terms with his own self-ignorance, and on the occasions that Charles goes to the house of his childhood sweetheart, set on a distant hill, the desperate hope he has of recaptivating her and the intense emotional conflict he feels is mirrored in the coastal landscape: "From the hillside one could see the distant headlands of the bay couchant in a light brownish heat haze" (122–123). Later in the novel, the landscape reflects the same feeling: "the rise of the blue sea receding into a heat haze and never had a pretty view looked so sinister" (419). Charles reaches an understanding of the other characters through his interactions with the sea, which he records in his diary entries. Hartley, now a shapeless, passive lump, is married to man described by Charles with brute-like images. She allows herself to be kidnapped, but only for a time. Both Charles and Hartley suffer from some form of mental aberration—Charles in his fanatical perseverance in disallowing the truth concerning Hartley's disinterest in him and Hartley in becoming the drooling idiot she reverts to in her dealings with Charles.

The vast scope of the sea and sky, as Charles views it, has a profound effect upon him. After James, his cousin, returns to London, where he finally dies, Charles lies at night like a newborn child on the lawn beside his house: "And I saw into the vast soft interior of the universe which was slowly and gently turning itself inside out. I went to sleep, and in my sleep I seemed to hear the sound of singing" (474). This cosmic kind of union, set against the soft eternal slapping of the sea, experienced by Charles as his transformation becomes complete, is very different from the sinister sea that he describes at the beginning of his retreat: "I could hear the soft grating sound of the waves, like a gentle scratching of fingers upon a soft surface. And I felt upon the empty darkening road a shuddering sense of my utter solitude, my vulnerability, among these silent rocks, beside this self-absorbed and alien sea" (101). The energy that Charles finds in the sea charges the entire story; it seems to enter his body and mind of its own volition, and because of this, he gives it characteristics of its own, able to do so through his absorbing relationship with it. In this sense, character and landscape are woven together by the constant presence of the sea and done so through the rhythmic movement of the waves, as each specific incident recorded by Charles in his diary is followed by an alternating description of the sea and coast in a pattern much like the one used by Virginia Woolf to describe the movement of the sea in *The Waves*.

In Graham Swift's short story "Learning to Swim," the sea is as crucial in the search for an understanding of love and human relationships as it is in W. B. Yeats' "Fighting the Waves." However, unlike Emer's insight, which enables her to reach spiritual freedom, the relationship between Mr. and Mrs. Singleton in Swift's story is a destructive one; neither husband nor wife is able to move towards each other. This inability to respond to each other's worlds results in a stalemate from which the only survivor is their six-year-old son, Paul. The idea of getting into the sea as a metaphor for developing an understanding of one's self in relationship to others is used in this story to describe the ordeal suffered by the young Paul as his father teaches him to swim. Mrs. Singleton understands the power of the sea and will never submit. She fears its timelessness and the inevitability of its pull: "It never struck her, hot as she was, to get up and join her husband and son in the sea.... They did not bathe as a family; nor did Mrs. Singleton swim with Mr. Singleton ... and she was somehow afraid that while Paul splashed and kicked around her he would suddenly learn how to swim ... Mrs. Singleton thought: All the best statues they had seen in Greece seemed to have been dredged up by the sea" (22, 24). In contrast, Mr. Singleton, an expert swimmer, is at peace only when he is in the sea. For him, swimming offers an escape from reality; he finds it painful to function on land. Both he and his wife are unable and unwilling to move across the barrier that lies between them. Because of this situation, there is no real unity in their marriage, even in their lovemaking: "When he made love to his wife her body got in the way; he wanted to swim through her" (16).

The escape that the sea offers to Mr. Singleton is not a journey into self-consciousness but the reverse; in divorcing him so from reality, it denies him human characteristics, and he becomes like a machine: "His shoulders shone like wet metal" (16). For him, the very act of swimming is a programmed response, the antithesis of his son's frantic churning: "He knew about mechanics and engineering because he knew how to make his body move through water..." (23). These two seemingly irreconcilable worlds of sea and land reflect the couple's own spiritual estrangement: "Mrs. Singleton looked at her husband. She felt afraid. The water's edge was like a dividing line between them that marked off the territory in which each existed. Perhaps they could never cross over" (26). And in her isolation, she understands the deathly stasis involved in it through the coastal setting: "She stood on the sand like a marooned woman watching for ships. The sea, in the sheltered bay, was almost flat calm. A few glassy waves idled in but were smoothed out before they could break" (26). The sense of pathos with which Mrs. Singleton views her life is not shared by her husband, who seeks only to escape further and further into the peace and isolation afforded him by the sea: "... in Mr. Singleton's dreams, there was no one else on the untouched shore he swam to" (26). In fact, he teaches Paul, a reluctant novice, to swim only because he will then be able to free himself from the marriage: "He thought, If Paul could swim, then I could leave her" (26).

Mrs. Singleton understands that the sea offers her husband escape from her and from reality, but she fears most the possibility that, in learning to swim, her son, too, will leave. The sea does offer an escape for Paul, albeit a very different one than his father's. As he finally learns how to swim, he surprises both parents by kicking off in his own direction—away from his mother's petrified world rooted on the shores of reality and away from his father's world of inarticulate fantasy. Paul's new world, achieved through his own choosing and attended by pain and terror, will continue to keep him on the edge, for he will have constantly to define his life through each anguished decision he makes: "He was terrified of water. Every time he entered it he had to fight down fear.... There was no way out; there were all these things to be afraid of and no weapons.... But then, perhaps he was not afraid of his mother nor his father, nor of water, but of something else.... He lowered his chin into the water ... he kicked and struck, half in panic, half in pride, away from his father, away from the shore, away, in this strange new element that seemed all his own" (27–28). It is a situation described by Canetti in *Crowds and Power*:

> The sea is all-embracing; nor can it ever be filled. If all the streams and rivers and clouds, all the waters of the earth, flowed into it, they would not really increase it; it would remain unchanged; we should still feel that it was the same sea. Thus in size, too, it serves a model for the crowd, which always wants to grow, and would like to become as large as the sea and, in order to do so, draws in more and more people. The word "ocean" is the final expression of the solemn dignity of the sea. The ocean is universal, it reaches everywhere, it touches all lands; the ancients believed that the earth itself swam on it. If it were possible, once and for always, to fill the ocean, the crowd would have no image of its own insatiability, of its deepest and darkest urge, which is to absorb more and more people. The ocean lies before its eyes as the mythical justification for its own unconquerable urge towards universality.[22]

Another work in which the powerful forces of the rural seashore infuse the story is Susan Hill's *The Woman in Black*, about which Hill comments: "I have always enjoyed and admired the classic English ghost story.... I discover, though, that apart from some very famous ones.... there are very few full length true ghost stories. Even short ghost stories are not written so much now.... In 1982, I decided I wanted to try and write a full length ghost story in the traditional English style."[23] Like Hill's *The Mist in the Mirror*, this is a ghost story which is set within the narrative framework of the narrator's present life and relates to circumstances occurring thirty-odd years earlier. The two settings of river and seashore, present and past, are suggest by the two main locales: Monk's Piece, the narrator's home by the River Nee from which the story is told, and Eel Marsh House, where the past events take place. The inner story begins with the railway station as Arthur begins his journey north where the terrain reflects the journey inward. The train enters the last stage of the journey at night through Gapemouth Tunnel, about which he is informed by a fellow passenger: "The hill it runs through is the last bit of high ground for miles. You've come to the flatlands, Mr. Kripps." Arthur responds, "I've come to the land of curious place-names, certainly. This morning, I heard of Nine Lives Causeway, and Eel Marsh, tonight of Gapemouth Tunnel." (31) Isolated Nine Lives Causeway on the northeast coast of England is the site of the bizarre events that take place. It is a topography governed, like Graham Swift's *Waterland*, by the tides, where lost villages and ruined abbeys rise appear at low tide: "As we drew nearer, I saw that the water was lying only shallowly over the rippling sand on either side of us, and that the line was in fact a narrow track leading directly ahead, as if into the estuary itself. As we slipped into it, I realized that this must be the Nine Lives Causeway—this and nothing more—and saw how, when the tide came in, it would quickly be quite submerged and untraceable" (54). "How long will the causeway remain passable?" he asks. "Till five" is the reply (55). The wind arises which, says W. H. Auden in *The Enchafèd Flood*, in literature signifies change,[24] and the narrator's senses intensify as his involvement with the story begins: "I wanted to drink in all the silence and the mysterious, shimmering beauty, to smell the strange, salt smell that was borne faintly on the wind, to listen for the slightest murmur" (57).

The story concerns a young solicitor, Arthur Kipps, who had been charged with the job of attending a deceased client's funeral, a widow named Mrs. Drablow, and settling her estate, Eel Marsh House. Now empty and secretive behind its shutters, this remote house with only a graveyard as a neighbor is reminiscent of a Poe setting. It overlooks the seemingly infinite stretches of the flat salt marshes around the Nine Lives Causeway which "lay silent, still and shining under the November sky, and they seemed to stretch in every direction, as far as I could see, and to merge without a break into the waters of the estuary, and the line of the horizon" (54). What Arthur anticipates to be an ordinary task turns out to be a sinister and terrifying series of experiences connected to the landscape which concern the ghostly appearances of a young woman, cadaverous in appearance and dressed entirely in black clothing of an earlier age, once at the funeral of Mrs. Drablow and another time in the old graveyard next to Eel Marsh House.

The narrator's story describes a search for truth concerning the ghostly figure which, in turn, becomes an existential search concerning questions of identity and purpose with its attendant aspects of confusion, isolation, fear, and revelation suggestive through the landscape of the rural seashore setting that relates to his own life: "I could no longer see very far in front of me ... because of a thick, damp sea-mist that had come rolling in over the marshes and enveloped everything" (69). When he gets lost he describes the "nightmare" in relation to the setting: "I was obliged to go step by slow step, for fear of veering off onto the marsh, and then into the rising water." He hears the crying of a young child: "It had somehow lost the causeway path and fallen into the marsh and was being dragged under by the quicksand and the pull of the incoming tide" (71). After his ordeal, he says in recognition of the change that has come over him: "All was so changed, so utterly changed that I might have been re-born into another world and all the rest been some fevered dream" (75–76). And like a newborn child, when Keckwick drives him back in the pony cart, "I fell into a sort of trance, half sleeping, half waking, rocked by the motion of the cart" (77).

During his stay overnight stay at Eel Marsh House, he tries to rescue the little dog that has been lent him for company, and the land reflects the danger and sinking into the subconscious:

> At first the path was firm, though muddy, beneath my feet.... The wind coming across the estuary was bitingly cold on my face and I felt my eyes begin to smart and water, so that I had to wipe them in order to see my way clearly.... Then I ... began to feel the stickiness and unsteadiness of the ground as it became boggier. Once I plunged my leg down and it stuck fast in a watery hole.... All around me the water was swollen and murky, the tide of the estuary was now high, running across the marshes themselves, and I was obliged to wade rather than walk.... I felt a second of pure despair, alone in the middle of the wild marsh, under the fast-moving, stormy sky, with only water all around me and that dreadful house the only solid thing for miles around" [129–130].

In this work, the causeway is the topological link between land and sea and signifies also the link between past and present as well as between the mind and actions of the narrator as he reaches a new level of self-awareness.

This is also the situation in *Crusoe's Daughter*, the most widely acclaimed of Jane Gardam's works, about which Gardam says, "...the landscape which includes the wide sands of Coatham where the poor children danced beside the cold North Sea ... is my mother's landscape; the novel is partly about my mother, who was never able to leave it for a fuller life and yet lived more influentially to her family, it seems to me, than any paid-up feminist."[25] The story describes the life of a woman, Polly Flint, from the time she is a six-year-old motherless child into late middle age, and her extraordinary relationship with the remote landscape of the Yorkshire coast: "Sometimes the marsh dazzled. Sometimes it was so pale and unnoticeable that it seemed only an extension of the sea.... But living on the marsh it was visible enough and had great beauty. Blue-green salt-marsh grasses, shadowy fields of sea-lavender reflected and were reflected in the sky, and the buildings between the salt and fresh-water flats and the rolling skies gave definition and authority to what otherwise would have seemed in the power of the haphazard" (21). It is a landscape similar to the one described by Dante Gabriel Rossetti in his poem "The Sea Limits" which is concerned with the concrete expression of beauty itself as the outward expression of the soul. Rossetti, like Gardam, reveals emotion through the natural setting. In the opening lines, the ocean amplifies the movement of the world: "Consider the sea's listless chime; / Time's self it is, made audible—/ The murmur of the earth's own shell" (589). In the second stanza, the organic metaphor: "Its painful pulse is on the sands" is described, and the horizon, like Matthew Arnold's in "Dover Beach," is eternal and unknown. The organic image appears again in the third stanza: "Listen alone beside the sea / Listen alone among the woods;" and ends with an organic continuance of life: "Hark where the murmurs of thronged men / Surge and sink back and surge again—/ Still the one voice of wave and tree" (589). The final stanza opens with an image of death, presenting it as a natural occurrence of life: "Gather a shell from the strown beach...."

Polly Flint is first taken to this setting by her 'father,' Captain Flint, who dies at sea shortly after. It is 1903 and she is six years old when she begins to her life at Oversands, the yellow house that stands alone on the sea marsh. Here, she lives with her two unmarried aunts, Frances and Mar; their maid, Charlotte, who becomes her friend; as well as the aunts' companion, the malignant Mrs. Woods, who delights in torturing her to vent her frustration, jealous from the start of Polly Flint because of her own secret passion for Aunt Frances; and finally, and most important, the landscape.

From the start, Polly Flint is drawn into the magic of the setting: "It was the light at first that was troublesome—the light and the space of the yellow house. Light flowed in from all sides and down from the enormous sky ... the wind knocked the clouds about over the hills and the marsh and the dunes and the sea, until the house seemed to toss like a ship. I remember that I clutched on to things a good deal" (12). And she begins to notice the difference between this landscape and the urban setting of her first home: "On the northern horizon there was a kind of bruise in the sky which was the Iron-Works, the demon kitchens my father and I had clattered through in the train, and when the wind was from the north these made alarming roaring noises now and then, and great surging sounds like tidal waves; but usually the marsh and everyone who lived on it was very quiet" (20). Her relationship with the marsh is stronger than any relationship she has with the characters in the novel. She turns to it after making the astounding decision not be confirmed in the church: "Greek and solemn music, and hour-long sermon and a sort of tribal dance in the wind at the church-door with Father Pocock bending about towards us all and all of us bending about towards him. Laughter and little hand-shakes. Big stupid smiles. Guilt at disdain. The home over the marsh again—no guilt there. No guilt ever on the marsh, just joy" (29). When she is twelve, she has a vision while she is walking across the marsh and decides afterwards never to go to church again: "When I was still twelve, not yet quite thirteen, one particular Sunday in March, we had embarked upon our journey over the marsh for the eleven o'clock service when I saw an angel. It was a huge gold man looking at me from the tower on the unfinished house.... He shone with comprehension and strength and I knew that he loved me and was on my side. So that at lunch-time later that day I said I wouldn't be able to go to church in the evening. Or probably again. Ever" (30–31).

The landscape of the rural coast, along with her love of reading, most importantly *Robinson Crusoe*, whose title character she identifies with, are the most powerful influences in her life as she moves towards adolescence: "The book was Robinson Crusoe, a book that I knew very well. Today it was going to where it and I would feel at home. I pushed it inside the front of my coat and set off, giving both inner and outer door a slam, for the wide sea shore" (37). The slamming of the door begins her spiritual transformation. It is marked by a strong wind, and Polly Flint feels this change sweeping over her: "The wind was tremendous over the dunes but the beach was in full sunlight and I walked fast and then ran and then walked again until I began to be aware of my fingers and toes again.... The aches and pains of the past few days had gone and I felt springy. Rather pleased with myself" (37). The end of this powerful scene marks for Polly the revelation that "I must be right. Somewhere inside we do know everything about ourselves. There is no real forgetting. Perhaps we know somewhere, too, about all that is to come" (38).

Throughout a series of subsequent revelations the landscape acts as her spiritual compass. She begins to see that the flat, fictitious life of Robin Crusoe, so admired by her up until this point, is a contrast of the lives of the people she grows up with, each of whom reveals a hidden side which is brought to light by the power of the landscape. With the maid, Charlotte, it is her illegitimate son, whose real identity is discovered when he catches a cold from Aunt Polly who, in turn, became ill after walking through the marshes during a violent storm. When the distraught Charlotte leaves the household, Aunt Polly, who blames herself, suffers a crippling sense of remorse which immobilizes her until she hears that her lover, also unrevealed until this point, the oily French. Peacock, who runs the church in the local village, had decided, unknown to her, to become a missionary in India. She insists he marry her so that she can go with him. She leaves, and Polly writes to her, and from her letters, none of which reach their destination, Polly marks the growing self-awareness that finds a parallel in the landscape around her: "I love the marsh and Oversands and I know that I live in a very compelling landscape as the Brontes did. But Aunt Frances I am not at all sure about the Brontes. I am not sure that we were ever meant to become knitted to the landscape. After all, I am in no way mystical. I don't even want to be confirmed. When Robinson Crusoe was married to a landscape you know, he had a hard time to keep sane. I am being dissolved into a landscape and all hope for me is that someone will come and marry me to make things complete and take me away" (77).

While abroad, Aunt Frances dies of amebic dysentery, and Aunt Mary, who is mentally unsound but whose insanity has always been coped with, disguised as eccentricity by the her sister, goes to live in a nunnery, and Polly Flint goes to stay for a while at her mother's ancestral home, Thwaite Hall. Here, she finds out that her mother, Gertrude, was the daughter of Arthur Thwaite, a man who was supposed to marry Aunt Mary had he not made Polly Flint's mother pregnant. This is the cause of Aunt Mary's lifetime descent into madness. And Polly Flint finds out that she is not who she thought she was, and, again, she draws a comparison between life and fiction.

She returns to the yellow house by the sea. When her aunt dies of a brain tumor and the companion, the insidious Mrs. Woods, who has never recovered from the death of Aunt Polly whom it is revealed she has loved passionately but unrequitedly all her life, also dies, Polly is left with the yellow house. "Married to the landscape," she lives on the marshlands and herself becomes increasingly eccentric in middle age.

Like Robinson Crusoe, she, too, is alone, but his character, so strong and simple, has not, she realizes, prepared her for dealing with the dark lives of those around her, including her own. It is her understanding, finally, of the distinction between fiction and reality that brings her peace, and by the end of the story, healed by the landscape of the marshlands, she becomes a surrogate mother and wife to an old childhood friend and his children who is now a war refugee from Germany and settles down to write a "spiritual biography."

These works that focus on the rural seashore may be understood in W. B. Yeats' world of "essences" that he talks about in relation to *The Waves*: "Certain typical books—Mrs. Woolf's *The Waves*—suggest a philosophy like that of the Samkarra school of ancient India, mental and physical objects alike material, a deluge of experience breaking over us and within us, melting limits whether of line or tint; man no hard bright mirror dawdling by the dry sticks of a hedge, but a swimmer, or rather the waves themselves."[26] In each of the novels and stories discussed, both the real and the tropistic presence of the sea become the catalyst by which each character is able to establish a connection with the past and embrace the present, as in *The Woman in Black* and *Crusoe's Daughter*. In *The Waves*, for instance, the actual condition of the sea reflects the psychological states of its seven characters. The sea also works as the catalyst for Jimeen's memory in "The Great Wave," and in "Fighting the Waves" the sea represents the power and force of love. In "Learning to Swim," the sea becomes a reflection of marital dysfunction as well as a desire for autonomy as it does in "Beside the Seaside." The sea affects and unites humanity in a shared experience, a linear movement of retrospective and perspective which is imaged in the sea's horizontal motion as it does in Thomas Hardy's *A Pair of Blue Eyes* and John Fowles' *The French Lieutenant's Woman*. The rural coastal setting with its cliffs, Martello towers, lighthouses, and the constant movement of the sea, is both the site and the catalyst that brings characters to a new level of self-awareness and an understanding of one another. For Mr. Ramsay, in *To the Lighthouse*, this is brought about when he achieves his goal of reaching the lighthouse. In "Beside the Seaside," Margaret is able to embrace life through asserting her choice attended by the symbols of the Martello tower and the lighthouse, and for Charles Arrowby in *The Sea, the Sea*, it is his ability to master the sides of the Martello tower which leads him to a realization of self-truth.

Chapter Five

The Urban Shore

Matthew Arnold's "Dover Beach" and "The Forsaken Merman," Jane Austen's *Persuasion*, Graham Greene's *Brighton Rock*, Patrick Hamilton's *The West Pier*, Samuel Beckett's *Embers*, Alan Bennett's "All Day on the Sands," Alan Sillitoe's "The Road," Edward Bond's *The Sea*, and Susan Hill's *The Albatross*

> "But the sea has, in addition, the constancy which the crowd lacks. It is always there; it does not ooze away from time to time and disappear. To remain in existence is the greatest, though as yet fruitless, desire of the crowd; and this desire is seen fulfilled in the sea"
> —*Crowds and Power*, Elias Canetti.

Nathaniel Hawthorne describes the English resort town in *English Note-Books* as "...a place where everybody seems to be a transitory guest, nobody at home."[1] When Matthew Arnold describes the urban shore of the seaside town Dover in his poem "Dover Beach" the description of the landscape—the conflicting perspectives of horizon and towering cliffs—suggests the speaker's inner conflicts generated by the rapid changes in Victorian society in which he lived, primarily the conflict between science and religion, and the shore and the sea—the constant ebb and flow of the waves—signifies this. The poem has a peaceful image of the sea at full tide and the moon shining on the Straits. Only a distant light suggests the presence of man. The cliffs, like Hardy's, shelter the bay and in their vast impenetrability seem to take on a presence of their own: "The sea is calm tonight. / The tide is full, the moon lies fair / Upon the straits; on the French coast the light / Gleams and is gone; the cliffs of England stand, / Glimmering and vast, out in the tranquil bay." The reader discovers that the description of beauty in the landscape is an illusion as the scene changes and the poem becomes more subjective. The landscape now becomes the vehicle for the speaker's own growing despair and loss of faith, which is paralleled by the retreat of the sea as he describes the tragedy of human experience. The perspective changes from one-dimensional horizontal to a linear descent into the imagination—a movement which is accompanied by the "grating" noise of the pebbles being dragged and thrown against the shore as his psyche is being bombarded by the intrusions of the industrial age.

The second part of the poem focuses on human history. Each human experiences the sea with imaginative difference. Sophocles heard it as "the turbid ebb and flow of human misery." To the speaker, the sea represents a slow retreat of Christian faith. Faith and the sea are presented as one comforting unified image: "The sea of Faith / Was once, too, at the full, and round the earth's shore / Lay like the folds of a bright girdle furled." In modern times, that comfort has withdrawn from the beach, and in the final section the sea has vanished and left man stranded on a "darkling plain" of naked shingles.

The urban shore is the focus of all human pain and suffering in another of Arnold's poems, "The Forsaken Merman," wherein the sea is an image of the womb where the children, "wild with pain," swim in safety until they surface, calling to their mother, who has made her home in the town on the shore, to return to them and the sea. But she, deafened by the various distractions of human life, cannot hear them. The stage through which child each passes as he or she reaches the shore is signified by the surf that crashes on the shore as the waves crest and break, much like the waves in Virginia Woolf's *The Waves*. The urban shore with church, castle, and academic hall symbolizes the fragmentation and shattered unity of preindustrial times: "She sits at her wheel in the humming town, / Singing most joyfully / ... For priest, And the bell, and the holy well, / For the wheel where I spun." Like contemporary writer Alan Sillitoe, for Arnold, the wheel represented the numbing routine of the industrialized world: "Turn to chamfer, then to drill, then to blade chamfer"[2] says the factory worker, Arthur

Seaton, in *Saturday Night and Sunday Morning*, with a self-detached mechanism, and when the wife of the merman makes her home on the urban shore it is her "whizzing wheel" like Arthur Seaton's carborundum wheel, that signifies her life, filled with action but dead beneath the surface.

Both of these poems set on the urban shore suggest both a reversal in historical time from the ideal past to the brutal present in "Dover Beach" and a reversal of nature in "The Forsaken Merman"—from the comforting womb-like world of the sea to the utilitarian world of the urban shore. They suggest a sense of movement particular to the urban shore—a movement of unrest that is the focus of many later works set on the urban shore.

Unlike the tranquil setting of the rural seashore where the solitary individual experiences a personal revelation, the noisy urban seaside offers a carnivaleque atmosphere attended by the all-important crowd often at a time of religious or social significance such as Whitsuntide/Bank Holiday or even an ordinary vacation, during which time the promenades and beaches become sites for spectacle and revelation as they do, for example, in Graham Greene's *Brighton Rock* (1938), Patrick Hamilton's *The West Pier* (1951), Susan Hill's "The Albatross" (1971), Edward Bond's *The Sea* (1973), Alan Sillitoe's "The Road" (1978), and Alan Bennett's "All Day on the Sands" (1985). Here, the seaside crowds of visitors, implied or real, reflect the waves themselves as they gather, surge and break during the peak of the holiday season and disperse at the end of the summer, but there is no sense of spiritual regeneration in this almost mechanical movement of humanity.

"Oh I do like to be beside the seaside / Oh I do like to be beside the sea / Oh I do like to stroll along the prom prom prom / Where the brass band plays Tid-de-ly-om-pom-pom!" These words from a popular English music hall song still hold true. There is a strong element of the carnivalesque in literature, or in Mikhail Bakhtin's terms "the carnivalization of literature,"[3] that uses the urban coastal setting in a blending of the ordinary with the not-so-ordinary, for since the mid-nineteenth century, British seaside resorts have presented themselves as unique and distinct locales unlike any other geographical settings, as Howard Grey comments in *The Victorians by the Sea*: "Lower fares, special excursion tickets for families and parties of people, and a general rise in the standard of living, meant that a different sort of person could now afford an occasional holiday at the coast—the railway had democratized the seaside resort."[4]

Jane Austen, for instance, remarks about the town of Lyme Regis in a letter to her sister: "I continue quite well, in proof of which I have bathed again this morning.... Hitherto the weather has been just what we could wish;—the continuance of the dry Season is very necessary to our comfort."[5] She uses the setting of Lyme Regis as a site for spectacle and revelation in her novel *Persuasion*, in which, "The young people were all wild to see Lyme..." (69). In this, her final novel, the story follows the romance of Anne Elliot and Frederick Wentworth, who have broken off their earlier affection because, upon the advice of his late wife's friend, Anne's father forbids it. When she is twenty-six, the relationship is rekindled after some romantic reversals in a dramatic event that takes place in Lyme Regis when Wentworth begins to realize that he is tiring of his current romantic interest, Louisa Musgrove. The situation is marked by a dramatic event that takes place on the Cobb, about halfway through the novel, and is the turning point, a reversal, on which the plot revolves: "The conclusion of her visit, however, was diversified in a way which she had not at all imagined" (69). Jane Austen writes about the Cobb in the letter to her sister: "We afterwards walked together for an hour on the Cobb."[6]

A coastal feature crucial in the seaside resort town is the front, often referred to as the promenade, parade, or strand. In *Persuasion*, it is the Cobb, part front, part stone pier, that finds its counterpart in the embankment of the river setting. Hawthorne describes the front or promenade: "The main street leads directly down to the seashore, along which there is an elevated embankment, with a promenade on the top, and seats."[7] Like the pier, the front was first built in the middle of the nineteenth century for specific reasons explained by John Walton in *The English Seaside Resort*:

> At many resorts it was obvious that some sort of bulwark was needed against the high tides, floods, and storms. As a result seawalls were constructed and it is interesting that even they came to be utilized for pleasure, for they provide a firm roadway for walking or riding along. Gradually the seaside promenade, like the piers, became a feature of the resorts.... Defending the seashore by walls and promenades was an inevitable consequence of the growth of seaside towns and meant that visitors were increasingly subjected to an urban environment, though one which, by being perched on the water's edge, seemed quite different from the inland towns."[8]

In *Persuasion* the Cobb is described through the perceptions of the characters, seeming to exert an almost magnetic quality over them as it draws them to the sea: "The party ... still descending, soon found themselves on the sea shore, and lingering only, as all must linger and gaze on a first return to the sea, who ever deserve to look on it at all, proceeded toward the Cobb..." (70). And here, on the Cobb, begins the revelation of truth: "When they came to the steps, leading upwards from the beach, a gentleman at the same moment preparing to come down, politely drew back, and stopped to give them way. They ascended and passed him; and as they passed, Anne's face caught his eye, and he looked at her with a degree of earnest admiration" (77). Attended by the wind of change the dramatic scene takes place and is marked by the change of direction Louisa makes as she jumps down and falls: "There was too much wind to make the high part of the new Cobb pleasant for the ladies, and all were contented to pass quietly and carefully down the steep flight, excepting Louisa; she must be jumped down them by Captain Wentworth.... He advised her against it, thought the jar was too great; but no, he reasoned and talked in vain; she smiled and said, 'I am determined I will:' he put out his hands; she was too precipitate by half a second, she fell on the pavement on the Lower Cobb, and was taken up lifeless!" (81).

The seaside resorts, says John Walton, in *The British Seaside*, are "peripheral sites" ideal for "socially marginal activities—carnivals of desire and explosions of unrest":

> The seaside puts the "civilising process" temporarily into reverse (although the participants understand that they are defying its conventions) and conjures up the spirit of carnival, in the sense of upturning the social order and celebrating the rude, the excessive, the anarchic, the hidden and the gross, in ways which generate tension and put respectability on the defensive, generating culture wars in settings where the prim and the Rabelaisian sides of British character come into maritime confrontation, and where the genteel, controlled, symmetrical front of the resort finds itself invaded by the disorder, untidiness, and misrule of the back.[9]

Bakhtin discusses the idea of carnival in relation to the medieval figure Rabelais, stating its function is "to consecrate inventive freedom, to permit the combination of a variety of different elements and their rapprochement, to liberate from the prevailing point of view of the world, from conventions and established truths, from clichés, from all that is humdrum and universally accepted. This carnival spirit offers the change to have a new outlook on the world, to realize the relative nature of all that exists, and to enter a completely new order of things."[10] During such time, ordinary events are temporarily suspended for a carnivalesque celebration which, in literature, signifies a reversal that brings about a disclosure of truth. Stuart Hall describes the idea of the carnivaleque in *Carnival, Hysteria, and Writing* as, "a metaphor for the temporary licensed suspension and reversal of order, the time when the low shall be high and the high, low, the moment of upturning, of 'the world turned upside-down.'"[11] The carnivalesque reversal that takes place in the urban seaside resort is suggested in W. H. Auden's poem "The Way to the Sea": "Do what you will: / Be extravagant, / Be lucky, / Be clairvoyant, / Be amazing. Be a sport or an angel, / Imagine yourself as a courtier, or as a queen. / Accept your freedom."[12]

In the literary carnivalesque of the urban seaside, certain artificial topographical features such as the pier, the promenade, and the railway station take on important functions within the movement of the plot. Cyril Bainbridge comments on the pier in his interesting and informative book, *Pavilions on the Sea: A History of the Seaside Pleasure Pier*: "Turbulent and colourful: carefree gaiety contrasting with grim, sad battles against economic, social and meteorological elements.... The pier became a half-mile or a mile of temptation to those who were lured into its arcades. The click of the ratchet mechanism of the turnstile was the key providing entry into a cast-iron springboard which led to a world of mystery, and excitement and daring unmatched."[13] In general terms the pier represents a bridge, a transition, that reaches across from the shore—humanity—to the sea—nature. It is viewed by the populace with reverence, almost like a shrine that takes the place of a church. Specifically, the pier is a place where something extraordinary happens—where communication between characters takes on a special meaning—where man is closest to nature and his inner feeling because he is closest to life and death—the sea.

The railway station with its maps and timetables, what Auden calls "rituals of space and time,"[14] is another vital feature of the seaside resort town, for it here that the all-important crowds disembark and, through its conventions and schedules, it presents both the necessary contrast to the swarming crowds and Rabelaisian air as well as an emphasis on the carnivalesque. *The Times* of 30 August 1860 comments: "Our seaside towns have been turned inside out. So infallible and unchanging are the attractions of the ocean that it is enough for any place to stand on our shore. That one recommendation is sufficient. Down comes the excursion train with its thousands, some with a month's range others tethered to a six hours limit, but all rushing with one impulse to the water's edge."[15]

With its seaside setting and the seasonal ritualistic activities enjoyed there by crowds of holiday makers, writers have often set their works in Brighton, one of England's largest urban resorts, located on England's south coast. Graham Greene's *Brighton Rock* and Patrick Hamilton's *The West Pier* use the seaside resort town of Brighton as setting as these writers develop themes of moral decay and corruption as well as the carnivalesque reversal of innocence and evil and reflect Allon White's statement in *Carnival, Hysteria, and Writing*: "...the carnivalesque forces, which were suppressed by bourgeois elites in their protracted withdrawal from popular culture, re-emerged in displaced and distorted form as objects of phobic disgust and repressed desire in both literature and psychopathology."[16] These novels are not only at geographical counter poles to Woolf's *To the Lighthouse*—the setting of noisy Brighton in southern England is the opposite of the quiet Hebrides islands in the north, but in its artificiality, Brighton seems to represent as much of a rejection of nature as Woolf's island is a celebration of it. Even the sea seems to resent the holidaymakers, mostly day-trippers, and offers no sense of regeneration to the transient crowds.

Brighton Rock opens as a thriller, and the first paragraph introduces several images related to the urban resort and to the carnivalesque, such as the festival of Whitsun, the wind of change, the crowds, the railway station, the piers, the sea, and the music of the band. These images recur throughout, taking on symbolic aspects as they do so. We first see Brighton through the eyes of Hale, and if, in one sense, Brighton is represented by the crowds of visitors, Hale is representative of the individual lost, guilty of existential bad faith in his inability and unwillingness to choose, suffering from a spiritual exhaustion and finally meeting a nihilistic kind of death with no sense of renewal, for he is murdered. His murder is the nemesis for Pinkie Brown, the central character, generating in him a paranoia and revulsion for life that finally ends in his own death, for as Canetti says, "Man petrifies and darkens in the distance he has created."[17]

Instead of acting for himself, Hale allows others—his employers and his friend Ida—to make decisions for him. His brief odyssey around Brighton, lost, confused, and terrified of what might lie ahead as he leaves clue cards at different locales, seems like an absurd parody of

Homer's tale of heroism. Hale's round of calls is repeated in each seaside town he visits until someone finds the clue he has left. The irony is that he works under a pseudonym, "Kolley Kibber," and has literally as well as spiritually given up his identity. In more general terms, in his endless, pathetic trips around Brighton, Southend, and other "ports of call" required by his job as "sentry go" for a newspaper aptly named *The Messenger*, Hale may be seen as the precursor of many of the wandering and confused heroes of twentieth century fiction. Rob Shields says in *Places on the Margin*: "The status of Brighton as a liminal zone made any and all rumours of transgression, decadence, crime, and degeneration the basis for sensational newspaper reporting."[18]

Also introduced in the opening paragraph are the contrasting elements of life and death—flow and stasis—and the theme of the outsider in the crowd as, with the "Whitsun wind off the sea" and the music of the band, the stage is set for the emergence of Pinkie Brown, the central character, himself a kind of modern-day Orpheus. The fictional, unreal world of Brighton finds its counterpart in the inner world of the seventeen-year-old killer and gang leader Pinkie Brown who, as Terry Eagleton says in *Exiles and Émigrés*, has no sense of human reality: "Brighton, a seedy, flashy, candy-floss world, is seen by the novel with a coldly dehumanizing perception which parallels Pinkie's own responses.... Pinkie's view of experience is time and again confirmed by the novel itself; his revolted rejection of life is underpinned by the book's mood and imagery, which remorselessly elaborates the selective sordidities of Brighton to the status of the entire human condition."[19] And Canetti's explanation of the relationship between the solitary individual and the crowd may be understood in the character of Pinkie Brown as well as the carnivalesque reversal: "It is only in the crowd that man can overcome fear of being touched.... As soon as a man has surrendered himself to the crowd, he ceases to fear its touch.... This reversal of the fear of being touched belongs to the nature of crowds."[20] Unlike the formless crowds that do not congregate at the seaside and resemble more the medieval crowd described by Bakhtin's medieval carnival is the closed crowd, which nonetheless still retains the carnivalesque loss of identity. These closed crowds appear at promenade, pier and beach, sites limited by access, often a gate or turnstile, and specific boundaries. It is the type of crowd described by Canetti in *Crowds and Power*: "The first thing to be noticed about it is that it has a boundary. It establishes itself by accepting its limitation. It creates a space for itself which it will fill.... The entrances to this space are limited in number, and only these entrances can be used; the boundary is respected where it consists of stone, of solid wall, or of some special act of acceptance, or entrance fee."[21] In *Brighton Rock,* Greene uses these crowds as background for the individual, for in their determined pursuit of easy gratification they make a fine contrast for such existential themes as personal choice and self-truth which are presented against a coastal background where wind and storm and intense sunlight contrasted with deep shadows comprise the setting.

Greene also uses the pier in much the same way as Woolf uses the lighthouse—as a symbol of reality that withstands time and through which the individual is able to reconnect with nature and, ultimately, his fellow man. However, given the types of characters in *Brighton Rock*—killers, mobsters, has-beens, and moral degenerates—this growing sense of communication experienced by them when they visit the pier or its vicinities often generates in them an unease. On the pier, Pinkie suppresses any likely sign of communication, often heralded by music, with violent anger, feeling the pain of life through the music he denies himself as he descends into his own private hell. When he meets the members of his gang on the pier to plan how to terrorize young Rose, who knows of Pinkie's connection in the murder of Hale, the sea beneath reflects the evil intention of the group: "The water washed around the piles at the end of the pier, dark poison-bottle green, mottled with seaweed, and the salt wind smarted on his lips" (22). And that Pinkie knows the pier is a very different place from the town is apparent in his comment: "All clocks on this pier are fast." As the town clock strikes twice, emphasizing the difference in the temporal space between the two worlds of pier and town, Pinkie waits for his sidekicks to appear and feels his anger, like the sea, "grinding in his guts like the tide at the piles below" (23). During another visit to the pier to meet his friends, the temporal and transitory aspect of life is also marked by the town clock, which strikes eleven times as another recurring image is introduced: the thunderstorm which represents the intensity of Pinkie's emotions at these meetings. This time he meets Spicer, an old "has been" who, to delay the discovery of the murder, will take the place of the dead Hale and distribute around Brighton the identification cards that bear the photo of him. Now, ironically, the holidaymakers will be searching for a dead man. At this meeting, Pinkie stares out to sea and tries to suppress the feelings aroused in him by the music he hears. Music unites and humanizes, and it can bring alive the imagination; in *Brighton Rock*, it is a threat to Pinkie's stronghold of isolation. And as Pinkie dismisses Spicer and waits for Rose to arrive so that he can put into motion his plan of coercion and intimidation, the elements of time, thunder, and the sea come together, and the music painfully stirs his innermost feelings: "In the town a clock struck eleven; three strokes were lost in the thunder coming down across the Channel.... He turned impatiently away from the sea and complained again. 'That music' (46). Taking her to the edge of the pier, Pinkie threatens Rose by recounting to her the story of a girl whose face was disfigured by vitriol for having known too much about a certain incident. The farther away from the music they move and the louder the storm becomes, so Pinkie's emotional state responds, reaching its most diabolical when he deceives the lonely and frightened Rose with intimations of love. As Pinkie watches Rose's horrified reaction to his story, he feels something akin to pity, and, for a brief moment, Rose becomes a symbol of hope for him, his possibility of salvation through her goodness. But he denies himself the opportunity, and with an action that foreshadows the ending of the story, he leads her back to the lights and the music of humanity.

The setting of beach and pier is used also to convey the question of self to Spicer shortly before his death at Pinkie's hands. After he disguises his voice on the phone to protect Pinkie, he symbolically loses his own identity in preparation for what is about to happen. The revelation of the enormity that has been committed dawns upon him as he walks the shoreline between asphalt and shingle—being and non-being. This displacement of self is emphasized in a strangely religious scene when Spicer goes down to the beach after his phone call, and a photographer who is walking under the pier takes a photograph of him. Simultaneously, a seagull flies up from the pier as a dove from a church, and Spicer reaches out for help. The first communicative expression between Rose and Pinkie when the two return to the pier, and the mortification felt by Pinkie through the fumbled kiss, is mirrored in the sea: "The Boy was staring over the side where the green tide sucked and slid like a wet mouth around the piles" (93). It is to the sea, as sour as his own life, that Pinkie returns after, with much trepidation, he arranges to marry Rose, as is affected in the true existential sense as "Fear and curiosity ate at the proud figure, he was aware of nausea and retched" (140). The condition of the sea and the gulls reflect his own spiritual sickness as he walks along the shore to take one last look at the slum where he spent his childhood, and the walk itself is a prefiguration of the reversal to infancy that takes place in the final scene. Pier and music, as an integral part of the urban seaside setting, are used here to develop the sense of drama and the impending carnivalesque reversal.

"All roads lead to the Front,"[22] says Greene, and he uses this setting for Rose and Pinkie when they express their ideas on good and evil as they run down to the parade during a thunderstorm: "...they were back on the parade in one of the empty glass shelters.... 'Of course there's hell. Flames and damnation,' he said with his eyes on the dark shifting water...." Later, when Pinkie takes one of his gang members to help him intimidate a criminal acquaintance, the two of them walk along the Front, and Pinkie's spiritual malaise is echoed in the grinding retreat of the sea and the striking, once again, of the town clock: "The rain had stopped; it was low tide and the shallow edge of the sea scraped far out at the rim of the shingle. A clock struck midnight" (55). After the pair have carried out their brutal threat, they return to Pinkie's dreary room where, from the window, the image of "the last lightning flapped across the grey roofs stretching to the sea" reflects Pinkie's growing paranoia stretching to the murky waters beneath the pier. The elements of time and the imagination, as represented by the monoliths and the moon, are now placed in a broader, more universal, historical context that counterpoises Pinkie's own deepening journey inward. The Front is also the setting used when Pinkie explains to his sidekick, Dallow, after he has killed Spicer, that the only way he can keep Rose quiet about his involvement in the murder of Hale is by marrying her.

Brighton Station, as it is described in *Brighton Rock*, is antithetical to the sea and the world of nature that it represents. The station is civilization at its most chaotic, bringing the hordes of people that swarm and surge down Queen's Road to the front, and for all the energy it represents, it is often viewed in a negative light. In *Brighton Rock*, the station with its sleazy side street and alleys, a neighborhood where only the underclass of Brighton's permanent citizens live in poverty and crime, including Rose, contrast to the rural areas that surround the city. As the story progresses, the setting broadens to include the nearby coastal village of Peacehaven. Pinkie, who represents the unreal, ineffable evil of Brighton, finds his counterpart in Rose, whose naive goodness represents the rather dull and dreary Peacehaven. The two go to Peacehaven on their first real date. Here, away from the disquiet of Brighton, they reach a tentative, awkward kind of closeness; Pinkie becomes his most vulnerable and Rose her most touching, and the walk on the cliff edge, where a fumbled attempt at a kiss is made, foreshadows the story's violent ending: "...hundreds of feet below the pale green sea washed into the scarred and shabby side of England" (93).

As the sea images Pinkie's sense of self as the story progresses, so his life becomes more and more troubled, and in his growing relationship with Rose, something he finds he cannot control, he fights his despair with viciousness. Pinkie experiences a sense of defiant despair such as Kierkegaard describes: "...with hatred for existence it wills to be itself, to be itself in terms of its misery; it does not even in defiance or defiancy will to be itself, but to be itself in spite.... Whereas the weak despairer will not hear about what comfort eternity had for him, so neither will such a despairer hear about it, but for a different reason, namely, because this comfort would be the destruction of him as an objection against the whole of existence."[23] Like Kierkegaard's despairer, Pinkie cannot accept the comfort of Rose's love because he senses an ensuing loss of control and a plunge into confusion. The climactic ending of the story takes place during a violent thunderstorm and is signaled by not one but several church clocks tolling the final hours for Pinkie: "Across the noisy sea the hours began to strike in Brighton churches: he counted one, two, three, four, and stopped" (235). Forcing Rose to write a suicide note, Pinkie has taken her back again to Peacehaven, to commit a double suicide, his part in which he plans to fake. As before, any steps towards love and communication between the two take place in the village by the sea where, in the pouring rain, Pinkie admits to himself that making love to Rose the night before had been "a kind of pleasure, a kind of—something else," and his spirit, like that of the gull that Rose saw in their earlier visit, now stirs; here on the shoreline, for a moment freedom might be realized—non-being seems about to become, but as Pinkie turns the car back around to Brighton, this hope dies. Parked again, this time between Peacehaven and Brighton, goodness and evil, on the edge of the cliff and about to embark on the suicide plan, Pinkie looks at the sea; "It's the world," he says, about to join it. And as the attempted suicide is foiled first by Rose as she comes into her own sense of being by exerting her choice— life over death—by throwing the gun away in defiance, and secondly by the intervention of Dallow and the policeman, the world intervening, Pinkie meets a very existential death in the downward plunge with its attendant symbols of the scream, breaking glass, blood, and a reversion to childhood to signify a death before coming alive. Turning the hands of the clock even further back, Pinkie leaps over the edge of the cliff and into the sea, the primal flux. Bachelard describes this kind of leap in *Water and Dreams*: "In point of fact, the *leap into the sea*, more than any other physical event, awakens echoes of a dangerous and hostile initiation. It is the only, exact, reasonable image, the only image that can be experienced of a *leap into the unknown*."[24] Pinkie's leap is a return to nature—nothing about to become: "...he was at the edge, he was over: they couldn't even hear a splash. It was as if he'd been withdrawn suddenly by a hand out of any existence—past or present, whipped away into zero—nothing" (243). The nothingness that Pinkie has become will, through his child which Rose is carrying, become being, and the cyclic process will ensure for him a type of reclamation from "that obscure countryside of death." Each death, Hale's and Pinkie's, is preceded by a journey, Hale's circular journey around Brighton and Pinkie's journey inward on which the participators' paths are marked by coastal images. The question of the recognition of the self, the first step in the regeneration of the spirit, is presented through these deaths: Hale's permanent, nihilistic death, as artificial as the stick of rock and its indelible letters, "Brighton," that he is choked with, that opens the story and Pinkie's suicide leap into nothingness with which the story concludes.

The carnivalesque setting of Brighton and the South Downs during Whitsuntide is also the setting for Patrick Hamilton's *The West Pier*, published thirteen years later. In *The West Pier* three young men on holiday from school meet up with two local girls. The action revolves around a particular couple, whose names, Ralph Gorse and Esther Downes, tie them into the landscape of the coastal area, the South Downs, that surround Brighton: "It's Gorse—isn't it? Like what you see on the Downs?" as Esther comments. Gorse is a young man totally without scruples who is vacationing with two of his friends in Brighton, and Esther Downes, like Rose in Greene's *Brighton Rock*, is a local girl, coming from the same slums near Brighton Station: "The lovely Esther lived in conditions of grave squalor" (72). What unfolds between these two in this psychological thriller, is a struggle between good and evil, for, as Murdoch says, "...fictional literature has a special moral dimension because it is about people and, I venture to say, it is in however covert, unclear, secret, ambiguous a way, about the struggle between good and evil."[25]

What takes place in this story, which Graham Greene says on the back cover is the best book written about Brighton, is much like the entrapment and exploitation of Rose by the boy killer Pinkie; here, Gorse exerts the same kind of perverse influence over Esther and finally takes off with her small savings of sixty-odd pounds. This insidious inveiglement of a young girl is taken to the point of malicious intent as the young protagonist, Ralph Gorse, in many ways a psychological parallel to Pinkie, takes moral and physical advantage of Esther, the naive working-class girl, in assignations that take place on the promenade and pier. Esther's job, selling the local candy, also brings to mind the setting and atmosphere of Greene's book: "She worked and served at the counter in a sweet shop—a rather large and low pink and white sweet shop—particularly pink and white because it specialized in Brighton Rock—and popular in the season because it was situated in the Queen's Road. Swarming day-trippers, arriving at Brighton Station, and desiring to reach the sea as soon as possible, were then, as they are now, compelled to use the Queen's Road" (75). While she spends some of her time with Gorse's friend, Ryan, it is Gorse who attracts and fascinates Esther. The jealous Gorse writes anonymous notes maligning his friend's character and sends them to Esther. She tells her mother who "knew that a great deal took place on the Brighton Front, and the West Pier," about them, but not that she has already lent Gorse two pounds during one of their meetings at the Hotel Metropole. Gorse continues writing the anonymous letters, and his goal is now to get at the sixty-eight pounds and fifteen shillings that amount to Esther's entire savings. His hints of marriage and the gift of a new purse ease the way as Gorse induces Esther into putting fifteen pounds of her savings into buying a car with him. The car is one he has borrowed for the evening and parked outside the Hotel Metropole for this purpose. To convince her, he takes her for a drive in it to the Downs. Here, Esther loses her inhibitions and freely chooses to go in with Gorse in buying the car, which brings about the final scenes of the story. In the hotel, Gorse tells Esther that he needs another sixty-five pounds to buy the car because his allowance won't be in until Monday, and the owner of the car will not hold the car past the weekend and that, in fact, if he doesn't come up with the money, they will lose the fifteen pounds deposit made on it. Esther is horrified at first with the idea of parting with all of her savings, but she finally agrees.

The West Pier functions as a crucial aspect of the carnivalesque reversal in this novel, as it does in *Brighton Rock*, and is described as a "sexual battleship." It is the meeting place for all five characters throughout the story:

> The Pier was intimately and intricately connected with the entire ritual of "getting off." Indeed, without the Pier, "getting off" would have been to some minds inconceivable, or at any rate a totally different thing. The Pier was at once the object and arena of "getting off" and usually the first subtle excuse made by the male for having been so bold as to "get off" was his saying that he thought it might be "nice" to go on the Pier. An invitation to go on the Pier was like an invitation to dance, it almost conferred upon "getting off" an air of respectability. And so now these three young men, by going on the Pier themselves, had, as it were, established their independence doubly—firstly by the act itself, and secondly by proving that they were in no way anxious to avail themselves of any excuse [47].

Stretching over the sea, reaching away from the coast and civilization, the pier represents a place where inhibitions are lost against the deep sea that surrounds. Esther's decision to go on the West Pier marks the loss of her innocence and the beginning of her downfall with Gorse; it begins her initiation into adulthood and reality and is signaled by the image of the young man playing a war game on the slot machine as she and her friend, Gertrude, go to the Pier in search of the three young men they have just seen on the front. On the West Pier, just as Rose succumbed to Pinkie and agreed to go along with his plan, in the dark, to a background of music and sibilant sea, so the same turning point in terms of choice arises for Esther. Esther chooses to take the stairs that necessitate she and Gertrude pass directly in front of the boys. When Gorse and his friends come upon Esther and Gertrude, and Esther looks to the sea, it is, like Pinkie and Rose's encounter, on the side of the Pier farthest away from the shore where instinct is at its strongest: "Something he could not name had led Gorse to lead the other two to the prow of the Pier" (59).

Promenade and station are also keys features in *The West Pier* and enhance the air of carnivalesque reversal as they do in *Brighton Rock*. Gorse and Esther have their first date at the Hotel Metropole on the front. They arrange to meet at the West Pier and walk to the hotel. This becomes a regular occurrence, and it is at the hotel, a public place like the café where Rose works as a waitress in Greene's *Brighton Rock* and where she and Pinkie make plans for marriage, that Gorse, with hints of marriage, slowly draws Esther into his plan for taking her money. After these meetings, the two often spend some time on the West Pier, where Gorse kisses her, and Esther's reaction is much the same as Pinkie's is when he first kisses Rose. And she discovers something new about the kissing and about her reaction to it. Like Rose in *Brighton Rock*, for Esther, "the lovely walker on the front" whose father works as a porter at the station, it is the "distressing audible background" that, living so close, she cannot escape. She is disturbed by "the noise of the engines, and the danger of the trippers bumping into them—so much so that she could hardly think" (31).

The breakup of the two "lovers" takes place outside Brighton, in a rural area, as it does for Rose and Pinkie in *Brighton Rock*. Here, it is the small seaside village of Shoreham where Gorse drives Esther in the car and deserts her in a tearoom after borrowing the last of her money to pay for their tea. Instead of using the money to pay for their meal, he takes off in the car for London, and Esther is left with no money to pay the bill or get home. She borrows ten shillings from the kindly waitress, leaving the purse that Gorse bought her as security, and returns, humiliated and wiser, to Brighton and reality where: "The West Pier, which brought them all together, wore its own peculiar air of indifference about their departure. This battleship—this sex battleship—was on this Sunday evening more crowded than usual. Sunday evening was one of its best, and the season was at its peak" (252).

Through a symbolic use of the urban/rural setting that involves music, crowds, a sense of drama and mystery, as well as places of public recognition such as the promenade, pier and station, all of which move against the background of the sea, *Brighton Rock* and *The West Pier* are fine examples of those novels, plays, and short stories that use the seaside resort setting to develop a carnivalesque inversion that allows, for a brief time, its participants a sense of freedom from restriction imposed by political and social order as well as by life and death. The dark side of the carnivalesque is also described in these works that use Brighton as setting because of, as Shields describes in *Places on the Margin*, "the reputation of Brighton as the scene of the carnivalesque lifting of social norms with consequent immorality, violent murder, and general lack of respect for decency."[26] This is especially true of *Brighton Rock* and *The West Pier*.

In Samuel Beckett's *Embers*, a play for radio broadcast, the crowds are represented through the listening audience. As the listeners are drawn into the action through the noise—the sound of the waves—they create their reality from images implied by the constant roar of the sea. The sea becomes, in a sense, a conscious reality which draws them from themselves and unites them in a shared, liberating experience which Victor Carrabino explains in "On the Shores of Nothingness: Beckett's *Embers*":

> This domination of the sea over the tumultuous voice that emanates with thunderous force from the abyss can be explained by Beckett's wish to purge man from his cowardice to act and to make him enter into true communication and discourse with himself and life in general.... The roaring of the sea is the language to which man must lend an ear and thus get to the very root of human existence. In this play Beckett's obsession with the core of human suffering is portrayed by the primordial roaring of the sea, which in fact is a positive symbol that spells liberty and infinite possibilities in human choices.[27]

Henry's memories surface as he sits on the strand, which symbolizes the border between being and non-being, facing the sea. As in Graham Swift's *Waterland* and Patrick McGrath's *Spider,* the form of communication is between past and present as Henry tries to come to terms with his memories, especially those of his dead father, who is himself represented by the noise of the sea. The sea, constantly intruding into the present and bringing with it the memory of his father, is something Henry must fight to overcome in order to live with. In this sense, the sea parallels the turmoil of Henry's spiritual landscape as he sits on the strand near where his father was drowned. "Henry's monologue by the sea," says Carrabino, "is the manifestation of both his conscious and unconscious reality. Having wandered throughout arid deserts and empty streets, this Beckettian character is now facing another endless abyss, the monstrous presence of the roaring sea, the cavernous tropistic voice of his unconscious."[28]

The play opens with the noise of the sea beginning a slow acceleration that corresponds with Henry's gradual confrontation of memories as he approaches it: "Sea scarcely audible" (95). The voice of Henry's father emanates from the sea, and the past comes roaring into the present through Henry's efforts to deal with it as he includes his audience in the experience: "I say that sound you hear is the sea, we are sitting on the strand" (96). The sea represents life, and when Henry tells the listeners, "I'm like you in that, can't stay away from it, but I never go in" (96), he is speaking for all who are torn between action and audience, those whose enervating psychological impotence negates a meaningful existence. "Man has always listened to the footsteps of other men," says Canetti in *Crowds and Power*: "Animals too have their familiar gait ... hoofed animals feel in herds, like regiments of drummers."[29] The catharsis for Henry's situation is in the symbolism of the thunder of the horses' hooves which, like the rhythmic pounding of the horses' hooves in Woolf's *The Waves* and in Yeats' "Fighting the Waves," signals an impending energy. But Henry fears life, and in his fear seeks only to confine this energy: "' Hooves!' (Pause. Louder.) 'Hooves!' (Sound of hooves walking on hard road. They die rapidly away. Pause.) 'Again!' (Hooves as before. Pause. Excitedly.) 'Train it to mark time! Shoe it with steel and tie it up in the yard, have it stamp all day!' (Pause.) 'A ten ton mammoth back from the dead, shoe it with steel and have it tramp the world down!'" (96). Henry is unable to free himself from the grip of inertia that is brought about by the inability to distance his present life from the past; he will always be "stranded," but as he sits alone with his evocations, kindling the embers of his memories, he is able, through the sea's presence, to give these embers universal aspects applicable to all of humanity so that, finally, it is the listener who brings his own understanding to the world that Henry has created and by doing so defines his own kind of freedom.

The ideas of freedom and constraint are also explored through the setting of the seashore in Alan Bennett's short dramatic piece "All Day on the Sands." In this piece the distant provocative glitter of the sea that opens and closes the play represents the inaccessible—that which is never to be realized, never to be achieved—in the lives of endless and seemingly pointless rituals of the Cooper family and other residents on holiday at the Miramar boardinghouse in the resort town of Morecambe where Mr. Cooper's words to his twelve-year-old son, Colin, "We haven't got anything for you to do," are a cry from the heart to all who suffer the indignities and petty privations that come with unemployment. The plot of "All Day on the Sands" concerns Colin's revolt against the boredom of his life and a feeling of uselessness that, no doubt, he sees in the eyes of his unemployed father. His revolt is to dangle his sister's shoe outside the boardinghouse window and to lose it on the roof below. Living, as they do, on unemployment benefits, the loss of the shoe poses a serious economic threat to the family. Colin tries to retrieve the sandal by stealing a length of fishing line from another boy with which to hoist the sandal back in the window, but he is caught and his small insurrection discovered before he has time to reverse it. Woven into this plot are several images, all related to the sea and coast, which reflect a kind of twentieth century malaise, a sense of entrapment and inertness, cloying in its viscosity, in which the characters are suspended, unable to act independently of their programmed routines which are dictated to them over the loudspeaker system by the proprietor of the Miramar each morning and evening: "Hi, all you leisure lovers. Eight o'clock, the temperature is 52 degrees and it's fair to cloudy in mid-town Morecambe. This is your Miramar host, Percy Cattley, saying hello again and welcome to another fun-packed day" (80). The inability to act, to break the routine, is seen in the response to Colin's request for a small change in his breakfast menu—he wants grapefruit segments *and* flakes. He wants a little more than he is offered and, typically, he is not going to get it. His valiant request is denied, foreshadowing his mother's bleak prophesy: "I don't think we'll get much further than the sands today" (86).

As the Coopers go onto the beach, the distant sea becomes symbolic of their own lives in that it is a disappointment; it doesn't live up their anticipation. The description of sea life represented in their daughter Jennifer's book, *Marine Life*, is not to be realized on the sands of reality: "*Dad.* (Picks up the book). '*Marine Life.* Crabs. Lobsters. Look at that! Sea-horses. I've never seen a sea-horse in my life. And starfish. It's not fair. Putting ideas into their heads. It makes them disappointed. Even the shells. There's none of them shells, is there'" (92). Mr. Cooper is familiar with disappointment. He equates it with the deadly routine of his life which is regulated by an unseen force that he likens to the rhythm of the sea tides controlled by the moon: "The tides are controlled by the moon.... It's up there somewhere, and it controls the tides" (92). The absence of mystery, of beauty, and of change in their bleak lives is echoed in Mrs. Cooper's answering remark: "Anyway, it doesn't do much of a job here, does it?" (92).

Colin's slow awakening to self-consciousness comes as he wanders down to the water's edge, where the dull quality of his life and the ennui that attends all the lives in the play is represented by the blurred conjunction of shoreline and sea. It is a vagueness that sees its counterpart in Colin's confusion: "Colin wanders down through the people sitting on the sands, trying to walk to the edge of the sea. Miles and miles of empty sand. The beach is very small and distant behind him. The very faint sound of the beach. Finally he reaches the edge of the sea. But he isn't sure whether it really is the edge, it's so gradual and undramatic" (96). Part one ends with the Coopers eating the prepackaged lunches labeled "Your Eats" that they collect from the boardinghouse as they leave each morning for the beach. As Mr. Cooper stares gloomily out to sea, Mrs. Cooper uses a tidal image to refer to both his unemployment and his boredom. It is an image that also references Mr. Cooper's earlier comment about the moon as it again ties their lives to the movement of the sea: "You'll find something when we get back. It's on the turn now. They all say that. It's in the paper" (98). As the first part of the play draws to an end, Mr. Cooper dozes intermittently on the beach, his sleep punctuated by Mrs. Cooper's slow, Proustian, seemingly pointless remembrances of sandwiches eaten on an earlier holiday, but in truth she not only defines her own existence by doing so but also that of her husband's as she draws him into the memory: "*Mam.* 'We had some right nice sandwiches once. Just after we were married. At Rhyl? Were they tomato?' *Dad.* 'I don't know.' *Mam.* 'I don't know either'" (98). As the tide begins to come in and the Coopers leave the sands and begin their return to the regime of Miramar, the pier and promenade function as places where communication takes place and where a new perspective is brought into view, suggested by Colin's view through the telescope. On the promenade, the confrontation takes place between the two fathers, Mr. Cooper and the father of the boy from whom Colin stole the fishing line. The energy created by the altercation stirs Mr. Cooper to positive action as he defends his son and draws the family closer by doing so. But the action, like his life, is easily negated as they reach the boardinghouse and he is summoned over the loudspeaker to Mr. Cattley's office, wherein Colin's misadventure with his sister's sandal is disclosed. Mr. Cooper turns his frustration against Colin. The dialogue ends with the voice of the loudspeaker announcing the evening meal, obliterating all human noise and emotion. The coastal setting is also symbolically significant in the second half of the play when Mrs. Cooper takes her daughter, Jennifer, across the sands to the water's edge. And in answer to Jennifer's question, "Is this the sea?" her answer, "I think so" reflects the insentience that surrounds her own life. It is Jennifer who leads her mother to the sea just as it is Colin who fires his father into action later on. If there is to be any hope for escape from the morass of spiritual inertia, Bennett suggests, it might possibly be through the children.

The theme of helpless frustration, of being locked into a system of survival from which there seems to be very little hope of escape is also presented through the coastal resort setting in Alan Sillitoe's short story "The Road" which also uses the perspective of the child figure. In this story, the three main characters, Stanley, Amy, and their five-year-old son, Ivan, spend a day on the beach at Skegness where the parents are shocked into a new awareness of life by a dramatic event that unifies the family, the temporary loss of Ivan, who wanders away from the beach during a violent argument between his parents. The argument is the turning point in the story, the peak to which it builds up, wavelike, through images of sea and coast that reflect the changing moods of Stanley and Amy as they confront their innermost feelings by making them public. The story begins, as does Alan Bennett's *All Day on the Sands*, on the beach, where the distant sea draws closer throughout the day as the parents search deeper into their inner selves. Stanley echoes Mr. Cooper's disappointment with the sea: "The sea was nowhere to be seen. They stood on the front and looked for it. Shining sand stretched left and right, and all the way to the horizon, pools and small salt rivers flickered under the sun now breaking through. The immense sky intimidated them, making Skegness seem small at their spines. It looked as if the ocean went on forever round the world and came right back to their heels. 'This is a rum bloody do,' he said, setting Ivan down. 'I thought we'd take a boat out on it. What a place to build a seaside resort'" (69).

As the argument develops between Stanley and Amy, instigated by Stanley's complaint about the crowdedness of the sands, Amy's response, "I suppose you wanted to dump us in the sea," is significant in that it suggests Stanley's desire for an awakening, a coming into being, for himself and his family. This desire intensifies as the argument develops and Stanley's inner turmoil is contrasted with the calm sea with its "beard of foam" suggestive, in the Woolfian sense, of birth—newness: "He was struck dumb by this irrational leap-frogging argument from someone he blindly loved. He stood and looked at the great space of sand and sky, birds, and a slight moving white beard of foam appearing on the far edge of the sand where the sea lay fallow and sleepy" (70). When Amy walks away in anger, leaving Stanley and Ivan stranded on the sands, an old man, a retired lifeboat man, who functions as a magus-like figure much like Evens in Edward Bond's *The Sea* and Phoebe in "Beside the Seaside," sits beside them. His words reflect his knowledge of the sea and the life and energy which it represents, and his description of it is also a description of Stanley's anger which he will shortly release when he strikes Amy: "'She'll be in a bit, don't worry. We're in the front line, so we'll have to move,' the old man said. 'Half an hour at the most. You can't stop it, and that's a fact. Comes in shoulder high, faster than a racehorse sometimes, and then you've got to watch out, even from this distance, my guy you have'" (72). With this advice, Stanley's confusion slowly gives way to inner revelation, and the vertical movement inward in his spiritual landscape is reflected in the horizontal perspectives of the coastal landscape through the surf's delineation of sea and shore: "If it weren't for a trace of white he'd hardly have known where the sky ended and the sand began, for the wetness under the line was light purple, a mellower of the midday lower horizon. The mark of white surf stopped them blending, a firm and quite definite dividing of earth and water and air" (72).

As the tide comes in, Amy returns, and the argument picks up again and comes to a head when Stanley strikes her three times with a violence that is counterpoised with the condition of the sea that has finally reached them: "In spite of the sea and the uprising wind, it could be heard.... A red leaf mark above her eye was slowly swelling.... It was the first time he had hit her in public, and the voices calling that he should have less on it, already sounded above the steady railing of the nerve-racking sea. An over-forward wave sent a line of spray that saturated one of her feet" (75). Amy's coming into being against a background of sea and wind is marked by the "wound" above her eye. The fight for spiritual freedom is paralleled in this very public fight and is followed by an occurrence—the loss of Ivan—that shocks and unites his parents. This newfound unity is emphasized through the sea to which they are now "closer than anyone else." When they look "into the sea" for Ivan, they find "the old lifeboat man had gone"—his purpose in steering Stanley toward being completed. And Ivan, too, has left the beach. He has returned to the road that brought them to the beach. His parents united, he sits in perfect peace on the steps of a nearby church after relinquishing, through the image of the rising seagull, the pain and confusion caused him by their argument: "A seagull sat at his feet, and when he sneezed it flew away. He stayed at peace even after they found him..." (76).

Themes of madness and magic, renewal of self through loss of identity, death through drowning, and love through self-knowledge also appear in Edward Bond's play *The Sea*, set in a small town and on the surrounding cliffs and shore of east coast of England during the First World War Bond explains the message behind his play in a letter to theatrical director William Woodman: "It's essentially about life's problems and how we go about trying to sort them out. Like the sea, the problems come and wash over us, whether we want them or not. We cannot avoid them, we must needs deal with them. And, again, like the sea, we come to grips with some of these problems, and some subside, again like the sea. It is also a play about insanity, chaos (as exemplified by Hatch and Mrs. Rafi), and sanity."[30]

Here, as in Samuel Beckett's radio play *Embers*, the crowd is represented by the audience that witnesses the disclosure of truth. The characters in *The Sea* are understood through their individual relationships with the sea and land. For example, whereas Evens, Willy and Rose are comfortable with the sea, the manipulative characters like Hatch, Hollarcut, and Mrs. Rafi prefer the land. Through the different worlds of sea and coast suggested by each character exists a tension, which is emphasized by the nation's state of war and the repetitive volleys of artillery in the background. This tension is described in the opening stage directions as the storm lashes the sea across the coast and creates a turmoil—a sense of energy and movement suggestive of change and newness, life and hope—that is the antithesis of the kind of negative chaos created by Mrs. Rafi and Hatch later on: "Beach. Empty stage. Darkness and thunder. Wind roars, whines, crashes and screams over the water. Masses of water swell up, rattle and churn, and crash back into the sea. Gravel and sand grind slowly. The earth trembles" (57). The wind, in this play the determining factor that brings about the loss of one life and the awakening of another, is described by W.H. Auden in "The Stone and the Shell" as "a force which the conscious will cannot cause or control ... it is also the source, good or bad, of all the movements of life."[31] Out of this wind and storm, this unrest, emerges Willy shouting for his lost friend, Colin. The audience never actually sees Colin; they hear about him from the other characters and see a corpse whose head is covered. In this light, we may see Colin as Willy's double—the old self from which the new is born, an idea Auden argues in his discussion of the types of wind described in Coleridge's "The Rime of the Ancient Mariner": "The roaring wind which is only heard and never touches the mariner or the ship, but brings rain, and at the sound of which angelic spirits occupy bodies of the dead crew. To hear and not feel, means to intuit the possibility and hope for the coming of the new life which one still does not know as an actuality."[32] Willy's cries for Colin are unheeded by the drunken Evens, who has reached a different level of consciousness from the other characters, one which he will maintain throughout the play and through which he will come to an understanding of Willy's situation. The duality in the Willy/Colin characters is reinforced through the sea as Willy comes out of the water "crying and pleading" for the life he has lost as he "stands on the edge of the sea." And as his identity is mistaken by the mad Hatch who thinks he is the enemy or an alien being, a threat to the world of sterility that Hatch inhabits, his cry of "help us" becomes a cry for humanity. Willy turns his back on the sea as he begins his new life, and Hatch delivers his diatribe to the noise of heavy artillery that signals the conflict between the stasis and change these two characters represent. The scene ends with Willy's voice raised in an anguished farewell as he beseeches the departed spirit: "Colin. Don't die. Not like this. Shout" (58).

The old man, Evens, who lives in a hut on the beach, is the sea itself; it is through his understanding of it that, like Murdoch's sea, it takes on human characteristics: "Mad woman in a grey bed / She struggles under the sheets / Threshing her grey hair." Mrs. Rafi, who, according to Bond, is Evens's social equal, recognizes the power of Evens' association and understanding of the sea even though she is incapable of the same: "Everything is washed up. Our coast is known for it" (64).

Scene three returns the setting to the beach. The storm has passed over, but the wind is blowing, and the sun is shining; the mood is set for change and enlightenment as Willy enters, searching for Evens, who comes up behind him as he tries the lock on the door of Evens' hut. Evens is described as looking like a holy man—a seer: "He is old, weathered and bearded" (67). Evens lives on the shoreline, the edge. When Willy asks him why he leads such a solitary existence, his answer, "Isn't that what everyone wants?" (69), is understandable, coming from one who is continually redefining his existence through choice. By living on the "razor's edge" Evens keeps himself alive spiritually, and his revealing speech to Willy explains his relationship with the sea in its representation of life. He begins with a cyclic image: "We're in the spring tides now" (70). Evens' knowledge is symbolized by the lantern—a source of light—that he carries; he passes this on to Willy and quotes from the Chinese poet Li Po: "you who are sated with life, now drink the dregs" (70).

The setting returns to the beach again in the sixth scene. Here, the body of Colin, his identity uncertain because, like the masked body of Yeats' Cuchulain, his face is hidden by his jersey, lies half in the sea and half on the shore. "It was dangerous to be there," says Willy of his boat ride with Colin. The idea of the double appears again as Rose immortalizes Colin's departed spirit with images of sea that take on the cyclic order of nature's time. Seen through the eyes of Hatch, the mad draper, the sea is a form of chaos, a threat to the permanency and stagnation in which his life is anchored. As a threat, it is a negative force that forms the catalyst for his consuming paranoia. When he creeps toward the corpse on the beach, the deathly aspects of his desire for stasis are present in his speech which carries images that are annihilative, not cyclical, and are presented with a description of sea monsters similar to the hallucinatory manifestations of Charles Arrowby's sick, obsessive mind in *The Sea, the Sea*: "Time runs and the enemy is closer.... This is the quiet place where the sea monsters breed and play and lie in the sun" (101).

Scene seven, Colin's funeral, takes place on a cliff and is fraught with danger. All the characters are present and drawn together through the effect each one has upon the other. In this surrealistic scene, Mrs. Rafi explains, after the vicar advises her not to go "too near the edge," what she represents, which is a sense of reality, a constant in the flux of life, and she does so through Woolfian images: "Sometimes I think I'm a lighthouse in their world. I give them a sense of order and security. My glare marks out a channel to the safe harbour" (112). Unlike Evens' light, Mrs. Rafi's is without change—it is a deathly light that allows no sense of mutability, admitting only to rigid order, as she herself admits: "There'll be chaos if I don't go and rule the tea room" (114). The contrast between sea and land, as represented by Evens and Mrs. Rafi, comes together on this cliff with a conflict that generates an energy in Willy and inspires him to go for a swim—to make a change and enter life. Through Willy and the other characters, all aspects of life encompassing birth and death, imprisonment and freedom, are present as Hatch and Hollarcut try to push the funeral party over the edge of the cliff and into the sea, a brutal act for which Hatch is sent to prison and Hollarcut made to dig in Mrs. Rafi's garden where, not surprisingly, nothing grows. With resignation, Mrs. Rafi comes to an understanding of what she has missed in her life, and she does so through an acknowledgment of the power of the sea: "Take me down to the beach. I want to see the sea" (113). In the final recognition of the sterility in her own life, she urges Rose, who was once in love with Colin, to leave with Willy, ending her role on a note of pathos: "But I shall be thinking of the sea and dead Colin, and how the world is full of things that have always been far away from me." (114).

The play completes its cycle, returning to the beach for the final scene, and Evens' words to Hollarcut and Willy takes on evolutionary aspects like those in *The French Lieutenant's Woman*: "I believe the universe lives. It teems with life. Men take themselves to be strong and cunning. But who can kill space or time or dust? They destroy everything but they only make the materials of life. All destruction is finally petty and in the end life laughs at death" (120). Evens' final words to Willy and Rose are advice to all who suffer the burden of choice: "Don't give up hope" (121). Through the use of the coastal setting, the ideas of conflict and hope are addressed in this play. With the guidance of Evens, as he affirms a continuity for humanity through his understanding of the sea and all it represents, Rose and Willy are able to take these new chances Bond speaks of, and in doing so they represent hope for all witnessed by the audience.

Another work set in a small seaside town is Susan Hill's novella "The Albatross." Here, the crowd image is represented by the townspeople who, like those in John Fowles' *The French Lieutenant's Woman*, govern the emotional well-being of the central character, the mentally slow Duncan Pike, and are responsible for his isolation from humanity. Pike, like the fish his name suggests, a fish which is thrown back into the water when it is caught because it is deemed useless, feels torn apart, gutted and tossed out, devoured by others, always wriggling on the hook of cruelty that he swallows each time he is sent out for errands and forced to face the other townspeople, many of whom are fishermen and unkindly call him "Dafty." He craves to see more of the world and break free of the confines of the small fishing village and the cramped cottage where he lives with his domineering crippled mother. Although he cares for his mother tenderly, carrying her upstairs to bed every night and cooking for her, she constantly humiliates and upbraids him: '... [but now he] only went and stood for hours on end, looking at the sea" (6). Throughout the story, which takes place during a winter of brutal gales and turbulent seas, the ever-present and often dangerous sea becomes a metaphor for the sudden destructive urges that surge through Duncan's mind. This reaches a breaking point during a violent storm when some of the local fisherman, including Ted Flint, whom Duncan greatly admires for his nonchalance and bravado, go out to rescue a ship offshore, and Ted Flint is killed. Throughout the story, Flint, as his name suggests, is the strength that Duncan draws from. Too shy to voice his silent admiration, Duncan nevertheless feels anguish at his death.

The reversal of the story comes the day after Ted Flint's death, and it is a violent act. Duncan drugs his mother with sleeping pills and takes her asleep in her wheelchair, to the edge of the cliff. The motion of the waves and the chair falling over the edge of the cliff reflect the physical inversion that necessarily accompanies the reversal: "Duncan hesitated, waiting. A wave built up, stirring the surface of the water, rising as it moved up towards the shingle. It lifted and tipped over, and as it came down, he pushed the wheelchair gently forward. It slipped at once, over the edge and out of sight, and the noise was lost in the suck and hiss of the waves" (88). As he runs away to a nearby town, he experiences an epiphany, and, for a brief moment, is free. This is Duncan's moment of existential awareness, the terror brought about by a sense of freedom and the realization of the outcome of his decision to kill his mother. He is soon picked up by the authorities, and the reader is left to assume that his life will pick up where it left off: incarcerated in a house, this time possibly a mental institution, subjected to the demands of others, except, for a while, during the carnivalesque reversal. The temporary reversal affords him a brief sense of self-realization. In the end, the landscape is what remains, as the closing statement of the story suggests a cyclic continuum much like that described in Ted Hughes' *River*: "Later that day, the wind veered west, blowing in soft-bellied rain clouds. The thaw began."

The landscape becomes a metaphor for the poignant, inarticulate longing for freedom for Duncan Pike. His growing desperation and his confusion are reflected in this landscape and in the Martello tower that signifies the war within him: "Walking along the sea wall, past the old quay and the martello tower, and then for miles across the pale stretches of shingle" (8). The sea reflects his desire for freedom: "He had never been, never been on the water.... And now, he longed for the sea, watched it and walked beside it, and thought of how it would be, to get away, like the men, in the early morning" (12, 13). The sea also represents death as Duncan analogizes Ted Flint's death with the death of the fish that are caught by the fishermen. He doesn't understand himself or his place in the world; instead, he is an outsider, always wanting to belong, finding love and warmth from nature, the sea, while longing to become part of the human community, the crowd. Canetti explains the relationship between the sea and the crowds in *Crowds and Power*: "In its impetus and its rage it brings to mind the one entity which shares these attributes in the same degree; that is, the crowd."[33]

Beginning with Jane Austen's *Persuasion*, each of these works set on the urban seashore suggests some elements of the carnivalesque. Each contains a reversal that takes place in a public setting and is witnessed by the crowd, small or large—in *Persuasion*, the group of friends on the Cobb. In later works, these crowds, all of whom have a relationship with the sea, are represented by such aspects of humanity as the holiday makers in Graham Greene's *Brighton Rock* and Patrick Hamilton's *The West Pier*, or the listeners in Samuel Beckett's *Embers*, or the live audience in Edward Bond's *The Sea*. An element also of danger, suggested by the topographical reversal of town to rural setting, is implied in these works. For instance, Pinkie Brown plunges to his death from the cliffs in *Brighton Rock*, and in *The Sea*, the coastal setting of cliff and beach also suggests danger that unites the characters and affords Rose and Willy a sense of hope in a violent world. The sea unites and offers a sense of freedom through which, for instance, the Cooper family in "All Day on the Sands" is able to transcend its worldly troubles, as are Stanley and Amy in "The Road," where the road that leads to the seaside and possible freedom is also, paradoxically, the road the leads away from it.

Evaluation

The Settings of Riverbank and Seashore

> "*Possibly more than any other element water is the complete poetic reality.*"
> —Gaston Bachelard

    As we look at these works, it becomes clear that the authors have demonstrated that the waters of river and sea and the landscape that surrounds them open to reveal an understanding of self, a "centering of consciousness" for their characters who seem to suffer from something that holds them back from self-truth and intellectual freedom. They are, in a sense, lost to themselves. Through their interaction with the waters of river and sea and through the power of the imagination, they are able to rectify this situation and not only recognize their own spiritual potential but also align themselves with the redemptive forces of nature. Some of these ideas find their genesis in Victorian literature, especially in those novels and poems that address, in various forms, the social and technological changes that were taking place too quickly for the adaptation of the human psyche, described by Matthew Arnold as one of historical transition, "between two worlds, / One dead, the other powerless to be born."

    The river, as it draws the self from isolation to a celebration of freedom, however brief, in Alfred Tennyson's great poem "The Lady of Shalott," is a theme that appears in several forms, all of which are connected to the rural river, in later works of the twentieth century. George

Eliot's novel *The Mill on the Floss* and Wilkie Collins' novella "The Guilty River" both demonstrate the powerful presence of the rural river in a utilitarian sense as it drives the mills with its force and enables a livelihood for the families that run them but also impels the characters into actions that eventually afford them revelations of self-truth. The intensely romantic theme of "The Guilty River" may also be found in H. E. Bates's *The Two Sisters,* where the rural setting of the River Ouse becomes the site of nearly all the action as a place from which the characters are able to embark upon journeys that lead to self-knowledge. The river in Charles Kingsley's *The Water Babies* moves the little chimney sweep, Tom, from imprisonment to freedom, signified by his metamorphosis from boy to piscine figure, as he escapes the working conditions of Victorian England. The River Ouse and its tributary, the River Leem, in Graham Swift's novel *Waterland,* also reflect history and foster knowledge through which the characters may gain an understanding of their lives and achieve a sense of liberty as does Tom Crick, the history teacher and narrator who demonstrates this as he relates his story which, in a sense, becomes the story of man, from what was once the time zone Greenwich Park, overlooking the River Thames, where past and present become one. Tom Crick also recognizes the metamorphic aspect of the very same river when he witnesses the transformation of his dull-witted brother, Dick, into a quick, eel-like form as he takes his final plunge into the river like Tom in *The Water Babies.* Tilda, the six-year-old girl in Penelope Lively's novel *Offshore,* represents this mutability and is viewed by her sister as a "strange aquatic creature" as they both prepare to search for treasure in the muddy waters of the urban Thames' tidal reach. The poet Ted Hughes uses the rural river setting in his remarkable collection of poems *River* to suggest, as one critic states, "...that those who passively accept the norms of our plastic and concrete urban environment have lost the capacity to perceive what nature can teach us about our limitations, a mutable universe, and the necessity of embracing life and savoring our moment to moment experience in the face of all this."[1] These ideas also appear as underlying archetypal themes in Kenneth Grahame's *The Wind in the Willows,* presented through the figures of Mole and Rat as they engage in their riparian adventures.

The powerful image of the urban River Thames in Charles Dickens' *Our Mutual Friend* may be found in several later works. In Joyce Cary's novel *The Horse's Mouth,* the urban River Thames is the extended trope for the creative mind of the artist, Gulley Jimson. If Jimson's freedom is threatened by incarceration, so is his imagination, and he is unable to paint. He goes to the river for affirmation of his freedom and confirmation of his artistic vision. In Alan Sillitoe's "A Scream of Toys," through stages marked by its embankment and bridge, the river suggests represents a boundary which the young girl must cross in order to reach maturity and freedom from the sadness surrounding her childhood. For Spider, the mentally disturbed man in Patrick McGrath's novel *Spider*, the Thames offers much the same kind of healing; from the perspective offered by its embankment, the river frees Spider from his dreadful memories. These memories he brings into the present as he sits beside the canal, the man-made counterpart of the river which symbolizes a conduit reaching back into his past, offering him hope and a way out toward truth and spiritual regeneration. The River Thames is the means by which the narrators of Iain Sinclair's *Downriver* and Susan Hill's *The Mist in the Mirror* travel into the past to gain an understanding of the present.

In these works, the journey of river to sea becomes the journey of each character toward spiritual freedom. The event, creative and exhilarating, as it is in H. E. Bates' *Down the River*, is also a never-ending process and marked in various ways that signify change, freedom, and renewal described in early works such as Tennyson's poem "A River," Jean Ingelow's poem "Four Bridges" and Charles Kingsley's *The Water Babies*. As river into sea is a never-ending process, so it may suggest in the postmodern sense the idea of "non-ending," a necessary lack of closure, as it does in such later works as Ted Hughes' *River*, Penelope Lively's *Offshore* and, as well, Graham Swift's *Waterland* and Iain Sinclair's *Downriver*.

With such novels as Thomas Hardy's *A Pair of Blue Eyes*, a new and innovative use of the rural coastal setting, one that has influenced succeeding writers, begins. For Virginia Woolf, the sea represents the continuity of life in *The Waves* and *To the Lighthouse*, and Iris Murdoch's novel *The Sea, the Sea*, set on the northeast coast of England, suggests, like Woolf's, this sense of eternity, or what Murdoch calls "an empty sea of eternal reality." However, Woolf's sea is full; it reflects the mystery and growth of humanity, whereas the emptiness of Murdoch's sea is changed by each character's interaction with it. As Woolf uses the coastal setting in *To the Lighthouse* to distance her characters from society in order to explore the relationships between them, so John Fowles in *The French Lieutenant's Woman*, Susan Hill in *The Woman in Black*, and Jane Gardam in *Crusoe's Daughter* use the same kind of perspective to enable a refocusing for their characters; and in W. B. Yeats' "Fighting the Waves," Stevie Smith's "Beside the Seaside," Mary Lavin's "The Great Wave," and Graham Swift's "Learning to Swim," the sea is an eternal force which galvanizes the characters into a true awareness of their lives.

Of those works set by sea and shore, often a kind of sea monster like Tennyson's Kraken and Charles Arrowby's monster in *The Sea, the Sea*, or those described in Edward Bond's drama *The Sea*, surfaces to represent the necessary confrontation with the subconscious—the past. Sometimes a spiritual guide, a magus-like figure who is in touch with the sea and aware of its potential, works as a kind of mediator or bridge between the subconscious and reality for the initiate, as in the person of James, Charles Arrowby's cousin in Iris Murdoch's *The Sea, the Sea*. Edward Bond's character Evens, in Bond's drama *The Sea*, also represents this type; he is the wise yet unpredictable man, one who has removed himself from society, living by the edge of the sea as he guides the neophyte, Willy, towards a sense of self-being. In Alan Sillitoe's short story "The Road," it is the old lifeboat captain who fills this role as he appears on the beach to witness, and thereby sanction by his presence, the imminent and crucial argument between Amy and Stanley. In his dance-drama "Fighting the Waves," W. B. Yeats uses the magical figure of Fand, the sea princess knowledgeable about love, to forge the union of Cuchulain and his mistress.

Tennyson's poems about the young mer-creatures, "The Merman" and "The Mermaid," suggest both isolation and a yearning for communication. In later works that develop the seaside setting, the child character often introduces a perspective from which is described the despair of the present as well as the theme of marital disunity, and the possibility of change as it does. The boy James Ramsay in *To the Lighthouse* introduces this possibility for his father as he guides him towards the realization of reality. In *The Waves*, the world of nascent possibility suggested in the dawn lyric is counterpoised with the prose description of the young children as they awake during the early morning hours in a house by the sea. In order to deal with the present, the bishop in Mary Lavin's short story "The Great Wave," summons the memory of a baptism through near-drowning that he experienced as a child. In Alan Bennett's short drama "All Day on the Sands," the young boy, Colin, demonstrates the need for personal choice in the denial of contingency, no matter how inconsequential the outcome may seem. Through a heroic assertion of choice, another young boy, Paul, in Graham Swift's short story "Learning to Swim," strikes out alone against all odds towards his own selfhood, and in "The Road," the character of six-year-old Ivan demonstrates the idea of love as the means by which the possibility of sincere communication between human beings may transpire.

The seaside setting is also the place where memory is evoked. These evocations take on the rhythm of the waves themselves, each born upon the retreat of the former, approaching and receding as past is brought into present. The pattern is clearly seen in *To the Lighthouse* as Mrs. Ramsay actively draws past into present through her reminiscences, and later in the story, after she dies, it is the actual memory of her that influences the lives of the family members as they each bring it to light. In *The Waves*, the lyric interludes compliment the growth of the characters' lives, resulting in a cyclic renewal of universal implications. The old man, Henry, in Beckett's radio drama "Embers" struggles to overcome the waves that bring the memory of his father as they wash over him with a strength that threatens to deny him participation in the present. John Fowles' *The French Lieutenant's Woman* is set in the past, but continuous intrusions from the present-day narrator bring it rhythmically into the present. In Mary Lavin's "The Great Wave" and in Iris Murdoch's novel *The Sea, the Sea*, the characters' evocations of their memories create for them both an understanding and an ability to accept their present situations. Attendant upon memories are symbols shared by these authors that are particular to the coastal setting. In Tennyson's powerful poem "The Kraken," the slumbering monster beneath the sea suggests the latent powers of the creative imagination harnessed by Victorian utilitarianism and a growing despair of imaginative faith. In later works, the sea itself, as it is used to represent the subconscious, brings the mind to reality by the wave and its promise of renewal that continually gathers force on the subliminal horizon before cresting through the results of specific symbolic actions, usually highly emotional, and dispersing on the shores of conscious self-knowledge. Any sense or possibility of change comes to these characters through their interactions with the sea. Matthew Arnold's poem "Dover Beach" describes the two worlds of imaginative nature and cold reality through the sea and urban shore with no hope of reconciliation between the two, a fact that is recognized by the merman and his children as they witness their mother's rejection of them and the world of the sea in favor of the industrialized world. In later works, however, the beach itself becomes a place where the individual comes into being through a recognition of self because it is a place where man is closest to nature and the forces of the tides, a place where man's emotions are drawn to the surface. A clear example of this is in the violent argument that erupts between Amy and Stanley in "The Road," one that leads them both to a new understanding and a closer bonding. The beach as a place of renewal is described in Edward Bond's drama *The Sea*, where, under the guidance of Evens, Colin's death and Willy's rebirth are witnessed. And the scene between Pinkie and Spicer in Graham Greene's novel *Brighton Rock* is one of the most powerful and revelatory in the story, suggestive of a possible spiritual redemption amid inescapable earthly conditions. The same kind of renewal is experienced by Margaret in Stevie Smith's short story "Beside the Seaside" as she walks along the beach at night and enjoys a spiritual freedom afforded her through her exertion of choice. And it is the memory of their embraces on the beach that Cuchulain's mistress uses to bring Cuchulain back to life and under her spell again in "Fighting the Waves."

Another aspect of the coastal setting, one that represents danger, is the cliff that overlooks both sea and beach. It appears in Thomas Hardy's *A Pair of Blue Eyes*, Graham Greene's *Brighton Rock*, Iris Murdoch's *The Sea, the Sea*, Mary Lavin's "The Great Wave," Edward Bond's *The Sea*, and John Fowles' *The French Lieutenant's Woman* as the site for an emotional, often crucial, turning point in the stories when certain characters obtain dramatic and disturbing news. The natural landscape parallels the landscape of these characters' spiritual lives and offers them insights which result for some, such as Pinkie in *Brighton Rock* in his final plunge from the cliff at Peacehaven, in a kind of "leap of faith" that brings them, however briefly, to a new awareness of self. The contrasting perspectives of parallel horizon and gradient shore are used by these authors most often to represent a spiritual conflict which occurs especially at times of choice as evinced in the actions of Elfride and Mr. Knight in *A Pair of Blue Eyes*, Mr. and Mrs. Ramsay in *To the Lighthouse*, Charles and Sarah in *The French Lieutenant's Woman*, Charles Arrowby in *The Sea, the Sea*, and the bishop in "The Great Wave."

In the urban landscape of the shore, landmarks appear, constants, man-made and anticipated in a impermanent world of shifting crowds of holiday-makers such as the promenade, pier, and railway station, that function as places where communication between the self and the world becomes possible. These structures, which through film and fiction have often gained mythic status, perhaps none so clearly as the promenade and the railway station, suggest, as James Applewhite states in *Seas in Inland Journeys*, "[that] the collective source symbolized by the sea must be approached through a structure of consciousness that limits and orders its impact."[2] In this sense, the setting embraces the totality of the environment and subjects and objects establish a symbolic basis through which objects assume functions much more significant than their outward appearances. The promenade, such as the Cobb in Jane Austen's *Persuasion*, is often used as a type of stage upon which the characters are presented and viewed by the other players in the drama of their lives as well as by the audience or reader. In *The French Lieutenant's Woman*, it is also the Cobb that serves this purpose; in "Embers," it is the Strand where Henry sits to battle the past; in *Brighton Rock* and Patrick Hamilton's *The West Pier*, it is the pier, and "All Day on the Sands" it is the promenade where certain truths about the characters' lives come to light. The lighthouses in *To the Lighthouse* and "Beside the Seaside" represent a new sense of reality that the characters strive for and do finally attain in their outer, public searches. The counterpart of the lighthouse, the Martello tower, is used in *The Sea, the Sea* and "Beside the Seaside" to represent the inner struggle for self-knowledge, and the pier in *Brighton Rock* and *The West Pier*, as it bridges the two worlds of land and sea, is also symbolic of a union between man and nature as well as the conscious and the subconscious.

A crucial aspect of the urban seaside setting, one that distinguishes it most clearly from the rural seaside setting, is its sense of carnival. In *Problems of Dostoevsky's Poetics*, Mikhail Bakhtin affirms that the carnival, or as it appears in literature, the carnivalesque, allows, "*a new mode of interrelationship between individuals*, counterpoised to the all-powerful socio-hierarchical relationships of non-carnival life in which the latent sides of human nature ... can reveal and express themselves."[3] The traditional settings for the carnival are the street and marketplace. David Danow, author of *The Spirit of the Carnival*, describes the setting of the carnivalesque in literature:

> The carnivalesque employs the familiar topoi of the marketplace (plaza) as setting, the sense of feast (fiesta), of music and celebration, the drawing of an immense crowd, resulting in general hilarity and excitement.... The role of the marketplace or central square

figures inherently as a principal feature of the carnivalesque. As such, the primary role inspires further consideration of a "poetics of the street" in acknowledgment of that place where virtually anything can happen, and often does, happen. The street is a real life stage upon which the most unexpected drama may be enacted, including the drama of carnival. On the individual plane, the street is where, potentially, one's fortune and destiny are ultimately played out. As part of the public domain, the street is also the stage for public demonstration.[4]

Street and plaza, these places of public recognition and social congress, become pier, promenade, and railway station in the novels that use the seaside resort setting and are closely associated with the rhythmic movement of the crowds of holiday-makers that in themselves reflect the pattern of the waves. Elias Canetti explains this relationship in *Crowds and Power*:

> Density is embodied in the formal recurrence of retreat and approach.... The dense coherence of the waves is something which men in a crowd know well. It entails a yielding to others as though they were oneself, as though there were no strict division between oneself and them. There is no escape from this compliance and thus the consequent impetus and feeling of strength is something engendered by all the units together. The specific nature of this coherence among men is unknown. The sea, while not explaining, expresses it.[5]

As separate entities, crowd and sea present powerful forces, which, united in the seaside resort through the carnivalesque, become even more potent. Novels such as *Brighton Rock* and *The West Pier* that use the theme of the carnivalesque take place during specific recognized times like the "traditional carnival"—public holidays—such as Whitsuntide, a celebration that begins the seventh Sunday after Easter celebrated as a festival in commemoration of the descent of the Holy Spirit on the day of Pentecost. Canetti explains: "They [crowds] always met for a special purpose of a religion, festal or martial kind; and this purpose seemed to sanctify their state."[6] In the urban seaside setting this is a time when the towns are filled with crowds of holiday-makers and an air of gaiety and symbolic inversion.

Although various critics have recognized the symbolic functions of riverbank and seashore in a general sense, it is a subject that has not been examined in depth. In this book, we have explored the influence of setting on characterization and plot as it symbolizes, intensifies, and illuminates these aspects of the twentieth century British novel, short story and drama. We have seen that the two distinct topoi of riverbank and seashore reinforce structural elements and divisions of fiction by working as transitional links between stages as well as by representing the psychological states of certain characters. And it is possible that as these fictional characters articulate their innermost thoughts through the waters of both river and sea they generate a similar response from the careful reader, for, "[e]ven when wise men talk to each other," says Murdoch, "it is beyond the words that the flame of understanding leaps. And with such considerations we move from ordinary commonsensical criticisms of art to a kind of metaphysical criticism."[7] We have also seen that the setting fulfills yet another important function in its representation of the vital sense of reality, and if we agree with the literary critic Jeremy Hawthorn's statement that "…any work which has enabled readers to understand their world and their own situation within the world better will have something to offer future readers in different times and places, for there are consistencies in the laws that govern the world, there are continuities in human life and experience,"[8] then, to the reader, the message is clear: if a person is to live freely and imaginatively he or she must first arrive at a position of self-truth and that imaginative freedom, the only true freedom, is internal.

Appendix A

About the Authors

Matthew Arnold, 1822–1888
Arnold worked for most of his life as an inspector of schools, traveling around England and establishing many lasting beneficial changes in the recently government-funded state school system. These days, Arnold is better known for his volumes of poetry, the first of these being *The Strayed Reveller and Other Poems* (1849), and his essays, the most important of which was a collection on literature, *Essays in Criticsm* (1865 and 1868).

Jane Austen, 1775–1817
Jane Austen, one of the most famous writers in English literature, was born at Steventon, Hampshire, where her father was the rector. Her first completed novel, *Sense and Sensibility*, was published in 1811. This was followed by *Pride and Prejudice* in 1813, *Mansfield Park* in 1814, and *Emma* in 1815. *Northanger Abbey* and *Persuasion* were published in 1818. Austen also wrote two other works: *Lady Susan* in about 1805, which was written in epistolary form, featuring Lady Susan Vernon, a designing coquette; and a fragment, *The Watsons*. Both were published in 1871, fifty-four years after her death. Another fragment, *Sanditon*, was published in 1925. *Jane Austen's Letters, Compiled and Edited* by Deidre Le Faye was first published in 1993. The writer Frank Morley quotes Austen's sister Cassandra in his discussion of Austen's ability to concentrate on writing when surrounded by family members and callers: "Her sole protections against the world were a door which creaked, whose hinges she asked might remain unattended to because they gave her warning that somebody was coming, and the blotting paper under which she slipped her small sheets of exquisitely written manuscript when a visitor was shown in."[1]

H(erbert) E(rnest) Bates, 1905-1974

One writer who uses the rural river setting consistently is H. E. Bates, whom Graham Greene once called Britain's successor to Chekhov. Bates was one of England's most popular novelists and short story writers of the 1930s and 1940s. His work includes the novels *The Two Sisters* (1926) and the well-known *Love for Lydia* (1952), as well as a collection of country comedies, *The Darling Buds of May* (1958), which, along with *Love for Lydia*, was televised by the BBC. Bates was a prolific writer whose works ranged from the countryside novels and short stories to government-commissioned war fiction such as *Fair Stood the Wind for France* (1944). As well as three collections of short stories, Bates also published three volumes of autobiographical work.

Samuel Beckett, 1906-1998

Samuel Beckett, playwright, novelist, short story writer and essayist, is one of the most famous writers in the English language. Although he is best known for his plays that are often classified under Theatre of the Absurd, plays such as *Waiting for Godot* (1953), *End Game* (1958), *Krapp's Last Tape* (1960), and *Happy Days* (1961), Beckett considered himself primarily a novelist with such novels as *Murphy* (1938) and the trilogy *Molloy* (1951), *Malone Dies* (1951), and *The Unnamable* (1960). He also wrote several short stories, including the frequently anthologized "Dante and the Lobster," collected in *More Pricks Than Kicks* (1934). Along with his friend and mentor, James Joyce, Beckett is considered to be one of the earliest and most significant of the postmodernists. Through his unique use of the stage and dramatic narrative, Beckett has greatly influenced such contemporary English playwrights as Tom Stoppard and Harold Pinter with works that are darkly humorous, excruciatingly bleak, yet oddly exhilarating. Beckett, who wrote nearly all of his work in French before translating it into English, was awarded the Nobel Prize in 1969.

Alan Bennett, 1934–

Born in Leeds, Yorkshire, Alan Bennett is an actor, playwright, and short story writer. In England, he first became famous for the satirical review "Beyond the Fringe" which he wrote and published for radio broadcast with Jonathan Miller in 1963. Following this, Bennett wrote a series of satirical comedies, including *Forty Years On* (1969), *Getting On* (1972), and *Habeas Corpus* (1973). Much of his work has been televised, including the hilarious monologues *A Crack in the Teacup*, *A Cream Cracker Under the Sofa*, delivered by himself, and *Bed Among the Lentils*, delivered by Maggie Smith. His play "All Day on the Sands" appears in a collection called *The*

Writer in Disguise, published in 1985. In a later work, the novella "The Clothes They Stood Up In" (2001), he continues his witty and sympathetic observations of human life, reflecting what David Nokes, in an article published in the *Times Literary Supplement*, writes about Bennett's work: "His characteristic style is unpretentious, small-scale and domestic. His genius lies in an unerring ear for the idioms of lower-middle-class life, the verbal doilies of self-respect and self-repression."[2] Bennett's most recent work is a collection of anecdotes published under the title *Rolling Home* in 2003.

Edward Bond, 1934–

A Londoner by birth, Edward Bond is a major English playwright. He uses dark humor as a vehicle for the themes of violence and injustice fostered through capitalism that appear in many of his works. His plays, which elicit extreme reactions from both critics and audiences, include *The Pope's Wedding* (performed in 1962) which focuses on violence in urban life, *Early Morning* (1962), and his two most famous, *Lear* (1971) which focuses on the violence in Shakespeare's *King Lear*, and *The Sea* (1973), structured, in part, on Shakespeare's *The Tempest*, about which Bond comments: "The basic idea behind *The Tempest*, I think, is the idea of conflict and resolution. The image of the sea conveys this very well—the storm is a destructive image, it reflects social and personal conflicts; the sea is finally able to resolve these into a powerful continuity. That's what Shakespeare, I think, had in mind." However, Bond also points out that in his play, "the image of the sea should be read as a symbol of hope and the character Evens considered a spokesman against philosophical pessimism."[3]

Joyce Cary, 1888–1957

Joyce Cary was born in Ireland. His greatest works are two trilogies. The first comprises *Herself Surprised* (1941), *To Be a Pilgrim* (1942), and *The Horse's Mouth* (1944) and focuses on art and explores the theme of individual freedom and choice; the second, which contains *Prisoner of Grace* (1932), *Except the Lord* (1953), and *Not Honour More* (1955), is a study of politics. Another popular work, *Art and Reality* (1958), is a series of essays Cary delivered at Oxford and Cambridge universities. In all, Cary wrote sixteen novels, more than sixty essays, nine volumes of occasional prose and two volumes of poetry.

Wilkie Collins, 1824–1889

The mystery writer Wilkie Collins was a contemporary of Charles Dickens and collaborated with him on several mysteries as well as other works. Collins was the first English novelist who dealt with the detection of crime. He established his reputation as a mystery writer with *The Woman in White* (1860).

Charles Dickens, 1812–1870

Charles Dickens, who ranks along with William Shakespeare as one of the greatest writers of English literature, was a Londoner whose father, a government clerk, was at one time imprisoned in the London prison Marshalsea because of his financial debts. It was an indelible experience for the young Charles, who had to forgo his education to help support his mother and siblings. He began writing in 1835 by becoming a reporter of political debates and wrote continuously until 1870. His fictional works, much of which appeared in installments, started with *Sketches by Boz, Illustrative of Every-Day Life and Every-Day People* and *The Posthumous Papers of the Pickwick Club* (1836–1837). His first novel, *Oliver Twist*, was published 1837–1838. His final novel, an unfinished work, *The Mystery of Edwin Drood*, was begun in 1870, but Dickens died before its completion. Among his most best-known novels are *Nicholas Nickleby* (1838–1839), *The Old Curiosity Shop* (1838–1839), *Barnaby Rudge* (1838–1839), *Martin Chuzzlewit* (1843–1844), *A Christmas Carol* (1843), *Dombey and Son* (1848), *David Copperfield* (1849–1850), *Beak House* (1852–1853), and *Hard Times* (1854). Critics agree that *Bleak House* and *Our Mutual Friend* represent Dickens' best works. Dickens also wrote a number of essays, letters, dictionaries, and stories, and collaborated with the mystery writer Wilkie Collins on some of the stories.

George Eliot (Mary Ann Cross, née Evans), 1819–1880

George Eliot lived her early life in Warwickshire where her father was an estate agent. She wrote for the *Westminster Review* and *Blackwood's Magazine* before turning to fiction writing. Her novels include *Adam Bede* (1859), *The Mill on the Floss* (1860), *Silas Marner* (1861), *Felix Holt* (1866), *Middlemarch*, published in installments from 1871 through 1872, and *Daniel Deronda*, published in installments from 1874 through 1876. Her novels contain all the humor and pathos of human life, along with her conviction of the purifying effect of human trials which she depicts via an extraordinary sense of setting. Eliot also wrote a number of well-known poems.

Penelope Fitzgerald, 1916–2000

Penelope Fitzgerald's novels, like Virginia Woolf's, are famous for their elegant prose style but, unlike Woolf, Fitzgerald often also uses humor. Her novels include *The Bookshop* (1978), *Offshore* (1979), which won the Booker Prize, *Human Voices* (1980), which draws on her experiences working for the BBC, *The Beginning of Spring* (1988), and *The Gate of Angels* (1990). *Means of Escape* is a collection of Fitzgerald's short stories published posthumously in 2000. She has also written books about Burne-Jones and Charlotte Mew and a study of her father and uncles, *The Knox Brothers*. In a review of Fitzgerald's works, Catherine Wells Cole comments: "Although her output to date is small and her novels are short, Penelope Fitzgerald is an important novelist. The significant critical response which her work has evoked derives from her ability to compress and intensify some of the traditional concerns of the novel: personal relationships, social institutions, the interactions between the two. On a superficial reading Fitzgerald's novels may appear slight, but their real strength lies in what has been pared away. Their skill and grace is not simply displayed technical achievement, but derives instead from Fitzgerald's absolute concern, often conveyed through humor and comedy, for the moral values of the tradition she follows so precisely."[4]

John Fowles, 1926–

John Fowles, who was born in 1926 at Leigh-on-Sea in Essex, established his reputation with *The French Lieutenant's Woman* in which, like Virginia Woolf and Iris Murdoch, he uses the rural coastal setting in truly symbolic ways to represent and enforce the drama associated with specific parts of the novel's plot. Like Murdoch, too, he often uses magic realism in conjunction with the coastal setting and leaves the reader to decipher what is "real" and what is not. Fowles' novels include *The Collector* (1963), a psychological thriller whose main theme, like Iris Murdoch's *The Sea, the Sea*, is kidnapping; *The Magus* (1966, revised edition 1978); *The French Lieutenant's Woman* (1969), which was made into a highly successful movie, *Daniel Martin* (1977); *Mantissa* (1982); and *A Maggot* (1985). His collections of short works include *The Aristos* (1965), *The Ebony Tower* (1974), and *Wormholes: Essays and Occasional Writings* (1998). Thomas C. Foster states in *Understanding John Fowles*: "Along with the intellectual and emotional appeal of his work, Fowles includes a powerful moral vision. The choices his characters make, and the choices his readers must also make, carry a strong ethical component. He is like his compatriot Iris Murdoch in his philosophical interests, investigating existence and identity, knowledge and experience of time, the nature of love, and issues of morality and conduct."[5]

Jane Gardam, 1928–

Jane Gardam was born in Coatham, Yorkshire, in 1928. She has written three novels, *Crusoe's Daughter* (1985), *The Queen of Tambourine* (1991, when she was sixty-one), and, at age sixty-seven, *The Flight of the Maidens*, published in 2000. Her latest novel, *Faith Fox*, was published in 2003. Gardam's collections of short stories include *The Pineapple Bay Hotel* (1976), *The Sidmouth Letters* (1980), *The Pangs of Love* (1983), *Showing the Flag* (1989), and *Going into a Dark House* (1994). She has also written numerous works for children as well as television scripts.

Kenneth Grahame, 1859–1932

Kenneth Grahame lived at Cookham, Berkshire, during his childhood, the setting for the rural River Thames. He wrote three memorable books: *The Golden Age* (1859), studies of childhood in a rural setting; its sequel, *Dream Days* (1898); and *The Wind in the Willows* (1908), whose enormous popularity with both children and adult still persists.

Graham Greene, 1904–1991

One of the most widely read of the major twentieth-century English novelists is Graham Greene. The central themes in many of his works deal with personal and political moral dilemmas. His characters often suffer guilt and despair against a background of urban decay or political nefariousness. When Greene became a Catholic in 1926, his works began to reflect his religious viewpoint. Some of his works, screenplays and novels, including thrillers, what he called "entertainments," also focus on the question of good and evil. His best-known works include *Brighton Rock* (1938), *The Power and the Glory* (1940), *The Third Man* (1950), *The End of the Affair* (1951), *The Quiet American* (1955), *Travels with My Aunt* (1969), and *The Honory Consul* (1973). *Strike it Rich*, which was based on his earlier novella, *Loser Takes All* (1955), was published in 1990, a year before Greene's death. Many of Greene's works were made into highly successful movies, including *Brighton Rock*.

Patrick Hamilton, 1904–1962

Patrick Hamilton was the son of an eccentric clergyman and died an alcoholic and manic depressive at age fifty-eight. Before becoming a novelist and a playwright, Hamilton was an actor. Both of his plays, *Rope* (1929) and *Gaslight* (1948), were made into popular films; *Rope* was directed by Alfred Hitchock. His novels, *Craven House* (1926), *Hangover Square* (1941), *The Slaves of Solitude* (1947), the trilogy *Twenty Thousand Streets Under the Sky* (1935), and *The West Pier* (1951), were also very popular at the times they were published. Tragicomedies with a strong sense of compassionate Marxism, all of Hamilton's works reflect various aspects of his own life and often describe the pleasures and dangers of alcohol as well as a sense of loneliness and despair.

Thomas Hardy, 1840–1928

Thomas Hardy was born near Dorchester, in Dorset, described in his novels as Wessex. His father was a builder, and Hardy worked as an architect when he was a young man. Hardy classifies his novels into three groups: "The Novels of Character and Environment" among which are *Far from the Madding Crowd* (1874), *The Return of the Native* (1878), *The Mayor of Casterbridge* (1886), *Tess of the D'Urbervilles* (1891), and *Jude the Obscure* (1896). Of the second group—"Romances and Fantasies"—*A Pair of Blue Eyes* (1873) is the most popular. The third group, "Novels of Ingenuity," includes collections of tales and reprints of earlier works as well as three lesser-known novels. Hardy also wrote poetry, seven volumes of which were published between 1898 and 1928. Hardy's underlying theme in his novels and poems is that of man's struggles against the neutral and seemingly indifferent force that rules the world, struggles that contain the ironies and disappointments of life, and, most of all, love.

Susan Hill, 1942–

Susan Hill published her first novel, *The Enclosure*, in 1961 when she was a student at London University. Since graduating with a degree in English from King's College, where she became a fellow in 1978, she has written more than thirty novels and collections of stories, many of which have been compared to the tradition of Charles Dickens and Thomas Hardy. In 1970, she won a Somerset Maugham Award for *I'm the King of the Castle*. Her other literary awards include the Whitbread Novel Award for *The Bird of Night* (1972), and the John Llewellyn Rhys Prize for *The Albatross* (1972). Her novels include *Strange Meeting* (1971), set during the First World War; *In the Springtime of the Year* (1974); *The Woman in Black* (1983) which was made into a successful stage and television presentation and is still running on the London stage; *Air and Angels* (1991); *The Service of Clouds* (1998); and her latest work, *The Boy Who Taught the Beekeeper to Read and Other Stories*, published in 2003. She has begun a new mystery series, featuring Simon Serrailler as the sleuth, with *The Various Haunts of Men* (2004), to be followed by *The Pure in Heart* in 2005. Hill has also written several nonfiction books and stories for children and is the editor of the literary magazine *Books and Company*. She has worked as a columnist for the *Daily Telegraph* since 1977. She established her own publishing company, Long Barn Books, in memory of Virginia Woolf and the Hogarth Press. About the major aspects of Hill's fictional works, biographer Dr. James Procter writes: "Viewed as a whole, certain patterns, images and devices can be seen recurring through Hill's varied fiction of the past forty years. Indeed, it is the repetition and recognition of familiar metaphors and tropes that constitutes one of the pleasures of her works. Typically Hill's writings revolve around wealthy, well-to-do families of the nineteenth and twentieth century. Many of these families are dysfunctional, broken, or about to be broken and the protagonists appear isolated, or awkward in the company of others."[6]

Ted Hughes, 1930–1998

Ted Hughes is often referred to as a "topographical poet." His first collection of poetry, *The Hawk in the Rain* (1957), established his reputation internationally. According to the biographer Robert B. Shaw, "Hughes's poetry signaled a dramatic departure from the prevailing modes of the period. The stereo-typical poem of the time was determined not to risk too much: politely domestic in its subject matter, understated and mildly ironic in style. By contrast, Hughes marshaled a language of nearly Shakespearean resonance to explore themes which were mythic and elemental."[7] Hughes' fascination with animals and his sense of beauty and violence in the natural world is a dominant theme in much of his work. Among the best-known are *Crow* (1970), a sequence of poems introducing the central symbol of the predatory, mocking, indestructible crow through which Hughes retells the myths of creation and birth, and *River*, a sequence of poems that describe the river and riverside life, including man. Hughes was appointed Poet Laureate of England in 1984.

Charles Kingsley, 1819–1875

Charles Kingsley was born in Devonshire. Like his father he became a curate and was rector of Eversley in Hampshire. He was a professor of modern history at Cambridge from 1860 to 1869, and he wrote a number of religious essays and sermons as well as poetry and ballads. Among his novels, a few continue to be read in present times; these include *Westward Ho!* (1857), *The Water Babies* (1863), and *Hereward the Wake* (1866).

Mary Lavin, 1902–1996

Born of Irish parents in 1902 in Massachusetts, Lavin returned to Ireland with her parents in 1921 and lived there until her death in 1996. She is well known for her thirteen collections of short stories which focus on internal conflict and change undergone by her protagonists, such as the bishop in "The Great Wave," the title story in *The Great Wave and Other Stories* (1961). Her biographer, A. A. Kelly, states: "Mary Lavin's work is often concerned with delicate social nuance; the play of mind on mind; with the contrast of thought and speech in the same character; the difference between the grand potential and the decrepit actual; the historic of philosophic ideal and the mundane enactment of it. She uses a carefully shaded pattern of meaning in which the strong reds and violets of dramatic tension appear but rarely."[8]

Patrick McGrath, 1950–

Patrick McGrath grew up in London at Broadmoor, an institution for the criminally insane, where his father worked as a superintendent. In an interview with Michael Coffey, McGrath, who now lives in New York and has gained a reputation as the master of the New Gothic, explains in an interview: "At first I think I was attracted purely to the furniture of gothic fiction ... the crumbling mansions, the dripping cellars, the gloomy attics.... Quite why it clicked I don't know. Certainly as I began to work in the genre the interest in purely gothic effects began to fade and I became much more intrigued in the application of the gothic mood to states of mind, to extreme states of psychological disturbance."[9] McGrath has written several short stories and novels, all of which are violently, and sometimes humorously, gothic. They include *The Grotesque* (1989), *Spider* (1990), *Dr. Haggard's Disease* (1993), *Asylum* (1997), *Martha Peake: A Novel of the Revolution* (2000), and *Port Mungo* (2004). His short story collections include *Blood and Water and Other Tales* (1998) and *The Angel and Other Stories* (1995). McGrath has also edited two anthologies of contemporary Gothic fiction.

Iris Murdoch, 1919–1999

For many years, Murdoch lectured in philosophy at Oxford University. In 1956, she married the literary critic and novelist John Bayley. Her philosophical works include *Sartre, Romantic Rationalist* (1953), *The Sovereignty of Good* (1970), *Metaphysics as a Guide to Morals* (1992), and a collection of essays on literature and philosophy written and presented from 1950 to 1997, *Existentialists and Mystics* (1998). Her novels, sometimes comic and often bizarre, have been described by critics as psychological detective stories which focus on the problem of how love, freedom and goodness can exist when surrounded by moral and intellectual ignorance. Murdoch won many awards for her writing before her death in 1999, including the prestigious Booker Prize for *The Sea, the Sea* (1978). Among her other novels are *The Bell* (1958), *A Severed Head* (1961, dramatized by J. B. Priestley in 1963), *A Fairly Honourable Defeat* (1970), *The Sacred and Profane Love Machine* (1974), and *The Good Apprentice* (1986). Like Virginia Woolf, Murdoch used the landscape in truly symbolic ways.

Alan Sillitoe, 1928–

Alan Sillitoe was born in Nottingham, England, in 1928. He established his reputation as a working-class writer, whom critics classified as part of the "Angry Young Men" movement of the 1960s, with two works: *Saturday Night and Sunday Morning* (1958), and *The Loneliness of the Long-Distance Runner* (1959), the title story of which, along with *Saturday Night and Sunday Morning*, were made into highly successful films. Since that time, Sillitoe has written many other novels, plays, and poetry collections that have been translated into many languages and continues to do so. With Nottingham as his birthplace, Sillitoe is recognized by many critics as the literary descendent of D. H. Lawrence while others align him with such writers as Charles Dickens and Arnold Bennett for his provincial realism. Of his latest novels, *The Broken Chariot* was published in 1998 and *The German Numbers Woman* in 1999. Two nonfiction works, *Leading the Blind: A Century of Guide Book Travel* and *Key Issues in Historical and Comparative Sociology* were published in 2001. In a letter to Gillian Hanson dated October 26, 2002, Sillitoe writes: "My novel is in and being read at Harper Collins [*A Man of His Time*, 600pp.]. Now I'm going through nearly twenty years of notes made for a possible third volume in the trilogy following 'A Start in Life' and 'Life Goes On.'"[10] *A Man of His Time* is scheduled to be published in 2005.

Iain Sinclair, 1943–

A poet, critic, and novelist, Iain Sinclair, an admitted "psychogeographer," established his reputation as a documentary film director and as a rare book collector, dealing with the beat poets and *noir* thrillers. His work is deeply involved with the history and topography of London. Sinclair's first novel, *White Chappell, Scarlet Tracings* (1987), involves the Jack the Ripper murders. It is followed by *Downriver* (1991) which won the 1992 Encore Award for best second novel and is described by critic Robert A. Morace as "...a work whose individual parts, everything from the twelve tales to single sentences, are so brilliantly (if often scabrously) conceived, so perfectly executed, and so wildly imaginative, at once timely and intertexually timeless." Sinclair's recent novels include *Dining on Stones* (2004) and *Journey out of London*, to be published in 2006. The writer Will Self said in *The New Statesman*: "The reach, integrity and beauty of Sinclair's writing is without parallel. [He is] the hierophant of English letters."[11]

Stevie Smith, 1902–1971

Stevie Smith was born in 1902 and grew up in north London, where she lived with her aunt, and eventually worked as a secretary for a publishing company. She began writing secretly, using the company's notepaper to produce *Novel on Yellow Notepaper* in 1936. This was followed by two other novels, but Smith considered herself primarily a poet. Her droll verse, often caustic and enigmatic, focusing on death and religion, was accompanied by her own distinctive pen-and-ink sketches and became very popular. She published several volumes of poetry, including *A Good Time Was Had by All* (1937), *Mother, What Is Man?* (1942) and *Not Waving But Drowning* (1957). Her *Collected Poems* was published in 1975. *Me Again: The Uncollected Writings of Stevie Smith* was published in 1982 and contains the short story "Beside the Seaside." Smith wrote her final novel, *The Holiday*, during World War II, and it was published in 1949. She died in 1971. Although she is considered a modernist, Smith drew much of her material from other fields, as Sanford Sternlicht explains in *Stevie Smith*: "As much as any twentieth-century writer, Stevie has a distinctive voice, there are obvious influences on her work.... William Blake seems to have been often on her mind. His religious nature, simple language, contrasting versions of heaven and hell, delicate shifts of stress, shadowy mythologies, and metaphysical gifts find distant echo in Stevie's verse. Samuel Taylor Coleridge's transcendental wisdom and his ability to lose himself in dreams and fantasies awed Stevie. Alfred, Lord Tennyson's narratives and Robert Browning's dramatic soliloquies, all well studied in her youth, worked on Stevie's mind too. With Emily Dickinson's life, art, and metaphysic there was clear sympathy and identification. Edward Lear's trick of juxtaposing humorous verse with illustrations inspired Stevie, as did James Thurber's technique."[12]

Graham Swift, 1949–

Graham Swift first became known through his short stories published in various magazines and collected in *Learning to Swim* (1982). He gained international renown for *Waterland*, which was made into a popular film and won several literary prizes. His other novels include *The Sweet Shop Owner* (1980), *Shuttlecock* (1981), and *Out of the World* (1988). Swift has also coauthored an anthology of fishing with the novelist and poet David Profumo entitled *The Magic Wheel* (1985). Swift's novel *Last Orders* (1996), which won the Booker Prize, was made into a successful movie in 2001. In 2003, Swift's latest work, a story of love and murder, *The Light of Day*, was published.

Alfred Tennyson, first Baron Tennyson, 1809–1892

Tennyson became Poet Laureate of England in 1850 after writing the famous poem "In Memoriam" in memory of his friend Arthur Hallam. Many of his poems, such as "The Lady of Shalott" and "The Holy Grail," are based on Arthurian legends, and others, such as "The Charge of the Light Brigade" are drawn from historical and sociological events of the

Victorian period. Tennyson is buried in Westminster Abbey. A life of him by his son was published in 1897.

Virginia Woolf, 1882–1941

One of the most influential writers of the twentieth century was Virginia Woolf. She was born in 1882 and committed suicide by drowning when she was fifty-nine years old. With such innovative works as *Mrs. Dalloway* (1925), *To the Lighthouse* (1927), and *The Waves* (1931), Woolf used the stream-of-consciousness method to investigate the minds of her characters rather than focusing on plot and action and eliminated the author as narrator or commentator. Much of Woolf's work, including *To the Lighthouse* and *The Waves*, addresses the question of the possibility of living a life of spiritual and imaginative fulfillment in a gradually dehumanizing world. Through essays, journalism, letters, and fiction, Woolf examines the nature of reality and the individual's place in a rapidly changing world through such themes as madness and sanity, sexuality, especially in terms of women, and the cyclic nature of life and death. Her first novel, *The Voyage Out*, was published in 1915; in this and subsequent works, Woolf's unceasing experimentation with the form of the novel examines the moment-by-moment experience of "being."

William Butler Yeats, 1869–1939

The Irish writer and poet W. B. Yeats received the Nobel Prize for his work as a poet, which included the early collection *The Wild Swans at Coole* (1917). His later poems were written in a sparse, colloquial style unlike his earlier works, which were influenced by his then interest in mystic religion and the supernatural. Yeats also wrote several plays and published collections of essays and edited many books. His personal letters are published in five collections. About Yeats' artistic accomplishments, one biographer states: "Yeats wanted poetry to engage the full complexity of life, but only insofar as the individual poet's imagination had direct access to experience or thought and only insofar as those materials were transformed by the energy of artistic articulation. He was, from first to last, a poet who tried to transform the local concerns of his own life by embodying them in the resonantly universal language of his poems. His brilliant rhetorical accomplishments, strengthened by his considerable powers of rhythm and poetic phrase, have earned wide praise from readers and, especially, from fellow poets, including W. H. Auden (who praised Yeats as the savior of English lyric poetry), Stephen Spender, Theodore Roethke, and Philip Larkin."[13]

Appendix B

Riverbank and Seashore in Quotation

The quotations below are listed in the order that the works from which they are taken appear in the text under the chapter headings of "The Rural River," "The Urban River," "The Rural Shore," and "The Urban Shore," with the exception of "River into Sea." In this section, I have included quotations from several different works discussed in other parts of the book, all of which relate to the passage of river into sea. Most of the excerpts do not appear in the main text, and all, I feel, add further interest for the reader to the topic of seashore and riverbank.

The Rural River

Just by the red red-roofed town the tributary Ripple flows with a lively current into the Floss. How lovely the little river is with its dark, changing wavelets! It seems to me like a living companion while I wander along the bank and listen to its low placid voice, as to the voice of one who is deaf and loving [*The Mill on the Floss*, 9].

The rush of the water and the booming of the mill bring a dreamy deafness which seems to heighten the peacefulness of the scene. They are like a great curtain of sound, shutting one out from the world beyond [*The Mill on the Floss*, 10].

She was floating in smooth water now—perhaps far on the over-flooded fields.... O how welcome, the widening of that dismal watery level—the gradual uplifting of the cloudy firmament—the slowly defining blackness of objects above the glassy dark! Yes—she must be out on the fields—those were the tops of hedgerow trees. Which way did the river lie? ... She seized an oar and began to paddle the boat forward with the energy of wakening hope ... [*The Mill on the Floss*, 538].

The spring at once reminded me of a greater body of water—a river, at some little distance farther on.... Unless my memory was at fault, this was the way that led to an old water-mill on the river-bank ["The Guilty River," 248].

Our gloomy trees and our repellent river presented an aspect superbly transfigured, under the shadows of the towering clouds, the fantastic wreaths of the mist, and the lurid reddening of the sun as it stooped to its setting.... The mist, rolling capriciously over the waters, revealed the grandly deliberate course of the flowing current, while it dimmed the turbid earthy yellow that discoloured and degraded the stream under the full glare of day ["The Guilty River," 314].

The dimly flowing river was at my feet; the river on which I had seen Cristel again, for the first time since we were children. Thus far, the dreadful loss of her had been a calamity, held away from me in some degree by events which had imperatively taken possession of my mind. In the darkness and the stillness, the misery of having lost her was free to crush me ["The Guilty River," 343].

"I want to be free!"... She began to walk rapidly in the direction of the river she could not see but whose distance and position she had become to know after so many hours of sojourn on its banks and on the edge of the valley through which it ran. That river! Tonight! [*The Two Sisters*, 30].

I was born not only within reach of one river valley, but two. I could almost reach out, with my two hands, and touch those twin but quite dissimilar streams flowing on almost parallel courses to the North Sea.... On the Nene I could watch the traffic of barges I could never see on the Ouse; on the Ouse I could see a richness of flower life that the Nene, being navigated, could not offer.... To one, the Ouse, I had nothing and needed nothing to attract me except its own placid but rich life; it was an idyllic and generous stream, flowery, unnavigated, watering a lovely valley. The other, the Nene, could offer me not merely an exciting life, but a life that had been and gone; it was a prosaic stream, flowerless, navigated, watering what was very often an ugly valley, but it had carried a rich traffic of life, during the late nineteenth century, that it no longer knew—the wild traffic of barges and bargees, the swaggering rough stuff of boozers and fancy but not too fancy ladies in the river-side pubs, the betting and boasting and comedy and often tragedy of hot summer evenings when the beer was served outside, under the chestnut trees, the sly slippery stuff or river-poachers, of eel-trappers, of night work [*Down the River*, 7–8].

Under her feet the ground began to slant river-wards, and she felt unable to do anything but follow it, whither it might lead.... The river was near at last. She had an uncanny sense of its nearness, and, listening, half-imagined she could hear its lap-lap against the banks and the wooden piles of its wharf.... She caught the smell of the river in her nostrils—a very thick definite smell, foul and heavy with rottenness that arises as a matter of course from sluggish streams. As she went farther down the slope she felt it overcoming her, overcoming the ascent, fighting to gain higher ground where the town lay.... And simultaneously with those first drops of slack rain, she tripped and fell ... [*The Two Sisters*, 72–75].

Ah, now comes the most wonderful part of this wonderful story. Tom, when he woke, for of course he woke—children always wake after they have slept exactly as long as is good for them—found himself swimming about, in the stream, being about four inches long or—that I may be accurate—3.87902 inches long, and having around the parotid region of his fauces a set of external gills (I hope you understand all those big words) just like those of a sucking eft, which he mistook for a lace frill, till he pulled at them, found he hurt himself, and made up his mind that they were part of himself, and best left alone.

    In fact, the fairies had turned him into a water-baby [*The Water Babies*, 50].

And all the while Tom was swimming about in the river, with a pretty lace collar of gills about his neck, as lively as a grig, and as clean as a fresh-run salmon [*The Water Babies*, 57].

But Tom was very happy in the water. He had been sadly overworked in the land-world; and so now, to make up for that, he had nothing but holidays in the water-world for a long, long time to come. He had nothing to do now but enjoy himself, and look at all the pretty things which are to be seen in the cool clear water-world, where the sun is never too hot, and the frost is never too cold [*The Water Babies*, 60–61].

My father kept the lock on the River Leem, two miles from where it empties into the Ouse. But because a lock-keeper's duties are irregular and his pay, set against the rent-free cottage in which he lives, is scant, and because, in any case, by the nineteen-thirties, the river-traffic on the Leem had dwindled, my father also grew vegetables, kept chickens and trapped eels. It was only in times of heavy rain or thaw that these secondary occupations were abandoned. Then he would have to watch and anticipate the water-level. Then he would have to raise the sluice which cut across the far side of the stream like a giant guillotine [*Waterland*, 2].

But under normal conditions the sluice remained lowered, almost to the river bottom, its firm blade holding back the slow-flowing Leem, making it fit for the passage of boats. Then the water in the enclosure above it, like the water in the lock-pen, would be smooth and placid and would give off that smell which is characteristic of places where fresh water and human ingenuity meet, and which is smelt over and over again in the Fens. A cool, slimy, but strangely poignant and nostalgic smell. A smell which is half man and half fish [*Waterland*, 2–3].

He thought his happiness was complete when, as he meandered aimlessly along, suddenly he stood by the edge of a full-fed river. Never in his life had he seen a river before—.... All was a-shake and a-shiver—glints and gleams and sparkles, rustle and swirl, chatter and bubble. The Mole was bewitched, entranced, fascinated [*The Wind in the Willows*, 4].

He glanced back and saw to his dismay that they were gaining on him.... Ceasing to heed where he was going, he struggled on blindly and wildly, looking back over his shoulder at the now triumphant enemy, when suddenly the earth failed under his feet, he grasped at the air, and, splash! He found himself head over ears in deep water, rapid water, water that bore him along with a force that he could not contend with; and he knew that in his blind panic he had run straight into the river! [*The Wind in the Willows*, 196].

The Urban River

The girl pulled the hood of a cloak she wore, over her head and over her face, and, looking towards so that the front folds of this hood turned down the river, kept the boat in that direction going before the tide. Until now, the boat had barely held her own, and had hovered about one spot; but now, the banks changed swiftly, and the deepening shadows and the kindling lights of London Bridge were passed, and the tiers of shipping lay on either hand [Our Mutual Friend, 14].

This description applies to the river-frontage of the Six Jolly Fellowship-Porters. The back of the establishment, though the chief entrance was there, so contracted that it merely represented in its connexion with the front, the handle of a flat iron set upright on its broadest end. This handle stood at the bottom of a wilderness of court and alley: which wilderness pressed so hard and close upon the Six Jolly Fellowship-Porters as to leave the hostelry not an inch of ground beyond its door. For this reason, in combination with the fact that the house was all but afloat at high water, when the Porters had a family wash the linen subjected to that operation might usually be seen drying on lines stretched across the reception-rooms and bed-chambers [Our Mutual Friend, 67].

It was about half-past six, too dark to paint, turning very cold. Clouds all streaming away like ghost fish under the ice. Evening sun turning reddish. Trees along the hard like old copper. Old willow leaves shaking up and down in the breeze, making shadows on the ones below, reflections on the ones above. Need a tricky bush to give the effect and what would be the good. Pissarro's job, not mine. Not nowadays. Lyric not epic [The Horse's Mouth, 14–15].

And I went out to get room for my grief. Thank God, it was a high sky on Greenbank. Darker than I expected. But the edge of the world was still a long way off. At least as far as Surrey. Under the cloudbank. Sun was in the bank. Streak of salmon below. Salmon trout above soaking into wash blue. River whirling along so fast that its skin was pulled into wrinkles like silk dragged over the floor [The Horse's Mouth, 44].

Surrey all in one blaze like a forest fire. Great clouds of dirty yellow smoke rising up. Nine carat gold. Sky water-green to lettuce-green. A few top clouds yellow and solid as lemons. River disappeared out of its hole [The Horse's Mouth, 48].

Franky and Walter were moving down the planks, and I went after them. The river came up to us and its surface dissolved away into the blue-glass sky [*The Horse's Mouth*, 53].

Beyond the old Church at Battersea the retreating flood had left exposed a wide shelf of mud and gravel. At intervals the dark driftwood lay piled. Near the draw dock some longshoremen had heaped it up and set light to it, to clear the area. Now the thick blue smoke gave out a villainous smell, the gross spirit of salt and fire. Tilda loved the smell, and stretched her nostrils wide.

Beyond the dock, an old wrecked barge lay upside down. It was shocking, even terrifying, to see her dark flat shining bottom, chine uppermost. A derelict ship turns over on her keel and lies gracefully at rest, but there is only one way up for a Thames barge if she is to maintain her dignity [*Offshore*, 57].

Above the river, the seagulls kept on the wing as long as they could, hoping the turbulence would bring them a good find, then, defeated and battered, they heeled and screamed away to find refuge. The rats on the wharf behaved strangely, creeping to the edge of the planking, and trying to cross over from dry land to the boats.

On the Reach itself, there could be no pretence that this would be an ordinary night. Tug skippers, who had never before acknowledged the presence of the moored barges, called out, or gave the danger signal—five rapid blasts in succession. Before slack tide the police launch went down the river, stopping at every boat to give fair warning.

"Excuse me, sir, have you checked your anchor recently?"

The barge anchors were unrecognizable as such, more like crustaceans, specimens of some giant type long since discarded by Nature, but still clinging to their old habitat, sunk in the deep pits they had made in the foreshore. But under the ground they were half rusted away. *Dreadnought*'s anchor had come easily enough when the salvage tug came to dispose of her. The mud which held so tenaciously could also give way in a moment, if conditions altered [*Offshore*, 124].

The wind brought a whiff from the glue factory, and the water smelled cold. A barge made an arrow, and a man at the front who steered it wore only a shirt and smoked a pipe, and stared at the bridge he had to go under ["A Scream of Toys," 95].

River into Sea

But he could not help thinking of what the otter had said about the great river and the broad sea. And, as he thought, he longed to go and see them ... [*The Water Babies*, 78].

And after a while he came to a place where the river spread out into broad still shallow reaches, so wide that little Tom, as he pulled his head out of the water, could hardly see across.
   And there he stopped. He got a little frightened. "This must be the sea," he thought [*The Water Babies*, 82].

A wide plain, where the broadening Floss hurries on between its green banks to the sea, and the loving tide, rushing to meet it, checks its passage with an impetuous embrace [*The Mill on the Floss*, 9].

... he sat down on the bank, while the river was still chattering on to him, a babbling procession of the best stories in the world, sent from the heart of the earth to be told at last to the insatiable sea [*The Wind in the Willows*, 4].

Now from the window of the tram I see masts among the chimneys; there is the river; there are ships that sail to India. I will walk by the river. I will pace this embankment, where an old man reads a newspaper in a glass shelter. I will pace this terrace and watch the ships bowling down the tide. A woman walks on deck, with a dog barking around her. Her skirts are blown; her hair is blown; they are going out to sea; they are leaving us; they are vanishing this summer evening. Now I will relinquish; now I will let loose. Now I will at last free the checked, the jerked back desire to be spent, to be consumed [*The Waves*, 164].

And having arrived, having reached the ultimate moment, what happens? We at once begin to look forward no more, but back. Having reached the point of fusion, we no longer want it. We look back instead to the middle reaches, the small beginnings [*Down the River*, 150–151].

Since he was a boy, he had grown used to all the sounds of the sea, and to those coming off the river and the marshes, he missed nothing [*The Albatross*, 19].

The Thames barges, built of living wood that gave and sprang back in the face of the wind, were as much at home as anything on the river. To their creaking and grumbling was added a new note, comparable to music. As the tide rose, the wind shredded the clouds above them and pushed a mighty swell across the water, so that they began to roll as they had once rolled at sea [*Offshore*, 125].

The dead match somersaulted over the parapet, and she thought she heard a sizzle as it hit the water and was carried away. It'll be in the sea by morning, she didn't wonder ["A Scream of Toys," 98].

The water of the estuary was the colour of dead fish. A dredger was chugging near the base of the pier. He thought, I could swim the estuary; but there is a bridge. Below him the yellow helmets of the workers moved over the girders for the roadway like beetles. He took his hands from the rail. He wasn't at all afraid. He had been away from his wife all week. He thought: She knows nothing of this. If he were to step out now into the grey air he would be quite by himself, no harm would come to him ... ["Learning to Swim," 13–14].

Today there were no clouds at all, but I could well imagine how magnificently the huge, brooding area of sky would look with grey, scudding rain and storm clouds lowering over the estuary, how it would be here in the floods of February time when the marshes turned to iron grey and the sky seeped into them, and in the high winds of March, when the light rippled, shadow casting shadow across the ploughed fields [*The Woman in Black*, 53].

Once the shallow, shift waters of the Wash did not stop at Boston and King's Lynn but licked southwards as far as Cambridge, Huntingdon, Peterborough and Bedford. What caused them to retreat? The answer can be given in a single syllable: Silt. The Fens were formed by silt. Silt: a word which when you utter it, letting the air slip thinly between your teeth, invokes a slow, sly, insinuating agency. Silt: which shapes and undermines continents; which demolishes as it builds; which is simultaneous accretion and erosion; neither progress nor decay.

It came first from the coast of Yorkshire and Lincolnshire, borne on the inshore currents which flowed southwards into the ancient Wash. In the blue-black clay which lies under the soil of Cambridgeshire are deposits of silt containing traces of shells of a type occurring on the beaches and cliff-beds of north-east England. Thus the first silts came from the sea. But to these marine salts were added the land silts carried by the rivers, the

Ouse, the Cam, the Welland, which drained and still drain, into the ever-diminishing Wash [*Waterland*, 7].

I turned then and gazed back down the long dark ribbon of London's river that led away to the sea, and felt for that moment utterly dejected, and as bleak-spirited and lonely as I had felt in my life [*The Mist in the Mirror*, 10].

The long march to the sea ends at Leyston, or as I keep calling it, Leytonston. There is nothing more.... This is the Last Redoubt, the final stand. Beyond the groined and squelching shore is the German Ocean ... [*Downriver*, 431].

This is the of the claims of civilization. The feeble encroachments of humanoid life-forms. From this point on we are free [*Downriver*, 433].

The Rural Shore

... they had formed an intention to go to St. Leonards for a few days at the end of the month....

The journey was along a road by neutral green hills, upon which hedgerows lay trailing like ropes on a quay. Gaps in these uplands revealed the blue sea, flecked with a few dashes of white and a solitary white sail, the whole brimming up to a keen horizon which lay like a line ruled from hill-side to hill-side....

They mounted the last crest, and the bay which was to be the end of their pilgrimage burst upon them. The ocean blueness deepened its colour as it stretched to the feet of the crags, where it terminated in a fringe of white—silent at this distance, though moving and heaving like a counterpane upon a restless sleeper [*A Pair of Blue Eyes*, 193].

The waves broke and spread their waters swiftly over the shore. One after another they massed themselves and fell; the spray tossed itself back with the energy of their fall. The waves were steeped deep-blue save for a pattern of diamond-pointed light on their backs which rippled as the backs of great horses ripple with muscles as they move. The waves fell; withdrew and fell again, like the thud of a great beast stamping [*The Waves*, 150].

My children will carry on; their teething, their crying, their going to school and coming back will be like the waves of the sea under me [*The Waves*, 132].

They came here regularly every evening drawn by some need. It was as if the water floated off and set sailing thoughts which had grown stagnant on dry land, and gave to their bodies even some sort of physical relief. First, the pulse of colour flooded the bay with blue, and the heart expanded with it and the body swam, only the next instant to be checked and chilled by the prickly blackness on the ruffled waves [*To the Lighthouse*, 33].

Then, being tired, her mind still rising and falling with the sea, the taste and smell that place have after long absence possessing her, the candles wavering in her eyes, she had lost herself and gone under. It was a wonderful night, starlit; the waves sounded as they went upstairs; the moon surprised them, enormous, pale, as they passed the staircase window. She had slept at once [*To the Lighthouse*, 222–223].

EMER. I think he loved as no man ever loved, for when he heard the name of the man he had killed, and the name of that man's mother, he went out of his senses utterly. He ran into the sea, and with shield before him and sword in hand he fought the deathless sea. Of all the many men who had stood there to look at the fight not one dared stop him or even call his name; they stood in a kind of stupor, collected together in a bunch like cattle in a storm, until, fixing his eyes it seemed as on some new enemy, he waded out further still and the waves swept over him [*Fighting the Waves*, lines 72–80].

The other currachs were far out in the bay already: the sea was running strong. For all that, there was a strange still look about the water, unbroken by any spray. Jimeen sat still, exulting in his luck. The waves did not slap against the sides of the currach like he'd have thought they would do, and they didn't even break into spray where the oars split their surface. Instead, they seemed to go lolloping under the currach and lollop up against the far side, till they might have been on great glass rollers they were slipping along ["The Great Wave," 12].

Were they blinded by the flash? Or had it suddenly gone as black as night over the whole sea? ["The Great Wave," 16].

Today there is a pleasant very light haze over the whole sky, and the sea has a misleadingly docile silvered look, as if the substantial wavelets were determined to stroke the rocks as hard as they could without showing any trace of foam. It is a compact radiant complacent sort of sea, very beautiful. There *ought* to be seals, the waves themselves are almost seals today, but still I scan the water in vain with my long-distance glasses. Enormous yellow-beaked gulls perch on the rocks and stare at me with brilliant glass eyes. A shadow-cormorant skims the glycerine sea. The rocks are thronged with butterflies. The temperature remains high. I wash my clothes and dry them on the lawn. I have been swimming every day and feel very fit and salty. Still no move from Lizzie, but I am not worried. I feel happy in my silence. If the gods have some treat in store for Lizzie and me, good. If not, also good. I feel innocent and free. Perhaps it is all that swimming [*The Sea, the Sea*, 67].

The bay itself is very beautiful, being fringed by rather remarkable, almost spherical boulders. It is known locally as "Raven's Bay" after the hotel, though it has some other name, something like "Shahore" in the local dialect. (Shore Bay? Why?) If followed to the left from Shruff End, the coast road passes through a curious narrow defile, which I have nicknamed "the Khyber Pass," where the way has been cut through a big outcrop of rock, which here invades the land to a considerable distance. Beyond this there is a very small stony beach; this is the only beach in the area, since elsewhere, a feature which originally attracted me to this coastland, there is deepish water up against the rocks at any state of the tide [*The Sea, the Sea*, 12].

Charles craned out of the window, and smelled the salt air, and saw on the beach some way to his right the square black silhouettes of the bathing-machines from which the nereids emerged. But the only music from the deep that night was the murmur of the tide on the shingles; and somewhere much farther out, the dimly raucous cries of the gulls roosting on the calm water [*The French Lieutenant's Woman*, 123].

Charles stared down at her for a few hurtling moments, then turned and resumed his seat, his heart beating, as if he had just stepped back from the brink of the bluff. Far out to sea, above the southernmost horizon, there had risen gently into view an armada of distant cloud [*The French Lieutenant's Woman*, 144].

Mr. Singleton was teaching Paul to swim. "Kick," he was saying. From here, against the gentle waves, they looked no more than rippling silhouettes ["Learning to Swim," 10].

He was trying to get Paul to hold his body straight and relaxed so he would float. But each time as Paul nearly succeeded he would panic, fearing his father would let go, and thrash wildly. When he calmed down and Mr. Singleton held him, Mrs. Singleton could see the water running off his face like tears ["Learning to Swim," 23].

Behind me, out on the marshes, all was still and silent ... [*The Woman in Black*, 71].

I felt a second of pure despair, alone in the middle of the wide marsh, under the fast-moving, stormy sky, with only water all around me and that dreadful house the only solid thing for miles around [*The Woman in Black*, 129–130].

I have no soul to speak to or relieve me ...
    Nobody was much about on my beach either. I saw a distant sea-coal gatherer with his hand-cart, then a far-away grass-hopper sitting up on a high bicycle with small children grasshoppers following on theirs—fashionable people from the terraces, "people we don't know socially," as the aunts said. Behind them was only the sea—the long, crocodile points.
    The wind dropped and the beach was full of small blue scallops of lights as the sun went lower in the sky, saucer shaped dents. A million, and each one of them shone. "Having now brought my mind a little to relish my condition," I read, "and given over looking at the sea..." and looked up myself and saw, far away towards the Works, a bouncing dark dot.
    I thought it was a bird at first, but then at once knew that it was too big. Up and down it danced on the sand, growing all the time, and soon I could hear something—perhaps just the clatter from the foundries blowing across unevenly in the wind [*Crusoe's Daughter*, 39].

Robinson Crusoe hard against my chest, I climbed the sea-wall and jumped down and began to run across the huge white beach. The wind battered me, the sun shone on me and the sea was far away with a silver line along the edge of it. The horizon was broken, so broken and curved that it seemed strange it had taken everyone so long to know that the world was round—smoke then ship came sailing towards me, ship then smoke went sailing away [*Crusoe's Daughter*, 37].

The Urban Shore

At many resorts it was obvious that some sort of bulwark was needed against the high tides, floods, and storms. As a result sea-walls were constructed

[*Rough sea. ADA cries out. Cry and sea amplified, cut off. End of evocation. Pause. Sea calm. He goes back up deeply shelving beach. Boots laborious on shingle. He halts. Pause. He moves on. He halts. Pause. Sea calm and faint.*]
[*Embers, Collected Shorter Plays*, 99–100; brackets in original].

Hi, all you leisure lovers. Eight o'clock, the temperature is 52 degrees and it's fair to cloudy in mid-town Morecambe. This is your Miramar host, Percy Cattley, saying hello again and welcome to another fun-packed day ["All Day on the Sands," 80].

Dad. (Picks up the book). "*Marine Life.*" Crabs. Lobsters. Look at that! Seahorses. I've never seen a sea-horse in my life. And starfish. It's not fair. Putting ideas into their heads. It makes them disappointed. Even the shells. There's none of them shells, is there ["All Day on the Sands," 92].

The tides are controlled by the moon.... It's up there somewhere, and it controls the tides ["All Day on the Sands," 92].

The sea was nowhere to be seen. They stood on the front and looked for it. Shining sand stretched left and right, and all the way to the horizon, pools and small salt rivers flickered under the sun now breaking through. The immense sky intimidated them, made Skegness seem small at their spines. It looked as if the ocean went on forever round the world and came right back to their heels ["The Road," 277].

A few people had been on the beach but now, on either side, hundreds advanced on to the sand, hair and dresses and white shirts moving against the wind, a shimmering film of blue and grey, red and yellow spreading from the funnel of the station avenue ["The Road," 277–278].

The thin white ray was coming towards them, feather-tips lifting from it, a few hundred yards away and suddenly no longer straight, pushed forward a little in the center, scarred by the out-jutting pier. It broke on the sand and went right back ["The Road," 279].

Beach
Empty stage. Darkness and thunder. Wind roars, whines, crashes and screams over the water. Masses of water swell up, rattle and churn, and crash back into the sea. Gravel and sand grind slowly. The earth trembles [stage directions for the opening scene of *The Sea*].
    EVENS (inside the hut). Is there a proper place? Perhaps not. We're

into the spring tides now. He'll be washed up where the coast turns in. [*Points.*] You see? People are cruel and boring and obsessed. If he goes past that point you've lost him. He should come in. He's hanging around there now. He could see us if he wasn't dead [Scene Two, *The Sea*].

Outside it was all but dark, the January sky like slate, and moving with clouds. The beacon flashed green, on-off, on-off, out to sea beyond the breakwater. Duncan walked down nearer to the waterline and then away, face into the wind, listening to the crunch and chop of his rubber as they bit into the shingle [*The Albatross*, 2–3].

He wished, after all, that there were another way, that he could walk down to the beach and get into a boat and go, as the fishermen all went, disappearing over the horizon. Though he knew that, in fact, none of them went far, only four or five miles out, to the sandbank. He had watched them for years, heard them talking about it and then tried to imagine how it would be, putting the boats out, nose facing the open sea. He had never been, never been on the water [*The Albatross*, 12].

He began to walk, away from the town, on and on, towards the Martello tower, looming up through the darkness. The air was raw upon his face, beginning to freeze. He had not stopped to put on a jacket or boots, the soles of his shoes made scarcely any noise on the flat concrete slabs of the wall. He would not have walked on the beach, not at night, the crunching of his steps in the shingle would have deadened his hearing of the other night sounds, and he must always be listening, ready for what might come...
     The wind had come roaring across the water, sending a sheet of spray slapping up into his face, blinding him.... After a moment he had opened his eyes. Humps of cloud moving fast one close behind the other, in front of the moon. The waves crashed over, like cannons booming up the beach [*The Albatross*, 18–19, 27–8].

Notes

Introduction

1. Iris Murdoch, *Existentialists and Mystics* 201.
2. Iris Murdoch, *Existentialists and Mystics* 181.
3. Gaston Bachelard, *Water and Dreams* 11.
4. H. E. Bates, *Down the River* 39.
5. W. H. Herendeen, "The Rhetoric of Rivers: The River and the Pursuit of Knowledge." *Studies in Philology*, 1981. Spring 78 (2) 107–127.
6. H. E. Bates, *Down the River* 150.
7. Iris Murdoch, *Existentialists and Mystics* 279.
8. Patricia Waugh, *Postmodernism* 5.
9. Patricia Waugh, *Postmodernism* 33.
10. Gaston Bachelard, *Water and Dreams* 193.

Chapter One

1. W. H. Herendeen, "The Rhetoric of Rivers: The River and the Pursuit of Knowledge." *Studies in Philology*, 1981. Spring 78 (2) 107–127.
2. Gaston Bachelard, *Water and Dreams* 6.
3. James Donald Welch, "Tennyson's Landscapes of Time and a Reading of 'The Kraken,'" *Victorian Poetry*, 197–204.
4. Gaston Bachelard, *Water and Dreams* 15.
5. Alfred Tennyson, *Memoirs* 117.
6. Gaston Bachelard, *Water and Dreams* 55.
7. Antonia Byatt, introduction to *The Mill on the Floss*, Penguin Edition, 2003, xvii.
8. Edward Garnett, foreword to *The Two Sisters* i.
9. H. E. Bates, *Down the River* 40.
10. Thomas Carlyle (see his discussion of the "Clothes Philosophy" in *Sartus Resartus*) 153–174.
11. Soren Kierkegaard, *Fear and Trembling and The Sickness unto Death* 202.
12. Jean Ingelow, *The Complete Poems* 1–2.
13. Gaston Bachelard, *Poetics of Space*, Introduction, xxxi–ii.
14. Pamela Cooper, "Imperial Topographies: The Spaces of History in Waterland" *Modern Fiction Studies*, 1996. Summer, 43 (2): 371–396. Baltimore, MD.
15. Gaston Bachelard, *Water and Dreams* 55.
16. Gaston Bachelard, *Water and Dreams* 12.
17. Pamela Cooper, "Imperial Topographies: The Spaces of History in Water-

land" *Modern Fiction Studies*. 1996. Summer 43 (2): 371–96.
18. Gaston Bachelard, *Poetics of Space* 152.
19. Peter Hunt, *The Wind in the Willows, A Fragmented Arcadia*.
20. Gaston Bachelard, *Poetics of Space*, Introduction, xxxi.
21. J. D. McClatchy, Review of *River*, *The New Republic* Sept. 3, 1984, vol. 191, 39.
22. Martin Heidegger, "The Nature of Language." *On the Way to Language*, Peter D. Hertz, translator, 181.
23. H. E. Bates, *Down the River* 13.
24. Gaston Bachelard, *L'eau et les rêves, Essai sur l'imagination matière* 155.

Chapter Two

1. Charles Dickens, *Dickens's Dictionary of the Thames from Oxford to the Nore. An Unconventional Handbook*, "Victoria Embankment" entry.
2. Algernon Swinburne, "Charles Dickens." *Quarterly Review*, July 1902.
3. Joyce Cary, *First Trilogy* xi.
4. H. E. Bates, *Down the River* 9.
5. R. May, editor, *Existence: A New Dimension in Psychiatry and Psychology* 22–41.
6. Katherine Dunn, *New York Times Book Review*, Sept. 23, 1990, 14.
7. Michael Coffey, "Patrick McGrath: A Purveyor of the Fantastic Makes a Foray into Madness." *Publishers Weekly*, Sept. 28, 1990, vol. 237, 39.
8. Michael Coffey, "Patrick McGrath: A Purveyor of the Fantastic Makes a Foray into Madness." *Publishers Weekly*, Sept. 28, 1990, vol. 237, 39.
9. W. H. Auden, "The Sea and the Desert," *The Enchaféd Flood*, 31–32.
10. Michael Moorcock, *New Statesman & Society*, March 8, 1991, (141)4, 36.

Chapter Three

1. Jean Ingelow. *The Complete Poems* 62.
2. H. E. Bates, *Down the River* 150.
3. Dale H. Porter, *The Thames Embankment* 25–26.

Chapter Four

1. Auden, *The Enchaféd Flood* 11.
2. James Applewhite, *Seas and Inland Journeys* 196.
3. Thomas Hardy, *Thomas Hardy's Personal Writings* 7.
4. Thomas Hardy, Preface to first edition of *A Pair of Blue Eyes*, published in serial form, 1832–1833, iii.
5. Susan Gorsky, *Virginia Woolf* 80.
6. Shelia Sutcliffe, *Martello Towers* 122.
7. William Cadbury, "The Utility of the Poetic Mask in Tennyson's 'Supposed Confessions.'" *Modern Language Quarterly*, 1963. 24, 374–385.
8. John Lehmann, *Virginia Woolf and Her World* 79.
9. Elias Canetti, *Crowds and Power* 80.
10. W. H. Auden, *The Enchaféd Flood* 11.
11. W. B. Yeats, "Prologue to Fighting the Waves," *Wheels and Butterflies* 73.
12. A. S. Knowland, *W. B. Yeats, Dramatist of Vision* 131.
13. W. B. Yeats, "Introduction to Fighting the Waves," *Wheels and Butterflies* 165.
14. W. B. Yeats, "Introduction to Fighting the Waves," *Wheels and Butterflies* 66–67.
15. Elias Canetti, *Crowds and Power* 81.
16. Edward Bond, letter to William Woodman in *Bond on File* 122, 123.
17. A. A. DeVitis and William J. Palmer, "*A Pair of Blue Eyes* Flash at *The French Lieutenant's Woman*." *Contemporary Literature*, 1974. 15 90–101.
18. Claude Lévi-Strauss, *The Savage Mind* 67.
19. Edward Bond, "Author's Program Note on *The Sea*," *Bingo & The Sea* 123–124.
20. Christopher Ricks, *Tennyson* 44–45.
21. Zoreth Sullivan, "Iris Murdoch and the Enchantment of Untruth" 161.

22. Elias Canetti, *Crowds and Power* 81.
23. Susan Hill, http://www.susan-hill.com/pages/books/the_books/the_woman_in_black.htm.
24. W. H. Auden, "The Stone and the Shell" *The Enchaféd Flood* 75.
25. Jane Gardam, *Something About the Author Series*, vol. 9, 179.
26. W. B. Yeats, "Introduction to Fighting the Waves," *Wheels and Butterflies* 65.

Chapter Five

1. Nathaniel Hawthorne, *English Notebooks* 344.
2. Alan Sillitoe, *Saturday Night and Sunday Morning* 34.
3. Mikhail Bakhtin, *Problems of Dostoevsky's Poetics* 122.
4. Howard Grey and Graham Stuart, *The Victorians by the Sea* 5.
5. Jane Austen, *Jane Austen's Letters* 94– 95.
6. Jane Austen, *Jane Austen's Letters* 94– 95.
7. Nathaniel Hawthorne, *English Notebooks* 344.
8. John Walton, *The English Seaside Resort, A Social History, 1750-1914* 50–52.
9. John Walton, *The British Seaside* 3–4.
10. Mikhail Bakhtin, *Problems of Dostoevsky's Poetics* 123.
11. Stuart Hall, "Metaphors of Transformation," introduction to Allon White's *Carnival, Hysteria, and Writing* 6.
12. W. H. Auden, "The Way to the Sea," *The Complete Works of Auden*, vol. 1, 432.
13. Cyril Bainbridge, *Pavilions on the Sea: A History of the Seaside Pleasure Pier* 7.
14. W. H. Auden, "The Way to the Sea," *The Complete Works of Auden*, vol. 1 432.
15. Anonymous, *The Times*, August 30, 1860.
16. Stuart Hall, "Metaphors of Transformation," introduction to Allon White's *Carnival, Hysteria, and Writing* 3.
17. Elias Canetti, *Crowds and Power* 18.
18. Rob Shields, *Places on the Margin* 102.
19. Terry Eagleton, *Exiles and Émigrés* 132.
20. Elias Canetti, *Crowds and Power* 15.
21. Elias Canetti, *Crowds and Power* 17.
22. Graham Greene, quoted cover note to Penguin paperback edition of *The West Pier*.
23. Soren Kierkegaard, *Fear and Trembling and The Sickness unto Death*, 207.
24. Gaston Bachelard, *Water and Dreams* 165.
25. Iris Murdoch, *Existentialists and Mystics* 255.
26. Rob Shields, *Places on the Margin* 102.
27. Victor Carrabino, "On the Shores of Nothingness: Beckett's Embers," *Poetics of the Elements in the Human Condition: The Sea*, 1985: 45–56.
28. Victor Carrabino, "On the Shores of Nothingness: Beckett's Embers," *Poetics of the Elements in the Human Condition: The Sea*, 1985: 45–56.
29. Elias Canetti, *Crowds and Power* 31.
30. Edward Bond, letter to William Woodman in *Bond on File* 122, 123.
31. W. H. Auden, *The Enchaféd Flood* 75.
32. W. H. Auden, *The Enchaféd Flood* 76.
33. Elias Canetti, *Crowds and Power* 80–81.

Evaluation

1. Leonard M. Scigaj, "The Ophiolatry of Ted Hughes." *Twentieth Century Literature*, 1985. Winter 31(4), 380–398.
2. James Applewhite, *Seas and Inland Journeys* 196.
3. Mikhail Bakhtin, *The Problems of Dostoevsky's Poetics* 123.
4. David Danow, *The Spirit of the Carnival* 19–20.
5. Elias Canetti, *Crowds and Power* 30, 80.
6. Elias Canetti, *Crowds and Power* 21.

7. Iris Murdoch, *Metaphysics as a Guide to Morals* 19.

8. Jeremy Hawthorn, *Unlocking the Text: Fundamental Issues in Literary Theory* 127.

Appendix A

1. Frank Morley, *Literary Britain: A Reader's Guide to Its Writers and Landmarks*, 177.

2. David Nokes, Review of *All Day on the Sands*, *Times Literary Supplement* Oct. 7, 1994, 38.

3. Edward Bond, "Author's Program Note on The Sea," *Bingo & The Sea* 122, 123.

4. Catherine Wells Cole, *Dictionary of Literary Biography, Volume 14: British Novelists Since 1960* 302–308.

5. Thomas C. Foster, *Understanding John Fowles* 27, 169–70.

6. Susan Hill, http://www.susan-hill.com/pages/books/the_woman_in_black.htm.

7. Robert B. Shaw, "Ted Hughes," *Dictionary of Literary Biography*, 40, 258–276.

8. A. A. Kelly, *Mary Lavin, Quiet Rebel* 123.

9. Sybil Steinberg, *Publishers Weekly*, Aug. 3, 1990, vol. 223, no. 31, 62.

10. Letter to Gillian Hanson dated May, 2001.

11. Robert A. Morace, Magill Book Review. Online database MagillOnLiterature Plus.

12. Sanford Sternlicht, *Stevie Smith*, 104.

13. *Contemporary Authors, New Revision Series*, vol. 15.

Bibliography

Fiction and Poems

Arnold, Matthew. *Poems*. Ed. Kenneth Allott, New York: Barnes and Noble, 1965.
Austen, Jane. *Persuasion*. (1817) New York: Dover, 1997.
Bates, H. E. *The Two Sisters*. New York: Viking Press, 1926.
Beckett, Samuel. "Krapp's Last Tape." *Krapp's Last Tape, and Other Dramatic Pieces*. New York: Grove Press, 1960.
Bennett, Alan. *Talking Heads*. Woodlands, London: BBC Books, 1988.
____. *The Writer in Disguise*. London: Faber, 1985.
Bond, Edward. *Bingo & The Sea*. New York: Hill and Wang, 1975.
Cary, Joyce. *First Trilogy: Herself Surprised. To Be a Pilgrim. The Horse's Mouth*. New York: Harper, 1958.
____. *The Horse's Mouth*. New York: Harper, 1944.
Collins, Wilkie. *Miss or Mrs?* [1870] *The Haunted Hotel* [1878] *The Guilty River* [1886]. Oxford: Oxford University Press, 1999.
Dickens, Charles. *Our Mutual Friend*. (1864–1865) Oxford: Oxford University Press, 1987.
Eliot, George. *The Mill on the Floss*. (1880) London: Penguin Classics, 2003.
Fitzgerald, Penelope. *Offshore*. London: Collins, 1979.
Fowles, John. *The French Lieutenant's Woman*. Boston: Little, Brown, 1969.
Gardam, Jane. *Crusoe's Daughter*. London: Hamish Hamilton Ltd., 1985.
Grahame, Kenneth. *The Wind in the Willows*. (1908) London: Penguin Classics, 1994.
Greene, Graham. *Brighton Rock*. New York: Viking Press, 1938.
Hamilton, Patrick. *The West Pier*. London: Constable, 1951.
Hardy, Thomas. *A Pair of Blue Eyes*. (1872–1873) London: Penguin Classics, 1998.
Hill, Susan. *The Albatross & Other Stories*. New York: E. P. Dutton, 1970, 1971.
____. *The Mist in the Mirror*.
____. *The Woman in Black*. London: Hamish Hamilton Ltd., 1983.

Hughes, Ted. *River.* (1983) New York: Harper & Row, 1984.
Ingelow, Jean. *The Complete Poems.* Toronto: R. Wilkenson, 1872.
Kingsley, Charles. *The Water Babies* (1863) London: Penguin Classics, 1994.
Lavin, Mary. "The Great Wave." *"The Great Wave" and Other Stories.* New York: Macmillan, 1961.
McGrath, Patrick. *Spider.* New York: Poseidon Press, 1990.
Murdoch, Iris. *The Sea, the Sea.* (1978) New York: Penguin Books, 2001.
Nicholson, D. H. S., and A. H. E. Lee, eds. *The Oxford Book of English Mystical Verse.* Oxford: Oxford University Press, 1917.
Sillitoe, Alan. "The Road." *Men Women and Children.* London: W. H. Allen, 1973.
____. *Saturday Night and Sunday Morning.* London: W. H. Allen, 1958.
____. "A Scream of Toys." *The Second Chance.* London: Jonathon Cape, 1981.
Sinclair, Iain. *Downriver.* New York: Random House, 1991.
Smith, Stevie. "Beside the Seaside." *Me Again: Uncollected Writings of Stevie Smith.* New York: Farrar, Straus & Giroux, 1982.
Swift, Graham. "Learning to Swim." *Learning to Swim.* (1982) New York: Washington Square Press, 1986.
____. *Waterland.* New York: Poseidon Press, 1983.
Tennyson, Alfred. *Works.* London: Macmillan, 1913.
Woolf, Virginia. *To the Lighthouse.* New York: Harcourt, Brace, 1927.
____. *The Waves.* New York: Harcourt, Brace, 1931.
Yeats, William Butler. "Fighting the Waves." *Wheels and Butterflies.* London: Macmillan and Company, 1934.

Secondary Sources

Adamson, Simon H. *Seaside Piers.* London: B.T. Batsford, 1977.
Applewhite, James. *Seas and Inland Journeys: Landscape and Consciousness from Wordsworth to Roethke.* Athens: University of Georgia Press, 1985.
Apter, T. E. *Virginia Woolf: A Study of Her Novels.* New York: New York University Press, 1979.
Auden, W. H. *The Enchafèd Flood, or The Romantic Iconography of the Sea.* (1950) Charlottesville: University Press of Virginia, 1979.
____. "The Guilty Vicarage." *The Dyer's Hand, and Other Essays.* New York: Random House, 1962.
____. "The Way to the Sea." *The Complete Works of W. H. Auden,* vol. 1. Ed. E. Mendleson. Princeton, 1998.
Bachelard, Gaston. *L'eau et les rêves, Essai sur l'imagination Matière.* Paris: Corti, 1942.
____. *Poetics of Space.* (1958) Boston: Beacon Press, 1959.
____. *Water and Dreams: An Essay on the Imagination of Matter.* (1942) Dallas: Pegasus Foundation, 1983.
Bainbridge, Cyril. *Pavilions on the Sea: A History of the Seaside Pleasure Pier.* London: Robert Hale, 1986.
Bakhtin, Mikhail. *Problems of Dostoevsky's Poetics.* Ed. Caryl Emerson. Minneapolis: University of Minnesota Press, 1984.

Barrett, William. *Irrational Man.* (1958) Garden City, N.Y.: Doubleday, 1962.
Bates, H. E. *Down the River.* (1937) London: Victor Gollancz, 1987.
Ben-Zvi, Linda. *Samuel Beckett.* Boston: Twayne Publishers, 1986.
Cadbury, William. "The Utility of the Poetic Mask in Tennyson's 'Supposed Confessions,'" *Modern Language Quarterly* 24 (1963): 374–385.
Canetti, Elias. *Crowds and Power.* New York: Viking Press, 1962.
Carrabino, Victor. "On the Shores of Nothingness: Beckett's *Embers.*" *Poetics of the Elements in the Human Condition: The Sea: From Elemental Stirrings to Symbolic Inspiration, Language and Life Significance in Literary Interpretation and Theory.* Ed. Anna Teresa Tymieniecka. Dordrecht, Holland: Reidel, 1985: 45–56.
Coffey, Michael. "Patrick McGrath: A Purveyor of the Fantastic Makes a Foray into Madness," *Publishers Weekly,* Sept. 28, 1990, vol. 237, 39.
Cooper, Pamela. "Imperial Topographies: The Spaces of History in *Waterland,*" *Modern Fiction Studies.* Summer 1996. 43 (2): 371–396.
Coult, Tony. *The Plays of Edward Bond: A Study.* London: Methuen, 1977.
Daiches, David. *The Novel and the Modern World.* (1939) Chicago: University of Chicago Press, 1960.
_____. *Virginia Woolf.* (1942) New York: New Directions, 1963.
Danow, David. *The Spirit of the Carnival: Magical Realism and the Grotesque.* Lexington: University Press of Kentucky, 1995.
DeVitis, A. A., and William J. Palmer. "A Pair of Blue Eyes Flash at The French Lieutenant's Woman," *Contemporary Literature* 15 (1974) 90–101.
Dickens, Charles. *Dickens's Dictionary of the Thames from Oxford to the Nore: An Unconventional Handbook.* London, 1880.
Dunn, Katherine. "The Child Is Father to the Mad." *New York Times Book Review,* Sept. 23, 1990, 14.
Eagleton, Terry. *Exiles and Émigrés.* New York: Schocken Books, 1970.
Forster, E. M. "Notes on the English Character." *Aspects of the Novel.* New York: Harcourt, Brace, 1927.
Foster, Thomas C. *Understanding John Fowles.* Columbia: University of South Carolina Press, 1994.
Gorsky, Susan Rubinow. *Virginia Woolf.* (1978) Boston: Twayne Publishers, 1989.
Gray, Nigel. *The Silent Majority: A Study of the Working Class in Post-War British Fiction.* New York: Barnes and Noble, 1973.
Grey, Howard, and Graham Stuart. *The Victorians by the Sea.* London: Academy Editions, 1973.
Gustavsson, Bo. "Ted Hughes' Quest for a Heirophany: A Reading of *River,*" *Critical Essays on Ted Hughes.* Ed. Leonard M. Scigaj. New York: G. K. Hall, 1992.
Halio, Jay L., ed. *Dictionary of Literary Biography, Volume 14: British Novelists Since 1960.* Detroit: Gale, 302–308.
Hanson, Gillian Mary. *Understanding Alan Sillitoe.* Columbia: University of South Carolina Press, 1999.
Hardy, Thomas. *Thomas Hardy's Personal Writings.* London: Macmillan, 1967.
Hawthorn, Jeremy, ed. *The British Working-Class Novel in the Twentieth Century.* London: Edward Arnold, 1984.

———. *Unlocking the Text: Fundamental Issues in Literary Theory.* (1987) New York: Routledge, Chapman and Hall, 1992.
Hawthorne, Nathaniel. *English Note-Books.* (1870) Boston: Houghton Mifflin, 1899.
Hay, Malcolm, and Phillip Roberts. *Bond: A Study of His Plays.* London: Eyre Methuen, 1980.
Heidegger, Martin. *On the Way to Language.* New York: Harper & Row, 1971.
Herendeen, W. H. "The Rhetoric of Rivers: The River and the Pursuit of Knowledge." *Studies in Philology,* Spring 1981, 78 (2).
Hunt, Peter. *The Wind in the Willows: A Fragmented Arcadia.* Boston: Twayne Publishers, 1994.
Kelly, A. A. *Mary Lavin, Quiet Rebel: A Study of Her Short Stories.* New York: Barnes & Noble Books, 1980.
Kierkegaard, Søren. *Fear and Trembling and The Sickness unto Death.* (1941) Garden City, N.Y.: Doubleday Books, 1954.
Knowland, A. S. *W. B. Yeats, Dramatist of Vision.* Gerrards Cross, Buckinghamshire: Colin Smythe, 1983.
Kronenberger, Louis. "A Return to the Novel of Essentials," *The New York Times Book Review,* September 26, 1926.
Lehmann, John. *Virginia Woolf and Her World.* New York: Harcourt Brace Jovanovich, 1975.
Lévi-Strauss, Claude. *The Savage Mind.* Chicago: University of Chicago Press, 1966.
May, Rollo, Ernest Angel, Henri F. Ellenberger, eds. *Existence: A New Dimension in Psychiatry and Psychology.* New York: Basic Books, 1958.
McClatchy, J. D. *The New Republic,* Sept. 3, 1984, vol. 191, 39.
McKinney, Ronald. "The Greening of Postmodernism: Graham Swift's *Waterland,*" *New Literary History:* Autumn 1997. 28(4): 821–832.
Michelet, Jules. *La Mer* [The Sea]. Lausanne: L'Age D'Homme, 1980.
Morgan, Nigel, and Annette Pritchard. *Power and Politics at the Seaside.* Exeter: University of Exeter Press, 1999.
Morley, Frank. *Literary Britain: A Reader's Guide to Its Writers and Landmarks.* New York: Harper & Row, 1980.
Murdoch, Iris. *Existentialists and Mystics: Writings on Philosophy and Literature.* New York: Allen Lane, 1998.
———. *Metaphysics as a Guide to Morals.* New York: Allen Lane, 1993.
———. *The Unicorn.* (1988) London: Penguin Books, 1996.
Nokes, David. *Times Literary Supplement,* Oct. 7, 1994, 38.
Orel, Howard. *Thomas Hardy's Personal Writings.* London: Macmillan, 1967.
Porter, Dale H. *The Thames Embankment: Environment, Technology, and Society in Victorian England.* Akron, Ohio: University of Akron Press, 1998.
Rai, Gangeshwar. *Graham Greene: An Existential Approach.* New Delhi: Associated Publishing House, 1983.
Ricks, Christopher. *Tennyson.* New York: Macmillan, 1972.
Roberts, Philip, comp. Letter to William Woodman, director of *The Sea. Bond on File.* London: Methuen Press, 1985.
Ruotolo, Lucio P. *The Interrupted Moment: A View of Virginia Woolf's Novels.* Stanford, Calif.: Stanford University Press, 1986.

Scigaj, Leonard M. "The Ophiolatry of Ted Hughes," *Twentieth Century Literature*, Winter 1985, 31(4): 380–398.
Sherry, Vincent B., Jr., ed. "Ted Hughes." *Dictionary of Literary Biography, Volume 40: Poets of Great Britain and Ireland Since 1960, Part Two: M–Z*. Detroit: Gale, 258–276.
Shields, Rob. *Places on the Margin: Alternative Geographics of Modernity*. London: Routledge,1991.
Steinberg, Sybil. Review of *Spider*. *Publishers Weekly*, Aug. 3, 1990, vol. 223 no. 31, 62.
Sternlicht, Sanford. *Stevie Smith*. Boston: Twayne Publishers, 1990.
Sullivan, Zoreth. "Iris Murdoch and the Enchantment of Untruth." *Old Lines, New Forces: Essays on the Contemporary British Novel, 1960-1970*. Ed. Robert K. Morris. Rutherford, N.J.: Fairleigh Dickinson University Press, 1976.
Sutcliffe, Shelia. *Martello Towers*. Devon, England: David & Charles, 1972.
Swinburne, Algernon Charles. "Charles Dickens," *Quarterly Review*, July 1902.
Vannatta, Dennis. *H. E. Bates*. Boston: Twayne Publishers, 1983.
Walton, John. *The British Seaside*. Manchester: Manchester University Press, 2002.
_____. *The English Seaside Resort: A Social History, 1750-1914*. Leicestershire: Leicester University Press, 1983.
Waugh, Patricia. *Postmodernism*. (1992) New York: Routledge, Chapman and Hall, 1993.
Welch, James Donald. "Tennyson's Landscapes of Time and a Reading of 'The Kraken,'" *Victorian Poetry*, 14, 1975, 197–204.
White, Allon. *Carnival, Hysteria, and Writing*. Oxford: Clarendon Press, 1993.
Wilson, Colin. *Introduction to the New Existentialism* (1966). Boston: Houghton Mifflin Company, 1967.
_____. *The Outsider*. Cambridge: Riverside Press, 1956.
Woodman, William. *Bond on File*. Compiled by Philip Roberts. London: Methuen, 1985.
Woolf, Virginia. *A Writer's Diary: Being Extracts from the Diary of Virginia Woolf*. London: Hogarth Press, 1953.

Index

The Albatross 6, 104, 127–29, 159, 168
"All Day on the Sands" 6, 104, 119–21, 129, 133, 167
Arnold, Matthew 1, 5, 66, 130, 139
Auden, W. H. 2, 65, 107, 124
Austen, Jane 6, 105, 139

Bachelard, George 2, 3, 5, 12, 13, 22, 27, 32, 130
Bakhtin, Mikhail 2, 104, 106
Bates, H. E. 2, 5, 9, 140
Beckett, Samuel 6, 140
Bennett, Alan 6, 140
"Beside the Seaside" 7, 83–84, 101, 133, 135
Bond, Edward 6, 88, 124, 141
"Break, Break, Break" 67
Brighton 108
Brighton Rock 2, 6, 104, 108, 114, 129, 135, 165–66
Brighton Station 112
The British Seaside 106
"By the Sea" 67

Canetti, Elias 2, 76, 108, 109–10, 129
Carey, Joyce 4, 141
Carnival, Hysteria, and Writing 107
carnivalesque 104
The Cobb 105, 136
Coleridge, S. T. 66
Collins, Wilkie 14, 141
Cooper, Pamela 25, 28
Crowds and Power 76, 83, 95, 102, 109–10, 119, 137
Crusoe's Daughter 5, 65, 97–101, 133, 164

Derrida, Jacques 61
Dickens, Charles 4, 34, 142

Dictionary of the Thames 34
"Divided" 22
"Dover Beach" 5, 67, 98, 102–3, 134
Down the River 4, 19, 31, 59, 132, 152–53, 159
Downriver 4, 45, 51–54, 60, 61, 132, 158, 161
"The Dying Swan" 12

Eagleton, Terry 109
Eliot, George 1, 5, 142
Embers 6, 117–19, 134, 166–67
The Enchafèd Flood 96
English Note-Books 102
The English Seaside Resort 105, 165
Exiles and Émigrés 109

The Fens 28
"Fighting the Waves" 5, 71, 81–82, 101, 133, 135, 162
Fitzgerald, Penelope 4, 142
"Flesh of Light" 59
"The Forsaken Merman" 5, 67, 68, 103
Forster, E. M. 63
"The Four Bridges" 5, 58, 132
Fowles, John 5, 86, 143
The French Lieutenant's Woman 5, 86–90, 101, 132, 134, 135, 163

Gardam, Jane 5, 97, 143
Grahame, Kenneth 144
"The Great Wave" 5, 71, 84–86, 101, 133, 134, 135, 162
Greene, Graham 2, 6, 14, 144
"The Guilty River" 14, 16–18, 131, 152

Hall, Stuart 107
Hamilton, Patrick 2, 6, 145
Hardy, Thomas 5, 67, 69, 144

Index

Hawthorne, Nathaniel 102
Heidegger, Martin 31, 45
Herendeen, W. H. 4, 11
Hill, Susan 6, 95, 145
Hopkins, Gerard Manley 76
The Horse's Mouth 4, 36, 37–40, 57, 131, 155–56
Hughes, Ted 5, 146

"Imperial Topographies: The Spaces of History in *Waterland*" 25
"Impression du Matin" 37
Ingelow, Jean 5, 58

Kierkegaard, Soren 21–22
Kingsley, Charles 4, 5, 146
"The Kraken" 5, 90, 134

"The Lady of Shalott" 3, 12, 13, 130
Lavin, Mary 5, 146
"Learning to Swim" 5, 93–95, 101, 133, 134, 160, 163–64
The Leem 24
lighthouses 71

Martello tower 71
Martello Towers 71
McGrath, Patrick 4, 147
McHale, Brian 61
"The Mermaid" 71, 133
"The Merman" 71, 133
The Mill on the Floss 4, 5, 14–16, 131, 151, 159
"The Miller's Daughter" 14
The Mist in the Mirror 4, 54–56, 132, 158, 161
Modern Painters 67

The Odyssey 65
Offshore 4, 37, 40–44, 50, 131, 132, 156, 160
"On the Shores of Nothingness: Beckett's *Embers*" 118
Our Mutual Friend 4, 17, 34–36, 131, 155
Ovidian themes 57

A Pair of Blue Eyes 5, 67–70, 101, 132, 135, 161
Pavilions on the Sea: A History of the Seaside Pleasure Pier 107, 165
Persuasion 6, 105–6, 129, 165
the pier 107, 135
Places on the Margin 109
Poetics of Space 22
Problems of Dostoevsky's Poetics 136
the promenade 105, 135
psychic disintegration 66

the railway station 107, 135
"The Rhetoric of Rivers" 4
"The Rime of the Ancient Mariner" 66
River 5, 14, 29, 30–32, 131, 132

"A River" 5, 58, 132
River Floss 14
River Nee 95
River Ouse 4, 5
"River Song" 58
River Thames 34
River Trent 37, 44
"The Road" 6, 104, 122–23, 129, 133, 135, 167
Robinson Crusoe 99
Rossetti, Christiana 67
Rossetti, Dante Gabriel 98
rural coastal setting 5
rural river 4, 11–32
Ruskin, John 67

Saturday Night and Sunday Morning 104
"A Scream of Toys" 4, 37, 44–45, 132, 156–57, 160
The Sea 6, 104, 124–27, 129, 133, 135, 167–68
"The Sea and the Skylark" 67
The Sea, the Sea 5, 90–93, 101, 132, 133, 134, 135, 162–63
Seas and Inland Journeys 66, 136
seaside crowds 104
Shelley, Mary 66
Sillitoe, Alan 4, 6, 103, 147
Sinclair, Iain 4, 5, 51, 148
"The Slave Ship" 67
Smith, Stevie 71, 148
The South Downs 114
Spider 4, 37, 46–51, 57, 60–61, 132, 157
Swift, Graham 5

The Tempest 65
Tennyson, Alfred 3, 13, 49
Thames Embankment 34
"Transformation" 66
To the Lighthouse 5, 70, 78–81, 101, 132, 133, 134, 135, 162
The Two Sisters 4, 5, 9, 18–22, 131, 152, 153

Water and Dreams 27, 28–30, 114
The Water Babies 4, 5, 11, 14, 22–24, 33, 131, 132, 153–54, 159
The Waves 5, 70, 72–77, 101, 132, 154, 161
"The Way to the Sea" 107
Wessex 68
The West Pier 114–17, 129, 166
Wilde, Oscar 37
The Wind in the Willows 4, 5, 14, 29, 131, 154, 159
The Woman in Black 5, 95–97, 101, 133, 160, 164
Woolf, Virginia 5, 70, 150

Yeats, W. B. 5, 71, 101, 150